Women Lawyers and the Origins of Professional Identity in America

Women Lawyers and the Origins of Professional Identity in America

The Letters of the Equity Club, 1887 to 1890

Virginia G. Drachman

Ann Arbor

The University of Michigan Press

Published in the United States of America by
The University of Michigan Press
Manufactured in the United States of America

1996 1995 1994 1993 4 3 2 1

*A CIP catalogue record for this book
is available from the British Library.*

Library of Congress Cataloging-in-Publication Data

Women lawyers and the origins of professional identity in America :
the letters of the Equity Club, 1887 to 1890 / Virginia G. Drachman.
p. cm.
Includes bibliographical references and index.
ISBN 0-472-10305-9 (alk. paper)
1. Women lawyers—United States—History. 2. Equity Club—
History. 3. Women lawyers—United States—Correspondence.
4. Women lawyers—United States—Biography. 5. Equity Club—
Biography. I. Drachman, Virginia G., 1948– . II. Equity Club.
KF299.W6W65 1993
349.73'082—dc20
[347.30082] 92-38987
CIP

For Douglas

Preface

I first discovered the letters of the Equity Club during my sabbatical in 1986 while beginning research at the Schlesinger Library of Radcliffe College for a project that I was just then contemplating on the history of women lawyers in America. The Equity Club was a correspondence club of nineteenth-century women lawyers whose membership and participation depended exclusively on letters they wrote and circulated among themselves. In an era when people lived their lives without the conveniences of modern transportation or modern communications systems, the letters of the Equity Club offered the only way for nineteenth-century women lawyers, who were scattered throughout the country, to come together.

As I read through the Equity Club letters, it became clear to me that they are a treasure for anyone interested in the history of women or the history of the legal profession in late nineteenth-century America. They provide a wealth of information, illuminating both the broad themes in the history of nineteenth-century women lawyers as well as the small details of their daily lives. Moreover, they proved what I had always suspected, that the professional and personal challenges that confront women lawyers today did not have their origins in the 1960s, as many have suggested. Rather, they reach back more than a century to the pioneer generation of women lawyers who were the first to articulate and grapple with the challenges facing women in the legal profession.

Over the course of the next few years I mined the letters of the Equity Club for a number of essays on the history of women lawyers in late nineteenth-century America.[1] But the more I strived to inter-

1. See Virginia G. Drachman, "Women Lawyers and the Quest for Professional Identity in Late Nineteenth-Century America," 88 *Michigan Law Review* 2414–43 (1990); "'My "Partner" in Law and Life': Marriage in the Lives of Women Lawyers in Late 19th- and Early 20th-Century America," 14 *Law and Social Inquiry* 221–

pret the letters, the more I came to realize that I could not fully convey the thoughts and feelings of their authors. Meanwhile, my husband, Douglas L. Jones, a legal historian and lawyer, had been urging me since I first discovered the Equity Club letters to publish them in a volume such as this. This book is the result of his gentle yet persistent prodding. I came to realize that my intellectual analyses should be augmented by the voices of the Equity Club members themselves. This book allows the women lawyers of the Equity Club to speak for themselves, giving the reader the opportunity to get to know, appreciate, and respect them as I have.

This book is comprised of three sections. Taken together, the sections provide a close-up of the Equity Club and its members as well as a broader view of the club set within the context of its time. The Introduction examines the history of the Equity Club and places it within the context of the history of women and the history of the legal profession in late nineteenth-century America. The central section contains the sixty letters written by the thirty-two members of the Equity Club during 1887–90, its four years of existence. Members wrote one letter per year. Some women contributed a letter each of the four years of the club's life. Others wrote letters during only one, two, or three years of the club's existence. The letters are organized by year beginning with the letters for 1887 and ending with those for 1890. Within each year, the letters are organized alphabetically by club member. The letters vary in length; some are but a few lines long while others are several pages in length. All are presented here in full, with annotations where necessary.

The Equity Club letters are part of the Lelia Josephine Robinson Series of the Mary Earhart Dillon Collection in the Arthur and Elizabeth Schlesinger Library on the History of Women in America, Radcliffe College, Cambridge, Massachusetts. The collection of letters exists in different forms for different years. The original manuscript letters exist for 1887. The letters of 1888 were published by the Equity Club under the title of the *Equity Club Annual*. The letters of 1889 and 1890 were transcribed by hand into journals that contain carbon copies of the transcriptions.

Because I am primarily concerned with producing a readable set

50 (1989); and "Entering the Male Domain: Women Lawyers in the Courtroom in Modern American History," 77 *Massachusetts Law Review* 44–50 (1992).

of letters rather than a precise duplication of the documents, I have edited the letters by eliminating crossed-out words and making grammatical changes for clarification only. In addition, I have listed the date and location of each letter in a uniform manner. In the few places where words were illegible, a black line appears in their place. Illegible words were more common in the journals of 1889 and 1890 where some of the transcribed letters were difficult, though by no means impossible, to decipher.

Accompanying the letters are explanatory notes. Some notes are elaborations of themes, ideas, or concerns that were raised by Equity Club members but that extended beyond their lives and were of importance within the broader parameters of late nineteenth-century American culture. Most of the notes briefly identify individuals, places, or institutions that may be unfamiliar to the reader. At the same time, I have chosen not to identify those individuals (such as William Shakespeare) with whom the general reader is familiar or remote people and places that would add little to the reader's understanding of the substance of a given letter.

The third section of the book contains biographical sketches of the individual members of the Equity Club. These sketches give information on both the private and professional lives of the women including family background, education, professional training and career, marriage and motherhood, and political and social activities. Given the diversity of women in the Equity Club—some were pioneers among women lawyers while others led private lives and were basically unknown—the available material on the women varied. For some I found a wealth of both primary and secondary material. For a few I was lucky enough to unearth papers in remote historical societies and libraries. For others I found very little information at all and had to content myself with a single obituary or a few facts culled from a city directory. As a result, the biographical sketches vary in the depth and breadth of information they provide, though they all attempt to acquaint the reader with the Equity Club members as individuals.

Over the course of editing this book, I have benefited from the help of many people and institutions. The research for this book was conducted in part with the aid of an ACLS/Ford Fellowship and grants from Tufts University. The staff of the Schlesinger Library gave me unrestricted access to the letters and helped me to uncover materials on various Equity Club members. The Equity Club Letters are published with the permission of the Schlesinger Library, Radcliffe College. The staff of the Bentley Library of the University of Michigan, and in particular Nancy Bartlett and Karan Jania, aided me in my pursuit of information on Equity Club graduates of the University of Michigan Law School. A number of people gave generously of their time in various stages of the project including David Chambers, Audrey Rogers, Janet Schulte, and Daneille Williams. In addition, I would like to thank the members of my senior history seminar at Tufts University in the spring of 1991, who include Christopher Carr, Stacey Druks, Nancy Duff, Michael Gilbert, Sarah Lowthian, Barbara Pajot, Jane Savoca, Marybeth Savicki, Lisa Schramm, Kristen Vagos, Stephen Woodward, and Julie Anne Zupan. Dianne Service was enormously patient and generous with me as she typed and retyped all the sections of this book several times over. My husband, Douglas L. Jones, to whom this book is dedicated, encouraged me in this project from the start and made many invaluable comments and suggestions. Finally, my children, Abigail and Eliza, inspired me in this work with their pride in their mother, and in turn made me proud to have two wonderful daughters.

Newton, Massachusetts V. G. D.

Contents

Introduction: The Equity Club in Historical Perspective 1

The Letters of the Equity Club

Letters from 1887 41

Letters from 1888 73

Letters from 1889 147

Letters from 1890 179

Profiles of the Members of the Equity Club 205

Index 285

Illustrations *facing page* 212

Introduction: The Equity Club in Historical Perspective

On the evening of October 6, 1886, seven women lawyers and law students at the University of Michigan in Ann Arbor met at the home of law student Letitia Burlingame for an all-women's dinner. The purpose of the evening was to honor the new female law students as they began their legal studies. By the end of the evening, this small group of women had formed the Equity Club. Though local at its founding, the Equity Club quickly developed into a correspondence club for women lawyers and law students throughout America and in other countries as well.[1]

Measured against large and powerful professional institutions and well-established women's organizations, the Equity Club was a modest venture. It lasted only four years and had only thirty-two members. But despite its short life and small size, the Equity Club was the first national organization of women lawyers in American history. Moreover, with several European members, the Equity Club was the first international association of women lawyers as well. Many larger and longer lasting women's legal institutions followed, including state and county women's bar associations, legal sororities, and the *Women Lawyers' Journal.* But the Equity Club was the first of these all-women's professional organizations in law. As such, its founding in 1886

1. Portions of this essay have been published in "Women Lawyers and the Quest for Professional Identity in Late Nineteenth-Century America," 88 *Michigan Law Review* 2414–43 (1990); "'My "Partner" in Law and Life': Marriage in the Lives of Women Lawyers in Late 19th- and Early 20th-Century America," 14 *Law and Social Inquiry* 221–50 (1989); and "Entering the Male Domain: Women Lawyers in the Courtroom in Modern American History," 77 *Massachusetts Law Review* 44–50 (1992). Though seven women attended the dinner at Letitia Burlingame's home, only six became members of the Equity Club. The seventh, Mrs. Bates, left law school because of ill health and did not participate in the club.

marked the budding of professional identity among women lawyers in the late nineteenth century.

The women of the University of Michigan founded the Equity Club in an age of organizational growth in the legal profession. The decade of the 1870s marked the beginning of this era. Lawyers organized city and state bar associations throughout the country to bring lawyers together at the local and state level while the American Bar Association [ABA] was founded in 1878, elevating this period of professional organization to the national level. The mission of these associations was to raise the standards of the legal profession through reforms, tightened educational requirements, and an elite membership of wealthy, white, American-born male lawyers.

The Equity Club was at once part of and apart from the legal associations of the era. Like the ABA, it was a national association that strove to unite lawyers throughout the country. At the same time, it functioned on an intimate, personal level like the local bar associations of the day. But unlike the mainstream legal associations, the Equity Club was inclusive, rather than exclusive, open to all women lawyers and law students. Its members, all women, were excluded from practically all of the professional organizations of the day. In an era when membership in legal associations became a new professional standard, the Equity Club was the only legal organization open to most women lawyers.

The women lawyers at Michigan founded the Equity Club in the midst of a decade when the number of women lawyers in America more than doubled from a sparse 75 in 1880 to 208 in 1890.[2] Scattered across the country, it was difficult, if not impossible, for these women to become acquainted with each other, much less to develop a sense of professional community and collective professional identity. The Equity Club provided women lawyers and law students with a way to transcend the geographic distance that separated them and to build a community of women with similar professional interests and concerns. In the span of only four years, its small membership identified and grappled with a range of pressing issues. These issues fell into three general categories: professional matters, the dilemma

2. United States Bureau of the Census, *The Tenth Census of the United States: 1880* (Washington, D.C., 1883) vol. 1, at 744; United States Bureau of the Census, *The Eleventh Census of the United States: 1890* (Washington, D.C., 1897) vol. 1, at 304.

of marriage and family, and the intimate details of health and sexuality. In grappling with the issues in these three areas, the women of the Equity Club defined the professional agenda for all women lawyers of their generation. Moreover, in doing so, they confronted their dual roles in the public arena of the workplace and the private arena of the home and identified the universal challenge that faced all professional women of their day—how to strike a balance between their femininity and their professional roles. This was the essential challenge that lay at the heart of all the issues the Equity Club members discussed and that defined the parameters of professional identity for women lawyers as it emerged in the late nineteenth century.[3]

The founders of the Equity Club were part of the first generation of women to enjoy the benefits of higher education. All of the original members—Letitia Burlingame, Corinne Douglas, Almeda Hitchcock, Rebecca May, Martha Pearce, and Margaret Wilcox—were graduates of the Law School of the University of Michigan. Their educational training set them apart from many young lawyers of their day—male or female—for formal legal education was typically not a requirement for admission to practice law in the late nineteenth century. Instead, most would-be nineteenth-century lawyers followed the route of apprenticeship into law practice. Under the apprenticeship system, an aspiring lawyer read law for several years with a practicing attorney before going out into practice on his or her own.

In the last quarter of the nineteenth century, legal education in law schools gradually became an alternative to the apprenticeship system. While elite law schools such as Harvard, Yale, and Columbia re-

3. In addition to my essays on the Equity Club cited in note 1, see also Joyce Antler, *The Educated Woman and Professionalization: The Struggle for a New Feminine Identity, 1890–1920* (New York, 1987); Karen Berger Morello, *The Invisible Bar: The Woman Lawyer in America: 1683 to the Present* (New York, 1986); Judy Jolley Mohraz, "The Equity Club: Community Building among Professional Women," 5 *Journal of American Culture* 34–39 (1982); and Beverly Cook, "Women Judges Organize: In the Footsteps of Women Lawyers," 66 *Women Lawyers Journal* 11–14 (1980). On professionalism and feminism in the lives of late nineteenth- and early twentieth-century women see Nancy F. Cott, *The Grounding of Modern Feminism* (New Haven, Conn., 1987), at 213–39. For an analysis of law as a manly profession in Victorian America see Michael Grossberg, "Institutionalizing Masculinity: The Law as a Masculine Profession," in Mark C. Carnes and Clyde Griffen, eds., *Meanings for Manhood, Constructions of Manhood in Victorian America* (Chicago, 1990), at 133–51. For a contemporary analysis of the tension women lawyers experienced between femininity and professional identity see David L. Chambers, "Accommodation and Satisfaction: Women and Men Lawyers and the Balance of Work and Family," 14 *Law and Social Inquiry* 251 (1989).

mained closed to women into the twentieth century, women made inroads into other university law schools in the late nineteenth century. Washington University in St. Louis and the University of Iowa led the way in 1869. Union College of Law (Northwestern) graduated the first woman lawyer, future Equity Club member Ada Kepley, in 1870. The University of Michigan and Boston University admitted women to their law schools in 1870 and 1872, respectively. Other law schools admitted women in the last third of the nineteenth century, including Hastings College of Law in San Francisco, Buffalo Law School, University of Pennsylvania, and New York University.[4]

It is no accident that the law department of the University of Michigan was the locus of the founding of the Equity Club. The University of Michigan was not only a pioneer institution in its early admission of women into the law school; it had a long record of admitting women throughout the university well before other institutions of higher learning. When it opened its doors to women in 1870, it was one of the first eight state universities in the country to become coeducational, and its medical department was the first university medical school to admit women.[5]

But the University of Michigan did not always embrace the idea of coeducation. Rather, the admission of women in 1870 was preceded by twenty years of debate and agitation. While the university's original statute of incorporation in 1837 provided that the university should be open to "all persons" regardless of sex, for decades women who applied to the university were rejected. Beginning in the 1850s, the question of accepting women at the University of Michigan became a widely debated topic. At its annual meeting in 1855, the state Teachers' Association, with its large female membership, officially

4. On the history of legal education see Robert Stevens, *Law School: Legal Education in America from the 1850s to the 1980s* (Chapel Hill, N.C., 1983).

5. On the history of the University of Michigan see Ruth Bordin, *The University of Michigan* (Ann Arbor, 1967) and Howard H. Peckham, *The Making of the University of Michigan, 1817–1967* (Ann Arbor, 1967). On women at the University of Michigan, see Dorothy Gies McGuigan, *A Dangerous Experiment: 100 Years of Women at the University of Michigan* (Ann Arbor, 1970) and Barbara Miller Solomon, *In the Company of Educated Women: A History of Women and Higher Education in America* (New Haven, 1985). On the University of Michigan Law School see Elizabeth G. Brown with William W. Blume, *Legal Education at Michigan, 1859–1959* (Ann Arbor, 1959) (hereinafter Brown, *Legal Education at Michigan*); Henry Wade Rogers, "The Law Department of Michigan University," 3 *Western Jurist* 129 (1869); and Henry Wade Rogers, "Law School of the University of Michigan," 1 *Green Bag* 189 (1889).

endorsed coeducation at the university. Over time they were joined by reformers—men and women—who supported the principle of coeducation, as well as taxpaying parents who wanted their daughters to enjoy the same educational opportunities as their sons. But the champions of coeducation faced formidable opposition from the Michigan State Board of Regents, a majority of the university's faculty, and university presidents Henry Tappan and Erastus Haven. After much debate, the University of Michigan opened its doors to women in 1870 under the temporary leadership of acting president Henry S. Frieze. Women finally had access to one of the most prestigious universities in the country.

In the fall of 1870, a total of thirty-four women studied at the University of Michigan, fourteen in the literary department, eighteen in the medical school, and two in the law department. Opposition to women on campus persisted, however. Initially, the faculty ridiculed or patronized the new female students, while residents of Ann Arbor often snubbed them in town and in church. The medical faculty vehemently opposed the presence of female medical students, arguing that the sensitive nature of medical topics required separate classes for the female students. Male students opposed female medical students as well, derisively referring to them as "hen-medics."[6]

Despite this resistance to coeducation at Michigan, the university, under the progressive leadership of President James Burrill Angell, emerged as one of the most popular institutions of higher learning for women in the late nineteenth century. Women flocked to the University of Michigan for liberal arts education as well as professional training. In 1871, Sarah Killgore Wertman, who later joined the Equity Club, became the first woman to graduate from the law school. Jane Slocum and Ellen Martin, also future Equity Club members, followed Wertman in 1874 and 1875, respectively. The founders of the Equity Club—Burlingame, Douglas, Hitchcock, May, Pearce, and Wilcox—were among the group of women who attended the law school in the 1880s.

While the acceptance of women into the University of Michigan provoked controversy, the actual experiences of the early female graduates of the law school revealed little of the acrimony that preceded their arrival. "The Law Department encountered no difficulty

6. McGuigan, *A Dangerous Experiment,* at 32–33.

in the admission of the new female students," Henry Frieze claimed in his President's Report in 1871.[7] Unlike the male students in the medical school who resisted the presence of women, most of the male law students welcomed women into their classes. The students of the Webster Society led the way.

The Webster Society was a literary club run by the law students at the University of Michigan. Committed to the idea that literary culture was essential to their success in professional life, the society met weekly for discussions, orations, and music. Its members were leaders in the law school. As early as 1874, they set an example for their male classmates regarding the acceptance of female law students into the student community when they invited Jane Slocum and her classmate, Mary Stockbridge, to join the Webster Society. Once they admitted women to the Webster Society, the male law students encouraged their female classmates to become active participants in its activities. In 1875, they elected one woman law student, Martha Strickland, secretary of the society, an acceptable position of responsibility for a woman of her day, and they chose her classmate, Mary Perry, to read an essay at the society's annual public exercises.[8] Keenly aware of the fair treatment women received from the Webster Society, Slocum wrote to the Equity Club years later that "every courtesy was ungrudgingly extended to us."[9]

Over the years, the male law students at the University of Michigan followed the lead of the Webster Society and welcomed the participation of their female classmates in student life. In 1885, they chose Letitia Burlingame to be class poet, and they elected her classmate, Mary Merrill, as class secretary.[10] In 1888, Equity Club member Almeda Hitchcock reflected on the consideration she received from

7. President's Report, 1871, at 18. Cited in Brown, *Legal Education at Michigan,* at 252.

8. Constitution and By-Laws of the Webster Literary Society of the University of Michigan (Ann Arbor, 1889) and Annual Public Exercises of the Webster Society, January 30, 1875, both at the Bentley Historical Library, University of Michigan Collection, University of Michigan, Ann Arbor, Michigan.

9. Jane M. Slocum to the Equity Club, 1887, Canadaigua, New York. Slocum's letter to the Equity Club is part of the letters of the Equity Club in the Lelia Josephine Robinson Series, Mary Earhart Dillon Collection, Arthur and Elizabeth Schlesinger Library on the History of Women in America, Radcliffe College, Cambridge, Massachusetts (hereinafter referred to as the Equity Club Letters, Dillon Collection).

10. O. C. Burlingame, ed., *Lettie Lavilla Burlingame: Her Life Pages, Stories, Poems and Essays* (Joliet, Ill., 1895), at 318.

her male classmates: "The life here at college has been all that one could ask for," she wrote shortly before she graduated. "My classmates have treated me with respect and kindness. Not an unpleasant thing has occurred in my college life."[11] Martha Pearce, one of the founders of the Equity Club, echoed Hitchcock's remarks when she described her experience as a law student at the University of Michigan in the early 1880s. "We had received a hearty welcome from our brothers in law to their moot courts and debating clubs and had found that they forgot all troublesome distinctions just to the degree that we ourselves ignored them."[12] In general, there appeared to be a smooth integration of women into all arenas of the law school in the 1870s and 1880s.

While the women law students were welcomed by their male classmates, they were graciously received by the faculty as well. Professor James V. Campbell and the dean of the law school, Judge Thomas M. Cooley, made them feel welcome and safe. "Judge Campbell's scholarly and benign face smiled upon us from the desk at regular intervals," Slocum recalled. Referring to Campbell and Cooley, she continued: "The generous interest of these distinguished jurists will never be forgotten by the grateful women who were treated not only as students who were welcome there, but as friends whom they were glad to aid in their life work."[13]

In reality, Cooley was condescending even as he was accepting of the women students. In a letter to the president of Cornell University in 1871, the year before Slocum arrived on campus, he revealed his ambivalence toward the new female students: "The number who come is small, and for the most part of the unlovely class, some of them afford the boys some amusement. . . ." Still, Cooley acknowledged that women not only could compete academically with the male students but were often held to higher standards than the men. "You are misinformed if you are told the standard for admission is lowered. The tendency has been in the other direction."[14]

But Cooley's ambivalent views did not seem to interfere with his

11. Almeda Hitchcock to the Equity Club, April 30, 1888, Hilo, Hawaii, *Equity Club Annual,* 1888, at 26, Equity Club Letters, Dillon Collection.

12. Martha K. Pearce, Report of the Corresponding Secretary, 1888, Bridgewater, Iowa, *Equity Club Annual,* 1888, at 6, Equity Club Letters, Dillon Collection.

13. Slocum to the Equity Club, 1887, Equity Club Letters, Dillon Collection.

14. Thomas Cooley to A. D. White, June 5, 1871, Thomas Cooley Collection, Michigan Historical Collections, Bentley Historical Library.

respectful treatment of the women law students. For her part, Slocum was aware of only courteous and kind treatment from Cooley. In a letter to him she freely expressed her deep gratitude for his respect and kindness toward her.

> It would in any case be impossible for me to express the gratitude which I feel for all your kindness and courtesy and for the advantages I have been permitted to enjoy here. One cannot know what a little cordial help is to any woman who tried to do something out of the beaten tracks, which makes people look with cold criticism if not with suspicion upon every motive and act, so you will never know how your abundant kindness will be treasured.[15]

Years after Cooley confessed his inner thoughts, female graduates of the law department continued to speak appreciatively of their treatment at the law school. In 1889, Cora Benneson, a graduate of the law school in 1880 and a member of the Equity Club, summarized the good will the women students enjoyed from both the faculty and male students. In an essay she wrote for the *Woman's Journal* entitled "Life of Women at Michigan University," she explained that the women students took their place beside their male classmates "as if no lengthy discussion had ever been held in regard to the fitness of co-education."[16]

While the spirits of the women law students at the University of Michigan were high, their numbers remained low. As President Angell reported in 1900, "the number of women in the law school is always small."[17] Throughout the nineteenth century, women law students were a remarkably small and isolated group within the large community of male students. In 1870, when the University of Michigan first accepted women, there were more than 300 male students in the law school. In 1872, Jane Slocum was one of only three female students among 327 men in the law school. In 1886, the year after Burlingame graduated, and the year that the Equity Club was founded, there were seven women in the law school, the largest num-

15. Jane M. Slocum to Judge Cooley, June 17, 18[73], Ann Arbor, Box 1, Thomas Cooley Collection, Bentley Historical Library.

16. Cora Agnes Benneson, "Life of Women at Michigan University," 21 *Woman's Journal* [n.p.] (1889).

17. President's Report, 1900, at 6, cited in Brown, *Legal Education at Michigan,* at 253.

ber of female students since women were first admitted in 1870. But for almost four decades thereafter, the number of women at the law school did not reach as high as seven again. It was not until 1924, when there were eleven women in the law school, that the number of women surpassed seven. By 1900, over 6,000 men had graduated from the law school. Ten years later, after forty years of coeducation, fewer than forty women had received law degrees from the University of Michigan.[18]

The University of Michigan was not alone in its low enrollment of women law students among law schools that accepted women. Boston University, from which came the next largest group of Equity Club members, was another example. From its founding in 1870, Boston University Law School was open to women. But no woman graduated from the law school until Equity Club member Lelia Robinson in 1881. Robinson was followed by Equity Club members Jessie Wright Whitcomb and Mary Anne Greene, who became the second and third female graduates of the law school in 1887 and 1888, respectively. Together, Robinson, Whitcomb, and Greene were part of a group of seventeen women and 985 men who graduated from Boston University Law School in the late nineteenth century. Like the women at the University of Michigan, they studied law among a sea of men.[19]

Despite the fact that most of the male law students at the University of Michigan accepted women into their school, it was not easy for most young women in the late nineteenth century to attend law school in an environment dominated by men. In 1884, shortly before she left her home in Joliet, Michigan, for Ann Arbor, Letitia Burlingame worried about going to the University of Michigan precisely because she knew there would be so few other women law students. "With my dreadful bashfulness, which age seems very little to banish, I realize what a trial a course in the University, in a large class with few, if any, ladies will be, but I guess grit will conquer shyness, for I feel that I can really make a successful lawyer let me once get admitted to the bar."[20]

18. Brown, *Legal Education at Michigan,* at 700–702, 735.

19. See *A Catalogue of the Graduates of the Boston University Law School, 1873–1905* (Boston, 1905) and *Annual Directory of Boston University* (Boston, 1924).

20. Pearce, Report of the Corresponding Secretary, 1888, *Equity Club Annual,* 1888, at 6, Equity Club Letters, Dillon Collection. Also Burlingame, *Lettie Lavilla Burlingame,* at 323–24.

But lack of female friendship was not the only problem women law students faced; at the same time that they had few other women to turn to, they also had to be careful to maintain a respectable distance from their male classmates. Burlingame resolved the matter of overcoming her loneliness and preserving her reputation in a way that was not unusual for other female University of Michigan students of her day; her mother went with her to live in Ann Arbor. While Letitia attended law school, her mother ran a boarding house for students of the university. In this way, Letitia's mother recreated a home away from home for her daughter, thereby protecting her from the loneliness and dangers young single women faced in a city alone. But in doing this for Letitia, the Burlingames temporarily broke up their nuclear family, for Letitia's mother left her husband for almost two years in order to stay with her daughter. This was no small sacrifice. Letitia recalled how difficult the breakup of her family was, particularly for her mother. "Such a general breaking up at home and leaving Papa behind awakened sad thoughts. . . . Thus sadness was mingled with joy, for I knew it was all done for me, and Mama cried for hours as if her heart would break."[21] The enormity of this sacrifice reveals the lengths to which the Burlingame family was willing to go to enable Letitia to attend law school at the University of Michigan.

The women law students at the University of Michigan were a very small group within the large community of male law students. But their isolation brought them closer to each other. While they enjoyed cordial relationships with most of their male classmates, they found their deepest friendships and their strongest support among themselves. Burlingame, for example, established strong friendships with several other women lawyers and law students, including Martha Pearce, Rebecca May, and Margaret Wilcox. During the summer after her first year at law school, Burlingame had the opportunity to spend some leisurely time with other women. "Those were golden hours," she recalled. "How I feel refreshed and strengthened by the sympathy of kindred minds. . . ."[22] The friendships Burlingame and the others built were deep and enduring. Burlingame was particularly close to Martha Pearce. "It will be a long while before I shall find

21. Burlingame, *Lettie Lavilla Burlingame,* at 316. Burlingame was not the only student to move to Ann Arbor with her mother. Other students did so as well. See Benneson, "Life of Women at Michigan University."

22. Burlingame, *Lettie Lavilla Burlingame,* at 323.

another friend in whom I can confide so unreservedly," she wrote in the midst of her second year of law school.[23] Moreover, these friendships lasted well beyond the days the women spent together in Ann Arbor. Three years after she graduated from law school Burlingame wrote to Rebecca May, who was practicing law in Topeka, Kansas, to invite May into joint practice. "I have some cases that it would be very difficult to manage alone," Burlingame wrote to May. "Would you at all consider a proposition to come here and go into partnership with me?"[24] Unfortunately, Burlingame and May never had the opportunity to work together because Burlingame became ill just two weeks after she had written to May and died seven months later.

But during their years together in Ann Arbor, Letitia Burlingame, Martha Pearce, Rebecca May, Margaret Wilcox, Almeda Hitchcock, and Corinne Douglas built a small community of women lawyers and law students. The heart of this community was the Equity Club. Its founders had often discussed the formation of a correspondence club. Catharine Waugh had written to the women at the University of Michigan and suggested the idea as well. With this goal in mind, Burlingame and Pearce invited the new female law students to dinner in 1886. They borrowed the idea for the dinner from the women of the literary department and the medical school, who traditionally invited the new female students of their respective departments to a special annual dinner. But the idea for a correspondence club was unique to the women in law, and they formed a local group to organize a correspondence club for women lawyers. They chose Burlingame as chair and Pearce as corresponding secretary.

The founders of the Equity Club made their organization as inclusive as possible, hoping to build a broad professional community for women lawyers. Their motto, "All the allies of each," reflected their commitment to bringing together as many women in law as they could. All women lawyers and law students, as well as nonpracticing women lawyers, were welcome to join. This set the Equity Club apart from the bar associations run by men, which were exclusionary in their admissions policies and hierarchical in their organizational structure. In contrast, the Equity Club, run by women for women, was a unique example of the women's institution building of its day.

23. Ibid., at 326.
24. Ibid., at 366.

In the second half of the nineteenth century, thousands of women, primarily, though by no means exclusively, white and middle class, began to form all-women's clubs, reform groups, and voluntary organizations. These groups were the product of the sexual discrimination nineteenth-century women encountered whenever they sought to participate in the world beyond the home. Women founded their own antislavery societies, colleges, medical schools, and hospitals because they were excluded from comparable institutions run by men. At the same time, women created separate organizations not only because they were excluded from those run by men, but because their own organizations were distinctly different from those of men. Inspired by female culture, that is, the values, customs, and experiences that nineteenth-century women shared simply because they were women, these women's clubs, schools, and professional organizations thrived, not only because of sexual discrimination, but precisely because they met women's unique needs.[25]

The Equity Club deviated somewhat from the model of sexual discrimination and female culture that lay at the heart of most nineteenth-century women's institutions. Its founders endured isolation within the male-dominated institution of the University of Michigan Law Department rather than outright exclusion from it. The creation of the Equity Club revealed women's attempt to nurture their female identity in a situation where, despite their acceptance into the law department at the University of Michigan, their numbers were so small that their presence was a matter "of entire indifference," according to Judge Cooley.[26]

Women's so-called benign isolation from the male lawyers and law students at the University of Michigan foreshadowed a situation that did not characterize that of women doctors until the early twentieth century when they began to attend male-run medical schools and hospitals instead of their own all-women's medical institutions. In

25. On women's institution building see Estelle Freedman, "Separatism as Strategy: Female Institution Building and American Feminism, 1870–1930," 5 *Feminist Studies* 512–29 (1979). On the women's club movement see Karen J. Blair, *The Clubwoman as Feminist: True Womanhood Redefined, 1868–1914* (New York, 1980). See also Ruth Bordin, *Women and Temperance: The Quest for Power and Liberty, 1873–1920* (Philadelphia, 1981); MariJo Buhle, *Woman and American Socialism, 1870–1920* (Urbana, 1981); and Virginia G. Drachman, *Hospital with a Heart: Women Doctors and the Paradox of Separatism at the New England Hospital for Women and Children, 1862–1969* (Ithaca, N.Y., 1984).

26. Cooley to White, June 5, 1871, Cooley Collection, Bentley Historical Library.

1905, the noted surgeon Dr. Bertha Van Hoosen, a graduate of the medical school at the University of Michigan, lamented the consequences of this new situation. "A generation earlier, women doctors were on the outside standing together, now they were on the inside sitting alone."[27] Women doctors responded to this isolation in much the same way as the women lawyers at the University of Michigan had years before, founding their own professional organizations to retain their female community. It is no accident that the all-women's American Medical Women's Association was founded in 1915, precisely the same year that the American Medical Association finally opened its doors to women.[28] In the early twentieth century, women doctors finally discovered what the women lawyers in the Equity Club understood years before—that entry into the male-dominated mainstream was only the first step on the long road for women who sought to make careers in a male-dominated profession.

While professional isolation rather than exclusion fueled the founding of the Equity Club, the club shared with other women's organizations of its day a strong commitment to the unique needs and values of women. In fact, its members made it clear that the very appeal of the Equity Club was that as an all-women's organization, it provided women lawyers with friendship and understanding from other women lawyers. Martha Pearce, the corresponding secretary of the club, expressed this sentiment in her letter to the club in 1887. "Our need of sympathy and encouragement has led each one of us at some time—at many times, perhaps,—to wish to clasp the hand and look into the eyes of someone who could understand without a word. . . . For what can be so refreshing to an aspiring soul, that has been stifled in a narrow conventionalism, as to be simply *understood*?"[29] These were compelling words to women such as Robinson, Whitcomb, and Greene, who had endured loneliness at Boston University Law School, as well as others who were lonely in their practice

27. Quoted from Mary Roth Walsh, *"Doctors Wanted: No Women Need Apply": Sexual Barriers in the Medical Profession, 1835–1969* (New Haven, 1977), at 213.

28. Drachman, *Hospital with a Heart.* On women doctors see also Walsh, *"Doctors Wanted"*; Regina Markell Morantz-Sanchez, *Sympathy and Science: Women Physicians in American Medicine* (New York, 1985); and Gloria Melnik Moldow, *Women Doctors in Gilded-Age Washington: Race, Gender and Professionalization* (Champaign, Ill., 1987).

29. Martha K. Pearce to the Equity Club, 1887, Ann Arbor, Equity Club Letters, Dillon Collection.

of the law. They were attracted by the female community and network of support the Equity Club offered them. Laura de Force Gordon, who had fought for women's right to study law at Hastings College of Law in San Francisco, spoke for all women lawyers when she confessed her need for the friendship and support she hoped to find from the women lawyers in the Equity Club. "Every woman in the Legal profession must feel that want of Professional companionship . . . as I have for years longed for expressions, or assurances of that close sympathy born of mutuality of interests, which women alone can extend to a woman."[30]

While the purpose of the Equity Club was to create a female professional community to address the unique needs of women in law, its founders at the University of Michigan took careful steps to ensure that they would not offend their male colleagues in the process. Appreciating the fair treatment they had received from men at the law school, and recognizing how dependent they were upon the good will of these men, the founders of the Equity Club wanted to continue to cultivate these friendly professional relationships. With this in mind, the selection of a name for their club demanded careful consideration. On the one hand, the founders wanted a name that would convey the club's special commitment to the needs of women lawyers. At the same time, they sought a name that would encourage support rather than ignite antagonism from their male colleagues. "We tried to avoid using any name that could raise a suspicion of opposition or rivalry," explained Pearce.[31] In particular, the founders wanted to avoid selecting a name that would convey the erroneous message that they had established a separate all-women's bar association. They feared that a women's bar would not only antagonize male lawyers, but would seem to exclude many potential members, particularly students and nonpracticing lawyers. With the number of women lawyers in the country so small, they needed a name that would welcome as many women in law as possible without alienating male lawyers in the process.

The founders of the Equity Club recognized the need to convey a message of moderation to male lawyers, and they also sought a name

30. Laura de Force Gordon to the Equity Club, April 26, 1887, Stockton, California, Equity Club Letters, Dillon Collection.

31. Pearce, Report of the Corresponding Secretary, 1888, *Equity Club Annual,* 1888, at 6, Equity Club Letters, Dillon Collection.

that would strike a balance for its members between their roles as women and their roles as lawyers. From this point of view, the very naming of the Equity Club was itself an example of women lawyers' perpetual struggle to balance their femininity with their professional identity. Ironically, it was a man, Harry Burns Hutchins, Professor of Equity at the University of Michigan, who provided the founders with the name they sought. His statement, "Equity has been the saviour of woman," conveyed precisely the message the founders wanted, and they seized upon it to name their group the Equity Club.[32]

In speaking of equity, Hutchins harked back to the historical roots of equity law in England during the fourteenth and fifteenth centuries. Equity courts emerged during this era of English legal history because the common law courts were unable to respond to the growing social and legal problems of an increasingly complex English society. The equity court was not an alternative system of justice designed to compete with the common law. Rather, the equity court was a complementary system of law, the purpose of which was to supplement the common law. The equity court had room for the flexibility and fairness that the rigidity of the common law courts made impossible. Thus, one sought fairness and justice from the equity court when the rigidity of the common law threatened a legal but heartless decision.[33]

When Hutchins spoke of equity as the savior of woman, it is likely that he did so because of the popular notion of the equity court as softening the hard and rigid rules of the common law court. Indeed, the equity court embodied the very qualities of femininity as Hutchins's generation conceived it. First, it complemented, rather than competed with, the common law courts. Second, with its emphasis on flexibility and fairness, it held out the hope of justice from the

32. Ibid., and Brown, *Legal Education at Michigan,* at 843.

33. I would like to thank David Chambers for suggesting to me the interpretive meaning of equity for the Equity Club. On the history of the equity courts see Stanley N. Katz, "The Politics of Law in Colonial America: Controversies over Chancery Courts and Equity Law in the Eighteenth Century," in Donald Fleming and Bernard Bailyn, eds., *Perspectives in American History: Law in American History* (Cambridge, 1971), at 257–84; Arthur R. Hogue, *Origins of the Common Law* (Bloomington, 1966), chaps. 7–8; and Bernard C. Gavit, ed., *Blackstone's Commentaries on the Law* (Washington, D.C., 1941). The standard treatise on equity law was published in 1881. See John Norton Pomeroy, LL.D., *A Treatise on Equity Jurisprudence, as Administered in the United States of America* (San Francisco, 1881).

heart, while the common law courts promised rigid and pure legal decisions of the head.

In their search for a name for their club, the founders of the Equity Club found a comfortable place within the boundaries of equity law. Burlingame, for one, decided early in her law school days to specialize in equity law precisely because she believed it to be "a very nice subject for a lady to pursue."[34] As a group, the founders of the Equity Club expanded Hutchins's notion of equity beyond his focus on the law and infused it with their vision of woman's professional place in law. Their interpretation of equity provided them with justification for their place within the male-dominated legal profession. Just as the equity court system supplemented the common law, so they envisioned themselves and other women lawyers as complementing, rather than competing with, male lawyers.

In the long run, the founders of the Equity Club did not seek pure equality with male lawyers, nor did they wish to sacrifice their ties to female culture as they established their professional identity. Rather they sought to bring their femininity to their professional lives. Whereas men claimed that the practice of law demanded an objective mind, most nineteenth-century women lawyers insisted that law required an understanding heart as well. By calling their organization the Equity Club, its founders invoked an age-old legal tradition and reassured men and women alike that women lawyers would complement their male colleagues, not compete with them.

Having settled on the name for their organization, the founders of the Equity Club sent invitations to sixty-two women to join. Requirements for membership were simple: an annual letter and annual dues of twenty-five cents. The dues covered the costs of postage, stationery, copyright, and printing. The letters formed the backbone of the club and were the primary requirement for membership. A woman who sent dues without a letter was not admitted as a member. On the other hand, if a woman sent a letter without dues, she was occasionally accepted depending on the circumstances.[35]

Of the sixty-two women invited to join, only fourteen women responded with letters for circulation in the first year. Significantly, ten

34. Burlingame, *Lettie Lavilla Burlingame,* at 322.

35. Pearce, Report of the Corresponding Secretary, 1888, *Equity Club Annual,* 1888, at 5, 9, Equity Club Letters, Dillon Collection.

were either alumnae or students of the University of Michigan Law School. Over the course of the four years of the Equity Club's life, a total of thirty-two women participated. Membership varied by year; while only fourteen women joined in 1887, twenty-two participated in 1888. Sixteen were new members, and six had been members the year before. Eight of the original group from 1887 dropped out. The year 1888 marked the peak of membership in the Equity Club. In 1889, there were no new members and ten women dropped out, leaving only twelve women in the Equity Club. In 1890, the last year of the Equity Club, two new members joined, but they were part of an even smaller group of eleven members.

Despite the turnover in membership, there was some continuity as well. Nine women were members for at least three years, five of whom were members all four years. Of this group of five, three—Martha Pearce, Almeda Hitchcock, and Margaret Wilcox—were among the original founders back in 1886. The other two were Lelia Robinson and Mary Greene, the first two graduates of Boston University Law School.

Altogether the thirty-two members of the Equity Club wrote sixty letters. They sent their letters to Martha Pearce who, as corresponding secretary, was responsible for collecting the letters and preparing them for circulation among the members. The original plan was to print the letters each year and to distribute a copy of the printed collection to each member. But the initial membership fee of twenty-five cents was too small to cover the cost of printing and mailing the letters. Hampered by a lack of funds in the club's first year, Pearce had to send out the original letters. One by one, individual club members received the collection of letters for 1887 and often held onto them until they made personal copies before they sent them on to others. In 1888, Pearce received twenty-two letters, many of which were significantly longer than any she had received the year before. With the dues increased to two dollars, Pearce was able to publish the letters as the *Equity Club Annual,* and she included an extensive secretary's report in which she detailed the history of the club's founding as well as its purpose, organization, and structure. In addition, Pearce raised issues and asked questions regarding social and professional matters, and she made suggestions for the future direction of the club. Her hope was that members would discuss these matters with each other in their future letters.

The time involved in producing the *Equity Club Annual* in 1888, plus the dramatic decline in the number of letters to twelve in 1889, combined to discourage Pearce from continuing in her position as corresponding secretary. At the same time, she was disheartened by the decline in members. "The letters she longed for never came," she lamented.[36] Moreover, she felt burdened by the time and responsibility her job as corresponding secretary demanded. In 1889, Pearce called for someone to replace her, but no one volunteered to take her place. As a result, the *Annual* was not published in 1889 and 1890. Instead, the letters were copied into a letter book and the original letters were circulated as in 1887.

The thirty-two women who comprised the membership of the Equity Club shared certain characteristics in common. All were white, American-born, and middle class. Women of color, different ethnic groups, or working-class backgrounds did not enter the legal profession in any measurable numbers until the turn of the century. The opening of part-time evening law schools such as Portia Law School in Boston and Washington College of Law in Washington, D.C., permitted working-class and immigrant women to study law at night while they continued to work during the day. In addition, the admission of women to the law school of Howard University in Washington, D.C., made it possible for a small number of African-American women to study law as well. But the Equity Club members were part of an earlier era when women lawyers, and male lawyers as well, comprised a homogeneous profession in terms of race, class, and ethnicity.[37]

In other ways, the members of the Equity Club were a diverse group. They came from urban centers such as Boston and Chicago, smaller cities like Omaha, Nebraska, and Iowa City, Iowa, and small towns such as Hutchinson, Kansas, and Tiffin, Ohio. In addition, there were three European members, one from England, France, and Switzerland, respectively. While they spanned the country from Massachusetts to California, a majority of twenty were from the Midwest and West, where law schools and state bars had a tradition of accept-

36. Martha Pearce, Report of the Corresponding Secretary, [1889], Equity Club Letters, Dillon Collection.

37. Charlotte Ray was unique in the era of the Equity Club. She was an African-American woman who graduated from the law school of Howard University in 1872 and was the first woman admitted to practice law in Washington, D.C. the same year.

ing women, while only seven lived in cities and towns in the East. Nine lived in large cities, three each from Boston, Chicago, and Washington, D.C., which were accustomed to women in professional work, social reform, and other activities in the public arena.

The members of the Equity Club ranged in age from their mid-twenties to their late fifties. At one end of the spectrum were young women such as Almeda Hitchcock, Jessie Wright Whitcomb, and Catharine Waugh McCulloch who, in their mid-twenties, were just embarking on their legal careers. Most of the Equity Club members were in their thirties and forties. They had completed their legal training and had settled into the pattern of their adult lives, whether it was legal practice, reform work, or care of home and family. Only two members, Belva Lockwood and Catharine Waite, were in their fifties. At the ages of fifty-seven and fifty-nine, respectively, they were the Equity Club's link with the first generation of the Woman Movement in antebellum America. Waite, a leader in the post–Civil War woman suffrage movement, did not enter law school until she was fifty-six. At the Union College of Law (Northwestern), she befriended a fellow student, young Catharine Waugh, and introduced her to another classmate, Frank McCulloch. Waugh married Frank McCulloch and became known as Catharine Waugh McCulloch. After Waite graduated, she went on to publish a legal journal, the *Chicago Law Times,* and became president of the International Woman's Bar Association.

Belva Lockwood was the first woman admitted to practice before the United State Supreme Court. She was the quintessential pioneer among nineteenth-century women lawyers, having overcome sexual discrimination to open the doors for herself and other women to the legal profession. She gave inspiration to younger women and served as the model of success for generations of women lawyers who followed after her.

While certainly the most well known of all nineteenth-century women lawyers, Lockwood was by no means the only pioneer among the Equity Club members. In fact, there was an impressive number of members who were the first among women to break barriers in the legal profession. Ada Kepley, a graduate of Union College of Law (Northwestern) in 1870, was the first woman to earn a law degree in America. Sarah Killgore Wertman was the first woman to graduate from the law school of the University of Michigan and the first woman admitted to the Michigan State Bar. Similarly, Lelia J. Robinson was the first woman to graduate from Boston University Law School and the first woman to gain admission to the bar of Massachusetts. Mary Wilkinson was the first woman to graduate from the University of Iowa Law School. Ada Bittenbender, Mary Greene, and Almeda Hitchcock were the first women to break the sexual barriers to the state bars of Nebraska, Rhode Island, and Hawaii, respectively. Several Equity Club members were ground breakers in other ways. Laura de Force Gordon, along with another California woman, Clara Foltz, brought a law suit against the University of California that opened the Hastings College of Law in San Francisco to women.[38] Emma Gillett, along with a friend of hers, Ellen Spencer Mussey, opened the Washington College of Law, a law school for women in Washington, D.C. Though Gillett and Mussey were willing to admit men to their law school, their primary goal was to provide legal education to women.[39] Catharine Waite managed and edited the *Chicago Law Times,* the law journal she owned with her husband.

With so many club members accomplishing so much, the women of the Equity Club were certainly an impressive group. In pursuing their own careers with conviction and persistence, they broke long-established barriers against women in the legal profession and opened the way for women to follow after them.

While more than a third of the American Equity Club members were part of this impressive group of pioneers and pathbreakers among women in the legal profession, most of the members made less notable accomplishments. But as they studied and practiced law, they too, in their own way, widened the pathway for women lawyers who came after them. All but a handful were graduates of law schools. In an age that predated the shift from apprenticeship to formal legal education, the Equity Club members were part of a small group within the legal profession who had gone to law school.

At the same time that they were unique among women and lawyers of their day, all of the Equity Club members, even the pioneers, led

38. On Laura de Force Gordon see the biographical sketch by Corinne L. Gibb in Edward T. James, ed., *Notable American Women, 1607–1950: A Biographical Dictionary* (Cambridge, Massachusetts, 1971), at 68–69 and Barbara Allen Babcock, "Clara Shortridge Foltz: Constitution Maker," 66 *Indiana Law Journal* 849–940 (1991).

39. On the Washington College of Law see Grace Hathaway, *Fate Rides a Tortoise: A Biography of Ellen Spencer Mussey* (Philadelphia, 1937).

lives that reflected the patterns of life for middle-class women in Victorian America. More than a third of the members had been teachers before they entered law. Because of the lack of opportunity for women in other professions, they flocked to teaching along with thousands of other women in the last quarter of the nineteenth century. A few, such as Cora Benneson and Jane Slocum, returned to the field of education after they completed their legal training. But most of those who taught, including Lockwood, Bittenbender, and Wertman, ultimately found it either unsatisfying or not lucrative enough and seized upon law as a preferable alternative.

While many Equity Club members shared the experience of teaching with other women of their day, they also participated with them in a number of reform activities. As thousands of women in the last decades of the nineteenth century left their homes to work on behalf of a wide range of reforms, many of the Equity Club members joined them in this Woman Movement, particularly to fight on behalf of suffrage and temperance. Some even took leadership roles. Bittenbender, for one, served as legal counsel for the Women's Christian Temperance Union, while McCulloch, Gillett, and Gordon were leaders in the suffrage movements in Illinois, Washington, D.C., and California, respectively. McCulloch, Robinson, and other women lawyers in the Equity Club also expanded the parameters of the Woman Movement by bringing their knowledge of the law to the question of women's legal rights, particularly property rights and custody rights. These were issues that only women lawyers, with their legal training, were qualified to address among all other nineteenth-century feminists. By contributing their legal expertise to the suffrage and temperance movements, the women lawyers of the Equity Club did more than participate in the Woman Movement; they took their place at its very center.

This diverse group of thirty-two women came together once a year through their letters. The Equity Club provided a way for them to ask questions, give advice, express their hopes and fears, and share the successes and setbacks in their professional and personal lives. While a few wrote tentatively, intimidated somewhat by the accomplishments of some of the members, they all participated enthusiastically and expectantly. The long silences between their annual letters tested their patience as they waited months to hear from one another. But their persistence revealed their need for each other and their commitment to the Equity Club at a time when they had few if any other opportunities to share their thoughts with other women lawyers. Moreover, their letters from year to year revealed a remarkable continuity in their subject matter as they responded to each other's queries, though twelve months later. At the same time, a great deal transpired in their lives over the course of a year, and members shared with each other some of the most significant professional and personal moments in their lives. Some graduated from law school, others passed the bar, while still others had important legal victories. A few married and one had a baby, while others had to stop work to care for sick relatives. As they communicated these events with each other from year to year, Equity Club members created a strong though short-lived network of support for each other. They were candid and trusting with each other as they addressed controversial professional matters and asked each other for advice. They were not afraid to disagree, but they always did so with respect and good humor. And they willingly shared some of the most intimate details of their personal lives.

The specific matters the Equity Club members discussed in their letters grew out of the realities of their public and private lives. They sought each other's advice on a range of issues including how to dress as lawyers while retaining their femininity, whether women lawyers belonged in the courtroom, whether they could succeed in the business of law while preserving their ties to charity and reform, how to balance marriage and career, and whether a woman had the physical constitution to withstand the demands of law practice. The diversity of these issues reveals the spectrum of concerns for women lawyers in the late nineteenth century. At the same time, at the heart of all of these issues was a common theme: how to be both a lady and a lawyer in the late nineteenth century. As women lawyers in the Equity Club corresponded about a range of issues, they simultaneously grappled with this dilemma of how to strike a balance between femininity and professional identity.

Lelia Robinson was one of the first members to raise the sticky problem of the place of femininity in women lawyers' professional lives. "*Do not take sex* into the practice," she wrote in her letter to the Equity Club in 1887. "Don't be 'lady lawyers.' Simply be *lawyers,* and recognize no distinction—no existence of any distinction between yourselves and the other members of the bar."[40] Robinson's straightforward advice launched a debate among the members of the Equity Club over how to balance their femininity and their professional identity. The letters from Ellen Martin and Emma Gillett the following year supported Robinson's advice to emphasize their responsibilities as lawyers over their roles as women. But others such as Ada Kepley and Sarah Killgore Wertman disagreed and urged their sister club members to emphasize their womanhood in their practice of the law. The result, Kepley claimed, would be "sweeter manners—purer laws."[41] But Kepley and Wertman did not have the final word. The dialogue continued in 1889 when Florence Cronise, in response to Kepley, declared herself "too matter of fact" to sympathize with her "sisters of the Equity Club who think woman's mission in the profession is to purify."[42]

In fact, the question of the role of femininity in their professional lives underscored every matter the Equity Club members discussed. From their debate over the professional question of the propriety of the bonnet in the courtroom to their discussion of the very private matter of the sexual rights of the married woman lawyer, the Equity Club members could not escape the gnawing problem of how to be at once a lady and a lawyer. For example, the matter lay at the very center of their debate over the place of philanthropy and reform in their professional lives. Victorian-American society created a clear distinction between business and charity. Business was defined as men's domain because it demanded the objectivity and hard-heartedness believed to be inherent to manhood. Charity and reform were accepted as part of women's domain because they relied on the supposedly womanly virtues of nurturance and sentimentality. This sharp division between men's business and women's charity and reform created another source of tension for women lawyers in the late nineteenth century. As women, it was appropriate for them to engage

40. Lelia J. Robinson to Equity Club, April 9, 1887, Calvert, Texas, Equity Club Letters, Dillon Collection.

41. Ada H. Kepley to the Equity Club, July 3, 1888, Effingham, Illinois, *Equity Club Annual,* 1888, at 30, Equity Club Letters, Dillon Collection.

42. Florence Cronise to the Equity Club, 1889, Equity Club Letters, Dillon Collection.

in charity and reform. But as lawyers, it was more acceptable for them to restrict themselves strictly to business and professional concerns.

There was little consensus among the women lawyers in the Equity Club over the place of charity and social reform in their professional lives. Some argued that law and charity could not mix. These women adopted the male lawyer's model of success. They believed that in order to succeed in law, they must follow a man's example and harden themselves to the urge to engage in philanthropy and charity. Cronise expressed this view when she wrote to the Equity Club: "No thought of being a public benefactor ever entered my head. I cannot accept sentimental views of woman's mission—This world is plain, hard facts."[43] Cronise's hard-hearted approach contrasted sharply with the image of the kind-hearted and nurturing woman of her day. But she was not alone among the Equity Club members in her impatience with charity and her rejection of sentimentality. Emma Gillett, for one, shared Cronise's view. "Nothing is more wearing than sympathy," she wrote. "I have cultivated a hardness of heart. . . . Charity clients should be shunned unless in extreme cases. . . ."[44]

Women like Gillett and Cronise linked charity with the sentimentality of True Womanhood and hard-heartedness with the objectivity of the law. In doing so, they created an equation that left no room for philanthropy in their professional lives. With a clear conscience and with women's best interest foremost in their minds, they chose career over compassion, and self-interest over social reform. But to these women, charity was not simply a matter for each woman lawyer to reconcile with professionalism on her own. Rather, they transformed the question of charity work into a political issue, making it a test of women's commitment to the cause of women lawyers. From their point of view, the survival of a woman lawyer's career came before the legal needs of an impoverished client. Charity work impeded the progress of an individual woman lawyer and by extension that of the community of women lawyers. Thus, the woman lawyer who took on charity work indulged in sentiment at the expense of her own professional advancement as well as the best interests of all women lawyers. In contrast, the woman lawyer who rejected charity work proved her

---

43. Ibid.

44. Emma M. Gillett to the Equity Club, April 27, 1889, Washington, D.C., Equity Club Letters, Dillon Collection.

personal commitment to her own professional success as well as her political allegiance to the larger cause of women in law.

Other members of the Equity Club posed an alternative model of practice rooted in the nineteenth-century values of ideal womanhood. They argued that the politically appropriate act was to incorporate charity and reform into their professional lives. Unlike Cronise and others who defined individual business success as the ultimate goal of the woman lawyer, these women lawyers shared the view that society came before self, and they urged others to put charity and reform at the heart of their professional lives. "There is something besides law to be studied," Marion Todd wrote to the Equity Club in 1888. "It is human justice." Referring to the poor women and children who toiled in factories and sweatshops, Todd insisted that women lawyers had an obligation to use their legal expertise to help the victims of industrial capitalism.[45] Todd was not alone in her call to women lawyers to help others. Catharine Waugh McCulloch confessed that "... it is difficult for me to resist outside pressure to help in church, temperance, and suffrage work."[46] Not only did she graciously accept women clients who were too poor to pay her, but throughout her professional life, McCulloch was a leader on behalf of a range of women's causes including temperance, suffrage, jury duty, and women's custody rights. Other women lawyers shared McCulloch's commitment to reform. Ada Kepley, the advocate of "sweeter manners—purer laws," was an ardent supporter of temperance who gave years of legal advice to the Women's Christian Temperance Union.[47] Ada Bittenbender combined her legal expertise with her commitment to reform and earned her livelihood as legal counsel to the Women's Christian Temperance Union [WCTU]. Bit-

45. Mrs. Marion Todd to the Equity Club, April 4, 1888, Albion, Michigan, *Equity Club Annual,* 1888, at 48, Equity Club Letters, Dillon Collection.

46. Catharine G. Waugh to the Equity Club, April 26, 1889, Rockford, Illinois, Equity Club Letters, Dillon Collection. On Catharine Waugh McCulloch see Nancy Cott, "Women as Law Clerks: Memoir of Catharine G. Waugh," in Domna Stanton, ed., *The Female Autograph* (New York Literary Forum, 1984), 12–13 and Paul S. Boyer, "Catharine Gouger Waugh McCulloch," in James, *Notable American Women, 1607–1950,* at 459–60.

47. On Ada H. Kepley see Mrs. Peggy Pulliam, "Effingham's Fighting Female," in Hilde Engbring Feldhake, ed., *Effingham County Illinois—Past and Present* (Effingham, Ill., 1968), at 299–310 and Ada H. Kepley, *A Farm Philosophy: A Love Story* (Teutopolis, Ill., 1912).

tenbender disagreed with women lawyers who believed that close ties to reform groups would detract from her professional advancement. "We who have taken up 'side issues' receive many a rap in the [Equity Club] Annual from you who have not or who have ceased to do so. . . ." She insisted that it was precisely because of her efforts on behalf of the WCTU that she met powerful male lawyers and politicians in Washington, D.C., men she would never have encountered without "'dabbling in side issues.'"[48]

While the women lawyers in the Equity Club grappled with the question of the place of charity and reform in their professional lives, they also tried to reconcile the problem of how to balance marriage and career. Lelia Robinson, perhaps contemplating marriage to her future husband, first brought up the issue in her letter to the Equity Club in 1889. "Is it practicable for a woman to successfully fulfill the duties of wife, mother, and lawyer at the same time? Especially a young married woman?" she asked.[49] Robinson's query was part of an ongoing discussion among Equity Club members about the relationship of marriage and family to their professional lives.

Single members of the Equity Club typically chose not to marry precisely because they believed that marriage imposed too many domestic obligations on women and was, therefore, incompatible with a serious career. "A glance through the [Equity Club] Annual," wrote Gillett, "would seem to indicate that the majority of the practitioners who are sticking to their work and plodding on in the sure and safe way to win success are unmarried."[50] Believing that they had to make a choice between marriage and career, single women sacrificed the former in hopes of establishing productive professional lives. Even Marion Todd, who had been married once but was a widow by the time she joined the Equity Club, insisted that she had no intention of remarrying, declaring that, from her experience, marriage was "too great a responsibility."[51]

While many Equity Club members followed the path of the single life that was typical of most nineteenth-century professional women,

48. Ada Bittenbender to the Equity Club, May 10, 1889, Washington, D.C., Equity Club Letters, Dillon Collection.

49. Lelia J. Robinson to the Equity Club, May 22, Boston, Mass., 1889, Equity Club Letters, Dillon Collection.

50. Gillett to the Equity Club, April 27, 1889, Equity Club Letters, Dillon Collection.

51. Todd to the Equity Club, April 4, 1888, *Equity Club Annual,* 1888, at 47, Equity Club Letters, Dillon Collection.

more than one-half (seventeen) of the members of the Equity Club were married. These married Equity Club members mirrored the marital patterns of women lawyers of their day. When Equity Club member Lelia Robinson sought to gather information on as many women lawyers in the country as possible, she found that one-half of the 120 women lawyers and law students she identified in 1890 were married. As Robinson concluded, the late nineteenth-century woman lawyer "exists to quite a numerical degree in the married state as in that of single blessedness."[52] Moreover, in contrast to the Victorian notion that marriage and career were incompatible for women, most of the seventeen married women in the Equity Club continued to practice after they married. Among this group of married, working women, eight were married to other lawyers and were in practice with their husbands. For these women, marriage enhanced rather than impeded their careers. In contrast to single women who typically had to confront sexual discrimination and the difficult search for work on their own, women lawyers who were married to lawyers usually found that their husbands not only shielded them from public disapproval but provided them with a secure and welcoming place in which to work.

Women lawyers whose husbands were lawyers typically shared a practice with them. In contrast to the idealistic notion that women should enter the law to help other women, most married women lawyers practiced law with the practical goal of helping their husbands. Married women lawyers such as Mary Haddock and Laura LeValley devoted their professional lives to assisting their husbands in their practice. Emma Haddock wrote to the Equity Club that her husband, a lawyer in solo practice, urged her to "enter the law school and prepare [herself] for office work."[53] Similarly, Corinne Douglas's husband explained to Lelia Robinson in a letter on his wife's behalf that "she studied law for the purpose of helping me and not for the practice generally."[54] Ironically, the Douglases settled in Atlanta,

52. Lelia J. Robinson, "Women Lawyers in the United States," 2 *Green Bag* 10–31 (1890), quote at 11. The numbers of women lawyers reported in my earlier essays were based on calculations from Robinson's "Women Lawyers in the United States" (1890). The numbers reported here reflect further research into the lives of the women lawyers after 1890.

53. Emma Haddock to the Equity Club, May 12, 1888, Iowa City, Iowa, *Equity Club Annual,* 1888, at 24, Equity Club Letters, Dillon Collection.

54. Robinson, "Women Lawyers in the United States," at 19.

Georgia, where women were not admitted to the bar. Despite the best intentions of Corinne Douglas and her husband, she was unable to practice law with him, and she ended up devoting her married life to the care of her family as well as charity and education.

In cases where husband and wife could practice together, both benefitted in important ways by sharing a law practice. For the husband in solo practice, as most lawyers were in the 1880s, the presence of a wife trained in the law could significantly reduce expenses as well as increase the ability of the law office to transact more business. Moreover, his wife was an assistant whom he could trust and who he knew would promote the welfare of the practice. For her part, the wife did not have to worry about the expenses of renting or furnishing an office, nor did she have to worry to the same extent as a single woman about the problem of attracting clients. But the advantages for the married woman of sharing a practice with her husband went well beyond financial concerns. By assisting her husband in his law practice, a married woman lawyer came close to personifying the image of the lady lawyer. Unlike single women lawyers who often had to go into court, whether they wanted to or not, a married woman lawyer could rely on her husband to bring cases before a judge or jury. As a result, she could avoid the public scrutiny of the courtroom and stay protected within the privacy of the office.

The debate over the appropriateness of courtroom work for the woman lawyer was a matter of great concern to the members of the Equity Club, whether they were married or single. The courtroom was considered the epitomy of the male domain in the legal profession. To most contemporary observers, this arena of legal combat where lawyers encountered "all the unclean issues of society" and where only the strongest of lawyers survived, was no place for a lady.[55] In contrast, the office was deemed the appropriate arena for women in the legal profession. While the courtroom duplicated the rough and tumble of the public arena, the office mirrored the privacy of the home. Office work demanded the same focus on organization, efficiency, and detail that was expected of the Victorian lady in her home. It was the site of negotiation, compromise, and settlement, the skills of the ideal wife and mother.

---

55. William P. Rogers, "Is Law a Field for Women's Work?" 24 *American Bar Association Report* 548–64 (1901), quote at 557.

Despite the prevailing view that the office was women lawyers' proper arena of work, the Equity Club members did not reach a consensus on the matter. Simply put, they were not all willing to turn over the courtroom to men. Some explained that they could not sufficiently service their clients from within their offices. Others admitted that they preferred the activity and publicity of the courtroom to the privacy of the office. Still others explained that courtroom work was more lucrative than office work.

But not all women lawyers in the Equity Club claimed equal rights to the courtroom. Many members preferred to restrict their practice to office work. Though they sometimes had to go to court, single women such as Gillett and Robinson tried to handle all their work in the office. In contrast, married women whose husbands were lawyers, such as Haddock, LeValley, and McCulloch, could rely on their husbands to handle courtroom matters while they stayed exclusively within the privacy of the office.

Emma Haddock, for one, explained that because she worked with her husband, she did not need "to take public part in the practice," and that, in fact, she "preferred the preparation of a case to its argument."[56] Laura LeValley described her situation similarly. "I have never made an effort to take an active part in court. In fact I never intended to do so, but have been assisting my husband in the office, and have given much time to stenography and office work. . . ."[57]

The professional arrangements women such as LeValley and Haddock made with their husbands mirrored the sexual division of labor that characterized Victorian-American marriages. Litigation and courtroom work tended to be the domain of the husband. This work demanded assertiveness, strength, and self-confidence, the perceived characteristics of nineteenth-century manhood. The office tasks the wife typically undertook, including legal research, the preparation of wills, real estate closings, case preparations, stenography, typing, and office management, mirrored her domestic role and demanded the same attention to detail and managerial skills as her housekeeping duties. This arrangement moderated the tension between marriage and career for women lawyers who were in practice with their husbands. The wife was the True Woman transposed into the safety of

56. Robinson, "Women Lawyers in the United States," at 19.

57. Laura LeValley to the Equity Club, April 20, 1888, East Saginaw, Mich., *Equity Club Annual,* 1888, at 31, Equity Club Letters, Dillon Collection.

her husband's office, working modestly and unobtrusively behind the scenes while he worked aggressively in the public eye.

The question of women's place in the courtroom led naturally to another matter of debate taken quite seriously by members of the club—the appropriate attire for the woman lawyer who had to go to court. Again, Lelia Robinson posed the question for the Equity Club. "Shall the woman attorney wear her hat when arguing a case or making a motion in court," she asked in 1888, "or shall she remove it?"[58] With this query, Robinson once again confronted her sisters in the Equity Club with the challenge of reconciling their traditional roles as women with their new roles as lawyers. From the point of view of social convention, which required a lady to wear a hat in public, it was appropriate for a woman lawyer to wear a hat when she ventured into the courtroom. But professional etiquette dictated that as a lawyer she remove her hat when she entered the courtroom, just as her male colleagues did. Thus, the matter of the hat, seemingly a frivolity of fashion, posed in actuality a perplexing problem for the woman lawyer seeking to balance her femininity and her professional identity.

The Equity Club members lined up on both sides of the question. Robinson spoke on behalf of the hat. She acknowledged that she followed her feelings on the matter and wore her hat in court because it made her feel more comfortable before the judge and jury. Catharine Waugh McCulloch objected to Robinson's willingness to succumb to sentiment and urged the Equity Club members "on principle" to remove their hats in the courtroom just as men did.[59] Other Equity Club members, including Burlingame and Wilcox, rejected both Robinson's ties to tradition and McCulloch's quest for equality and claimed, instead, every woman lawyer's right to make the decision for herself. "I maintain it is the inalienable right of each lady to follow her 'own sweet will,'" wrote Wilcox in her letter in 1889.[60]

The hat debate focused on the most public of arenas, the courtroom. In contrast, the issue of women lawyers' health and sexuality

58. Lelia J. Robinson to the Equity Club, April 7, 1888, Boston, Mass., *Equity Club Annual,* at 45, Equity Club Letters, Dillon Collection.

59. Catharine G. Waugh McCulloch to the Equity Club, May 2, 1888, Rockford, Ill., *Equity Club Annual,* at 51, Equity Club Letters, Dillon Collection.

60. Margaret L. Wilcox to the Equity Club, June 1, 1889, Chicago, Illinois, Equity Club Letters, Dillon Collection.

forced the Equity Club members to face the innermost sanctums of their private lives. More than any other issue, the matter of women's health and sexuality reveals how deeply the problem of balancing their dual roles as women and as lawyers penetrated women lawyers' personal lives. Female health was a highly controversial issue in the late nineteenth-century United States and one which the Equity Club took very seriously. Their debate about women's physiological ability to endure the strains of law practice occurred within the context of the larger social debate about the fragility of women's health.

Prevailing medical wisdom defined women as physiologically unsuited to undertake rigorous mental work after the onset of puberty. The physician most responsible for popularizing this view was Edward H. Clarke, a professor at Harvard Medical College. In 1873, he published *Sex in Education; or, a Fair Chance for the Girls,* which explained the supposed weaknesses of female physiology to the general reader. Wrapped in the banner of medical authority, *Sex in Education* was an assault on the new phenomenon of coeducation. Clarke warned that women's reproductive physiology made it unsafe for them to undertake any intellectual activity with the same rigor as men. Excessive study, he explained, diverted energy from the female reproductive organs to the brain, causing a breakdown in women's health and threatening the health of future generations.[61]

Sex in Education was widely read, placing advocates of education for women on the defensive. In the years immediately following the book's publication, the president of Smith College anxiously defended the school against Clarke's arguments in his annual report to the board of trustees. Even M. Carey Thomas, the first female president of Bryn Mawr College, acknowledged that she did not know when Bryn Mawr first opened "whether woman's health could stand the strain of education. We were haunted in those days by the clanging chains of that gloomy little specter, Dr. Edward H. Clarke's *Sex in Education.*"[62]

61. Edward H. Clarke, *Sex in Education; or, a Fair Chance for the Girls* (Boston, 1873).

62. M. Carey Thomas, "Present Tendencies in Women's Colleges and University Education," 25 *Educational Review* 68 (1908). In 1874, the year after *Sex in Education* was originally published, four books challenging Clarke appeared: Anna C. Brackett, ed., *The Education of American Girls Considered in a Series of Essays* (New York, 1874); Julia Ward Howe, ed., *Sex in Education: A Reply to Dr. E. H. Clarke's "Sex in Education"* (Boston, 1874); George Fisk Comfort and A. M. Comfort, *Woman's Education and Woman's*

Sex in Education reached beyond the boundaries of the elite women's colleges in the Northeast to large public universities such as the University of Michigan. The local bookseller in Ann Arbor sold over 200 copies of the book in a single day. Olive San Louie Anderson, one of the early female students at the University of Michigan, reminisced about the impact of the book on the university community. "Dr. Clarke's book was discussed by more than the girls in Clinton Street. The boys read it and delivered their opinion at length among themselves. The president and the faculty read it, and shook their heads doubtfully about the 'experiment in coeducation.'"[63]

In 1886, Charles C. Moore, a lawyer in Litchfield, Connecticut, and a frequent contributor to law journals such as *Law Notes, Case and Comment,* and the *Green Bag,* applied Clarke's theories about women's health specifically to women in law. In a short story entitled "The Woman Lawyer," Moore linked the personal matter of women's health with other issues the Equity Club would eventually confront, namely, the advantages of marriage and the place of women lawyers in the courtroom. Moore told the tale of a young woman lawyer, Mary Padelford, who moved to a small town in Connecticut to set up a solo law practice. Single and alone, Padelford's vulnerability was accentuated all the more by the fact that "her health had never been exceedingly rugged." As she struggled to build her law practice, her health gradually declined. One day she finally fainted from exhaustion in court. Diagnosed by the doctor as "seriously ill," she prepared to give up her career and leave town. But at the last moment, she married a local attorney and entered into a law partnership with him. It was clear to the reader that the new wife, under the protective

---

Health: Chiefly in Reply to "Sex in Education" (Syracuse, 1874); and Eliza Bisbee Duffey, *No Sex in Education; or an Equal Chance for Both Boys and Girls* (Philadelphia, 1874). The outrage of many nineteenth-century women at *Sex in Education* has been echoed by contemporary historians who have interpreted Clarke's book as a dangerous threat to women's rights. See Walsh, *"Doctors Wanted,"* chap. 4.

63. Olive San Louie Anderson, *An American Girl and Her Four Years in a Boys' College* (New York, 1878), at 96. Ironically, while men and women alike debated the question of women's health at the University of Michigan, the only incidents of students leaving the law school because of failing health from April, 1894, through June, 1895, involved four young men. See Faculty Minutes of Law Department, University of Michigan, April 27, 1894, to June 21, 1895, in Michigan University Law School Records, Box 49, Bentley Historical Library.

eye of her loving husband, would stay in the office and no longer exhaust herself in the courtroom.[64]

Stories such as "The Woman Lawyer" not only nourished the notion that women lawyers' proper place was in the office, they also popularized the medical arguments about the limits of women's health. The women lawyers of the Equity Club understood all too well that the warnings of Clarke and other physicians threatened their desires for professional careers. But, within the privacy of the Equity Club, where they could openly discuss their concerns about health, Equity Club members did not unanimously reject Clarke's ideas. Ellen Martin first brought the issue into the open in her letter to the Equity Club in 1888 when she warned her fellow club members about the delicacy of the female reproductive system. Sharing Clarke's view, she wrote: "I refer to the close relation between the brain and the organs peculiar to women, and to the fact that any trouble with those organs (and a celebrated anatomist says they seem made to get out of order) seriously affects the brain and the nervous system."[65]

Martin's view reflected the tragic death of her partner and beloved friend, Mary Fredrika Perry, in 1883. Perry, a young woman in her early thirties, had a reputation in Chicago for being a hardworking attorney who never lost a case. At the same time, she was well known for her kindhearted sympathy toward the needy. Not only did she devote much of her time to providing free legal services for poor women, but she was generous in other ways as well. Shortly before she became ill, she braved one of the coldest of Chicago's winter storms to give away warm clothing to the needy. To Martin, Perry was a small woman who could not withstand the demands of her rigorous work schedule or the imprudence of her charitable deeds, so she became weak and sick. There was no question in Martin's mind. "Miss Perry's death was caused by overwork," she wrote to the Equity Club, eerily echoing Clarke's own words.[66]

64. Charles C. Moore, "The Woman Lawyer," 26 *Green Bag* 525– 31 (1914), quotes at 527. See also D. Kelly Weisberg, "Barred from the Bar: Women and Legal Education in the United States 1870–1890," 28 *Journal of Legal Education* 485–507 (1977).

65. Ellen A. Martin to the Equity Club, May 25, 1888, Chicago, Ill., *Equity Club Annual,* 1888, at 34–35, Equity Club Letters, Dillon Collection.

66. "M. Fredrika Perry," 15 *Chicago Legal News* 825–26 (June 30, 1883) and "Chicago Women," 12 *Chicago Legal News* 434 (September 4, 1880).

Perry's death gave Martin reason to be cautious not to overwork in her own law practice. As a result, Martin preferred office work to the stress of the courtroom, and she gave money rather than her labor to charity cases. But when she warned her sisters in the Equity Club about the delicacy of female physiology, she touched off a debate about the impact of women's health on women lawyers' professional lives that placed her in the extreme minority.

In reading the club letters for the 1888 *Annual,* Corresponding Secretary Martha Pearce recognized the significance of Martin's views on women's delicate nature, and invited other members of the Equity Club to respond. "I am not sorry that she wrote it down," explained Pearce, "for when there is any evil abroad it is better to talk about it and find out why it exists, and how it can be overcome, than to leave it alone."[67] The Equity Club members responded enthusiastically to Pearce's call to debate the question of women's health. From their letters, it was clear that Martin's views were in a distinct minority. Only Emma Gillett acknowledged that she had a weak constitution and limited her practice to office work because of her delicate health. "I have never gone into jury cases and have done very little court work, but I deliberately chose this course at the beginning as I knew by experience that my nervous organism would break under the strain." But Gillett was quick to point out that her weak constitution was unique to her, not a natural condition of womanhood. "This lack of nervous endurance I do not count as a feminine failing," she wrote. Nor did she believe that her weak constitution was unchangeable. Instead, she explained that she had improved her health and strengthened her body through a steady regimen of exercise and diet.[68]

The Equity Club members overwhelmingly agreed with Gillett that it was the material conditions of women's lives, rather than a weakness inherent to women's reproductive physiology, that was responsible for their physical problems. In particular, they pointed to three components of women's life style that were crucial to women's health: a daily regimen of diet and exercise, meaningful work, and respectful sexual relations between husband and wife. While Clarke's *Sex in*

67. Pearce, Report of the Corresponding Secretary, 1888, *Equity Club Annual,* 1888, at 10–11, Equity Club Letters, Dillon Collection.

68. Gillett to Equity Club, April 27, 1889, Equity Club Letters, Dillon Collection.

Education carried the weight of medical theory, the opinions of the Equity Club members grew out of their personal experiences. Practical reality rather than ideology shaped their responses to Martin's letter.

Catharine Waugh McCulloch, then a young unmarried lawyer in Rockford, Illinois, echoed the wisdom of the health reformers in the antebellum period, and explained that she believed the key to health for women was exercise, diet, and sensible clothing. Moreover, she insisted that law was an ideal profession for women because there were few emergencies as in medicine, so women could postpone cases if necessary and "be sick in comfort."

Letitia Burlingame challenged Clarke's warning about the dangerous consequences of mental activity, and explained to the Equity Club that meaningful work had enhanced her physical and mental well-being. Burlingame, who had been sickly ever since childhood, continued to suffer ill health during twelve years of teaching. When she took up the study of law at the University of Michigan, her friends feared that her health would decline even further. But she became stronger and healthier in law school. "My health has steadily improved, so that I am now stronger than ever before," she wrote to the Equity Club.[69] Two years later, at the end of her first year of practice, Burlingame brought up the topic of her health once again. Referring directly to Martin's concerns about women's "delicate organization," Burlingame explained that her health had continued to thrive during the first year of her active law practice. "I am now stronger and able to endure more than at any other period of my life. Indeed I stand courtroom work better than many of the men," she wrote proudly.[70]

Tragically, despite her claims to health, Burlingame died a year and a half later from influenza. She was only thirty-one years old. And Burlingame was not the only member of the Equity Club to suffer an untimely death. Almeda Hitchcock died in 1895 at the age of thirty-two, and Lelia Robinson died in 1891 at the age of forty. While both deaths cut short the professional careers of two budding women lawyers, neither woman died as a result of her work. Hitchcock, in fact, had temporarily stopped her law practice, and suc-

69. Letitia L. Burlingame to the Equity Club, April 23, 1887, Ann Arbor, Equity Club Letters, Dillon Collection.

70. Lettie L. Burlingame to the Equity Club, April 22, 1889, Joliet, Ill., Equity Club Letters, Dillon Collection.

cumbed to an illness she contracted while accompanying her physician husband on his medical visits to natives in primitive parts of Hawaii. Robinson died from an accidental overdose of belladonna.

Other Equity Club members focused particularly on the importance of respectful sexual relations between husband and wife in preserving a woman's health. While Clarke described the female reproductive system as naturally delicate and prone to illness, the women of the Equity Club defined female reproductive physiology as naturally healthy but sensitive to abuse. Again, they argued that it was not the universal condition of female physiology but the material conditions of women's lives that determined their health. In an era when the only reliable method of birth control was abstinence, the women of the Equity Club embraced the prevalent medical wisdom that frequent sexual relations in marriage endangered the wife's health. To protect the wife's health, nineteenth-century physicians strongly urged married couples to refrain from sexual intercourse except when they wanted to reproduce. While doctors viewed the question of sexual relations between husband and wife as a matter of health, many women in the second half of the nineteenth century understood that it was also an important political issue between husband and wife. In an attempt to establish autonomy for the wife in marriage, they argued, not only should sexual relations occur solely for the purpose of procreation, but it was the right of the wife to accept or reject her husband's sexual advances.[71]

It was within the context of these contemporary views of sexual relations in marriage that several of the Equity Club members responded to Martin's letter. Again, they disputed the notion that the female reproductive organs were inherently delicate. Rather, they insisted that it was the history of abuse of those organs that caused women so much suffering. "Let us . . . put the blame for woman's diseases where it belongs—on the blind errors of our ancestors who in ages past abused the powers that nature designed for the holiest uses," wrote Pearce. "The results have been visited upon their daughters in weaknesses that have no parallel throughout the animal king-

71. See Linda Gordon, *Woman's Body, Woman's Right: A Social History of Birth Control in America* (New York, 1976); also James W. Reed, *From Private Vice to Public Virtue: The Birth Control Movement and American Society Since 1830* (New York, 1978).

dom."[72] While Pearce spoke in general terms, a prospective Equity Club member provided specific proof of the harmful effects of marital excess. The writer, who chose to remain anonymous, graduated with high standing from law school and had a promising legal career before she married. Her husband's sexual demands, however, ruined her health and destroyed her chances for a professional life. Her friends believed that she had fallen victim to too much mental work. "The few who know of me would wisely nod their heads and quote the old story of 'over study,'" she wrote. For a long time she listened quietly as they attributed her ills "to any cause but the true one." But the Equity Club gave her the support she needed finally to expose the truth. Confessing the real source of her private torment, she lamented that "with all my study, I did not study woman in the marriage relation."[73]

Greatly moved by the woman "who unburdened her heart," Ada Bittenbender generously shared with the Equity Club the intimacies of her own marital relationship. Unlike the anonymous writer who suffered silently from her husband's sexual demands, Ada Bittenbender explained that she openly discussed the issue with her husband. "I talked the matter over frankly with my husband as I do all other interests in life, and since have received his hearty consideration in this as in all efforts I make." To solve the problem, Bittenbender recommended that married couples sleep apart. "I would recommend the occupying of separate beds, and also of bed-chambers where convenient by married people."[74]

The willingness of Bittenbender and others in the Equity Club to discuss marriage and sex so openly is testimony to the trust they placed in each other and in the organization they built together. Moreover, it reveals the fact that the Equity Club members were keenly aware that they simply could not discuss their professional lives apart from their private lives. At every turn, they found that professional matters overlapped the boundaries of their personal lives.

Set against the rise of the legal profession in the late nineteenth

72. Pearce, Report of the Corresponding Secretary, 1888, *Equity Club Annual,* 1888, at 11, Equity Club Letters, Dillon Collection.

73. Ibid., at 11.

74. Ada M. Bittenbender to the Equity Club, May 10, 1889, Washington, D.C., Equity Club Letters, Dillon Collection.

century, the Equity Club was a small, little-known organization. But, to its members, each of whom had her own doubts and uncertainties about her place as a woman in the legal profession, it was an important source of strength and support. The Equity Club members overcame the limits of geographic distance and brought themselves together into an impressively close community of women lawyers through their letters. Within this community, women lawyers turned to each other for sympathetic advice and encouragement as they strived to carve out their professional identities and careers. Trusting in the respect they shared for each other, they confessed to their confusion and trepidation about their place as women in the legal profession.

While the Equity Club brought together women because of their common professional interests, its all-female membership made it a safe place for women lawyers to discuss their private lives as well. Protected by the confidentiality of the club, its members opened their hearts to each other about intimate, personal concerns including health, marriage, and sexuality.

Finally, the Equity Club provided a vehicle by which its members identified matters of professional importance for women lawyers in the late nineteenth century. Through their debates over issues such as court versus office practice, charity versus paying clients, professional versus political work, and marriage versus career, the women lawyers of the Equity Club not only identified their own professional concerns; they laid the groundwork for the professional agenda for women lawyers in the twentieth century. From this point of view, the Equity Club left an enduring legacy for women lawyers who followed them. As the first national organization of women lawyers in the United States, it sowed the seeds of their professional community. Today, as women lawyers grow in numbers and influence as they move into the twenty-first century, they may draw inspiration from the members of the Equity Club. They understood all too well the importance of creating what they proudly referred to as a community of "sisters in law" in a profession dominated by men.

The Letters of the Equity Club

Letters from 1887

Cora Agnes Benneson, December 12, 1887, Bryn Mawr, Pennsylvania

Letitia Lavilla A. Burlingame, April 23, 1887, Ann Arbor, Michigan

Eliza Anne Chambers, September 12, 1887, Washington, D.C.

Corinne Williams Douglas, May 7, 1887, Ann Arbor, Michigan

Laura de Force Gordon, April 26, 1887, Lodi, California

Mary Anne Greene, April 27, 1887, Jamaica Plain, Massachusetts

Almeda Emily Hitchcock [Moore], May 1, 1887, Ann Arbor, Michigan

Belva Ann Bennett McNall Lockwood, April 30, 1887, Dysart, Iowa

Leona Taylor Lounsbury, April 27, 1887, Omaha, Nebraska

Rebecca May, May 1, 1887, Ann Arbor, Michigan

Martha Kellum Pearce, n.d., Ann Arbor, Michigan

Lelia Josephine Robinson [Sawtelle], April 9, 1887, Calvert, Texas

Jane Mariah Slocum, n.d., Canandaigua, New York

Margaret Lyons Wilcox, May 2, 1887, Ann Arbor, Michigan

Radnor Hall, Bryn Mawr College, Bryn Mawr, Pennsylvania
December 12th, 1887
To the Members of the "Equity Club,"

As the letters of the "Equity Club" are to serve to introduce the members to one another, I trust that a short account of my varied experience since I began the study of law may not be without interest to them, and I give this in the hope that something may be found therein which will be helpful to others.

During the three years next succeeding my graduation from the Law School of Michigan University in March, 1880, I devoted myself to post-graduate studies, my work being directed by a Committee appointed from Michigan University, consisting of three professors from the Literary Department, in co-operation with two professors from the Law Department. I was permitted to do this as a non-resident, in consideration of having previously received from the same institution the degree of A.B. My subjects of study were Jurisprudence and German Literature. In recognition of this work, after examination in Jurisprudence by Judge Cooley[1] and in German by Prof. Walter[2] and public defence of a thesis of "Republican Constitutions," I received in June, 1883, the degree of A.M. from Michigan University.

Immediately after the close of these studies, I traveled for two years and four months, sailing from San Francisco, and visiting the Hawaiian Islands, Japan, China, India, Arabia, Egypt, Palestine and all of the principal countries of Europe. During this journey, I took especial pains to attend, when practicable, sessions of the different legislative bodies and the courts of various countries for the purpose of observing their legal forms and procedure. To enter into a detailed account of this experience would transcend the limits of this letter. Let me say only that, in my view, the two most interesting countries politically at the present time are Japan and Russia; Japan, because in 1890 its first parliament is to be elected and the Japanese are, in

1. Judge Thomas McIntyre Cooley, one of the first three professors appointed to the law school at its founding March 30, 1859, was the dean of the law school at the University of Michigan from 1871 through 1883. He was the author of *Constitutional Limitations* (1868), the most important treatise on constitutional law in its day.

2. Professor Edward Lorraine Walter taught ancient and modern language and literature at the University of Michigan from 1868 until his death in 1898.

consequence, very keen in the study of political science in order to qualify themselves to participate in the government; and Russia, because it is apparently on the eve of a revolution likely to be far-reaching in its influence.[3]

When I was in Italy, the question of the admission of women to the bar had recently been under discussion in the Italian courts. Miss Lydia Poët, of Pinerolo,[4] graduated in the legal course at the University of Turin on June 17, 1881. Subsequently, she studied two years in an office. She then passed an examination, receiving the approval of forty-five out of fifty of the judges. The Turin Council of Advocates considered her worthy to be enrolled on their books, but at the office of the "Procura Generale," she was objected to on the ground of sex. Miss Poët answered in a remarkable argument. The matter went up to the Court of Appeals in Turin on November 14, 1883, and thence to the Court of Cassation in Turin on April 18, 1884. Both courts decided against her admission, although Miss Poët had passed the examination successfully. An account of the question as presented before the courts, the arguments pro and con by distinguished persons, the expressions of public opinion in relation to the case have since been published by Signor Santoni de Sio, of the Court of Cassation in Italy, in a work entitled "La Donna e l'Avvocatura,"[5] in which he takes the ground that there is nothing in the laws of Italy to prevent a woman from following the profession of a lawyer.

For a woman desiring to study Jurisprudence abroad, the best opportunities are offered at Zurich, where there are some of the ablest professors on this subject, and where degrees are conferred irrespective of sex.[6]

---

3. As a result of her travels, Benneson wrote a twelve-part article on Palestine. See "Palestine Today," parts I-XII in 5 *The Unitarian*, nos. 1–12, Jan.-Dec., 1890, 15–17, 68–71, 132–34, 174–75, 228–31, 285–87, 336–39, 384–87, 431–32, 478–81, 532–34, 587–88.

4. After graduating from law school at the University of Turin, Lydia Poët passed the bar exam and unsuccessfully sought admission to the bar of the Turin Court of Cessation in 1883. Her denial was based on the argument that the legislature did not intend to admit women to practice law because it employed only the masculine term avvocato and did not also use the feminine term avvocata. Poët ultimately went on to practice law in her brother's office in Turin.

5. Santoni de Sio, *La Donna e l'Avvocatura; Studio giuridico-sociale.* Parte prima, La questione giurdica (Rome, 1884).

6. There was no federal legislation concerning the practice of law in Switzerland. Rather local laws regulated law practice in individual cities. In Zurich, Mme. Emilie

During the two years succeeding my return from my trip around the world, I have been almost constantly occupied in giving lectures and conversations on subjects connected therewith, speaking principally in Illinois, Minnesota, Michigan and Ohio. This I have found delightful and profitable. From August to November, 1886, however, I was engaged in law editorial work for the West Publishing Co. of St. Paul, Minn.

In May, 1887, I was honored with a fellowship in history at Bryn Mawr College, Bryn Mawr, Pa., and I am now residing there, continuing, under exceedingly favorable circumstances, my studies in Jurisprudence and political history.

Cordially yours,
Cora A. Benneson

* * *

Ann Arbor, Michigan

April 23rd, 1887

Dear Ladies of the Equity Club,

My connection with the legal sisterhood has been so brief and pleasant that like the old negro who was asked to give his experience in prayer-meeting I must say: "I'd like to mighty well, brevren, but de fac' is, I don't got no sperience."

As a child, being sickly and much alone, I acquired a taste for reading and thinking. After some twelve years in school, first as pupil and afterwards as *teacher* my health demanded a change, and I took up the study of law, for the broad philosophy of which I had great admiration. Several declared I would kill myself, but, on the contrary, my health has steadily improved, so that I am now stronger than ever before. Worry over fashion and misplaced ambition have wrecked more bodies than anything else but the wine-cup, while deep drinking at the fountains of knowledge refreshes the whole physical and moral system.

Kempin-Spyri was denied admission to the bar in 1886. In 1887, she opened a consultation practice in the office of Professor Meili, the foremost lawyer in Zurich, and built up a large clientele. Soon thereafter she contacted Martha Pearce and joined the Equity Club.

A few days after taking up the study I called on the wife of one of the elders in our church who was himself a lawyer. Almost her first words as she met me at the door were: "Is it true that you are studying law?" "Yes," I replied, half expecting a reproof. "Well," said she, "if I were a girl again I would do the same, for we need even in our everyday life to know more of these things." I shall always be so grateful for those kind words, for they gave me confidence.

The only direct reproof I ever received was from an uncle in the East. As he had taken considerable interest in me, I wrote him of my plans, and instead of answering my letter he wrote to Father: "Tell Lettie that I think good wives and mothers are much more interesting than lady lawyers and much more sought after. Women lawyers are at a discount in this country." As you observe this explosion of masculine opinion did not frighten me much. Some of our married sisters will no doubt ask what is to hinder a woman from being both a lawyer and a "good wife and mother?"

My liberal ideas as to the development of womanhood were inherited from my Father and Mother who have given me every encouragement possible.

After two years of study with a law firm in Joliet, I came to Ann Arbor, where I have spent two of the pleasantest years of my life. Not least has been the pleasure of finding so many ladies engaged in similar studies, not only in law, but in medicine and science.

The local branch of the Equity Club, which has held fort-nightly meetings for transacting business and discussing various questions of interest, has been a source of strength to me, for while I have the kindest feelings towards all men and women, it seems that we who have common aims should stand very close together, not merely for material assistance we may give each other, but for that sympathy and encouragement which shall better fit us all for whatever difficulties we may encounter. When I think of Miss May's strong common sense view of things, of Miss Pearce's earnestness of purpose and principle, of Mrs. Wilcox's broad charity, of Mrs. Douglas' bright flashes of thought, of Miss Hitchcock's quiet force, and, outside of the Club but no less of our number, of Miss Merrill's[1] generous nature and Mrs.

1. Mary Merrill graduated from the University of Michigan Law School in 1886, was admitted to the Michigan bar in 1887, and set up a law practice in Wichita, Kansas.

Whiting's[2] sturdy perseverance, I am so glad that we have all met, and so glad, through the general Club, to be able to greet our far-away sisters who have joined us in our efforts to bring about a better acquaintance among the women lawyers of our country.

The members of the local branch desire with me to return our sincere thanks to our Corresponding Secretary, Miss Pearce, for her untiring and well-directed efforts, which have assured the success of the Equity Club. Since I began this letter a lady asked me if I did not think the women of home and society were sweeter and more unselfish than those who went forth to battle with the world for their own fame. "No!" I said, for say what you please, many of the women whom you call homebodies and award rich medals of praise are greater intriguers and tricksters than any women office holders or suffragists who ever lived, and their influence is worse and is more abiding because exerted upon those whom they love and who love them. They tolerate and wink at political meannesses and immorality in the men at their side, not so much in the hope of seeing their husband's wishes gratified, as for themselves obtaining high social position and *admiration* of *men.* Unselfish? No! It is far easier to help someone else to become famous than to become so yourself, especially when you are a woman and under the limitations of custom at every turn. If she had said "*happier*" instead of "*unselfish*", I would have answered differently.

With best wishes for all members of the Equity Club, and hoping that it may grow and prosper, I am

Very sincerely,
Letitia L. Burlingame

* * *

2. Mary C. Whiting graduated from University of Michigan Law School in 1887, was immediately admitted to the Michigan bar, and set up a law practice in Ann Arbor.

803 F. St. N.W.
Washington, D.C.

September 12, 1887

To the Members of the Equity Club greeting,
Ladies:

It affords me most sincere pleasure to enroll my name on your list of co-workers in the Cause of woman.

Last June I was admitted to practice at the Bar, of the Supreme Court of the District of Columbia.

My experience thus far is but limited. One, by one, the doors are thrown open, very wide to woman; and, I am fully convinced, that the time is at hand, when woman's ability to fill the chair, of Professor of Law, in our colleges, sit beside her brother on the "wood-sack," and even grace the "White House" in our city, as the nation's choice and its Chief Executive.

Very Respectfully,
Eliza Anne Chambers, LL.B.

* * *

Ann Arbor

May 7, 1887

Friends of the Equity Club,

Woman's right to a professional training is no longer a mooted question. It is a settled fact. Our girls may now take a classical or professional education with scarcely a ripple of disapproval. The woman whose life is given to the arts may wonder at the task for the one who devotes herself to science or jurisprudence, but no longer is it said that woman has less right to devote herself to the one cause than to the other. Indeed, in the department of medicine, we find her not only tolerated but eagerly welcomed. Of her right, heaven given, to heal the sick, to soothe pain and suffering, there is, there can be no question. All the poetry of our nature, as well as all the common sense of an every-day world perceive the fitness of the combination, woman and physician. It is true that there does not exist the same urgent need of lady-lawyers, as lady-physicians, yet none the less they have a place and a work. I very much doubt whether in the nature of things, we ever see women form a very large percentage of the legal profession. I do not anticipate the day when a lady advocate pleading in police or criminal courts will be a common sight. Oftener will she be found arguing in those cases where a well-prepared brief is more important than browbeating a witness or hoodwinking a jury. The law business that will fall most naturally into her hands, is that not less honorable, and more remunerative if less public, class, known as "office-work." Here her careful attention to detail, added to equal training will give the average woman an advantage over the average man. Surely it is better to make a deed over which there can be no litigation than to twist a meaning favorable to one's client out of one unskillfully drawn.

Women as well as men have the duty laid upon them of making the world better, so far as in them lies of bringing happiness or comfort, or a lightening of burdens to the race. Sometimes there may come a conflict of duties. Between the home and the profession, between the duties of wife and mother and those that a professionally trained woman owes the world, there can be no hesitation as to which is the greater, the more imperative. I have no sympathy and but little patience with those who can say of a woman, no matter what her talent or how extended her researches, "She is burying herself in her home; throwing herself away upon the children." Thank God for the noble women who thus "throw themselves away" and the greater their genius and learning, the more shall their children rise up and call them blessed, and the more powerfully for good will their influence be felt in the next generation. To have made one happy household is to have made no small addition to the sum-total of human good. But not to all comes this choosing of paths. With many the two are not incompatible, and run so closely side by side that they can be merged in one: and with that large class of women, who do not marry, whose hearts are too completely filled with their chosen life-work to leave room or desire for marriage, there is not only no necessity of choosing but the added need of using the professions as a means of support. To other married women, more perhaps than we know of, professional study, in the schools or in private, is a means of becoming to their husbands more nearly what the word "help-meet" means. Recently I heard it related of the wife of one of America's greatest jurists, to whose generous and intelligent assistance he is said to be indebted for no small part of his fame, that when questioned concerning her unwearied, unselfish and silent work for him, which the world knew only by his name, she said, "Long ago I saw that we could not both be famous, and I resolved to help him to be so." It is such self-abnegation that shows the true nobility of our manhood and womanhood.

With many hearty wishes for the success of the members of the Equity Club, in whatever direction their work lies, I am,

Yours,
Corinne Williams Douglas

* * *

Lodi, California

April 26, 1887

To the members of the Equity Club,

My Dear Sisters-in-Law,

A pleasant note from your Secretary, inviting me to become one of you, and enclosing a brief printed circular setting forth the objects of this association, was received with pleasure, and responded to most cordially.

Every woman in the Legal profession must feel that want of Professional companionship, or in other words, must, at times (as I have for years) longed for expressions, or assurances of that close sympathy born of mutuality of interests, which women alone can extend to a woman.

There is a certain "moral support" in the confiding sympathy of brave-souled, warm-hearted women, who have dared and suffered in kind with ourselves, which becomes a *tower* of *strength* to nerve the heart and sustain the brain when both are taxed to the utmost as is often the case in the practice of our grand profession. I became convinced years ago, that the few women lawyers of the country should become better acquainted for their mutual benefit, and acting upon such conviction, wrote to several of my sisters in the profession, from which resulted a correspondence both pleasant and profitable.

That the excellent motto selected by the Equity Club may be fully realized, is my earnest desire, and it would give me great pleasure to correspond with such individual members of the Club with whom this feeling may be mutual.[1] I think it would be a most desirable object, if the Club could arrange for a Grand Annual Reunion of the Lady Lawyers of America, that we might be able, by personal acquaintance and the discussion of topics of grave importance to all women, not only benefit ourselves as members of a profession, but do much good for all woman kind. Our laws are, in many instances, inimical to the well being and interests of women, and to those of the Legal Profession must our sisters thus discriminated against, look for relief.

I should be pleased at some future time to relate personal incidents in the practice of Law, which have strengthened my belief in the absolute necessity of women having a woman Lawyer if they hope to secure a just and equitable interpretation of the statutes at the Bar of Justice, for the length of this self-introductory epistle, precludes me from so doing at this time.

With an earnest wish for the success of the Equity Club, and a speedy realization of its laudable objects,

I am my dear sisters-in-Law,

Yours Very Truly,
Laura de F. Gordon
(Residence) Lodi, California

* * *

#1 Warren Square
Jamaica Plain, Massachusetts

April 27, 1887

To the Members of the
Equity Club;
Greeting;—

A law student of very little individual experience comes among you, having had by reason of a long illness, very few thoughts on legal

1. The motto of the Equity Club was "All the allies of each."

topics since early in the winter. I feel that this club will aid me much in gathering up and knotting together the broken chains of thought.

My resolve to study law was so suddenly taken, and so quickly acted upon, that I have never become so familiar with what other women in the profession are doing, as I should have done, had I spent a longer time in inquiry before coming to a decision. Consequently I am very glad to embrace the opportunity here presented of knowing who my sisters in the profession are and what they are doing.

I had two reasons for taking up the study of law. First, because of a perplexing occurrance once in my own business affairs, which opened my eyes to the fact that I was most woefully ignorant of the very first principles of our Common law; secondly, because I had, within a very short time, heard of so many instances where women, when they had been left widowed, had been over reached, duped and deceived in money matters by those who should have been their most trust-worthy friends. These women, when it was too late for any remedy would say: "Oh if I had only known as much as I do now. If I could only have gone to some one who would give me sympathizing counsel, how much richer and happier I should be."[1] I felt convinced that here was a field for women, that just as many women would prefer to consult a woman physician because they could talk freely and be more sure of sympathy, so they would, for the same reasons, consult a woman lawyer. A remark of one of my fellow students has confirmed the opinion. He said that during the two years he was in a lawyer's office, he was surprised many times to learn how much women who came as clients had unnecessarily suffered, before seeking legal advice, because they dreaded to consult a lawyer. He felt sure that they might have been helped much sooner, had they had an opportunity to consult a *woman* in whose legal knowledge and ability they had confidence.

And thus the thought has been impressed upon me of the necessity of an exceptionally high moral standard, if women are to succeed in the law. For the women who are pioneers in any public movement are

1. This remark to Greene is strikingly similar to the remark made by a dying woman to Elizabeth Blackwell. In that case, the dying woman confessed to Blackwell that she would have sought medical attention for her ailments if she could have seen a woman doctor. The remark inspired Blackwell to seek medical education, and she subsequently became one of the pioneer woman doctors in mid-nineteenth-century America.

narrowly watched and keenly criticized, and the slight misstep of one brings suspicion on all. Then again the temptations to "sharpness" may easily lead on into dishonesty, and as the temptations are great so must the ideal be high.

I fear I have been "preaching" too much for such a beginner, but there is so much of the feeling among certain of our students that a lawyer need not be quite so particular in discriminating between right and wrong as the laity must be, that I have often been pained by it. And we all know the common talk about the trickery of lawyers.

An intelligent lady said to me the other day, "Whatever possessed you to study law? Was it the *justice* of it?" with a very sarcastic inflection upon the word "justice." I thereupon resolved that my professional conduct should be such that my friends should plainly realize the truth that the law of the land requires that lawyers and clients alike shall deal justly and live honestly.

Cordially yours,
Mary A. Greene
Law School of the Boston
University Class of '88.

* * *

Ann Arbor

May 1st, 1887

To the ladies of the Equity club,

Thinking that it might interest you to hear of the origin of the Sandwich or Hawaiian Island laws and how matters in reference thereto are conducted, I will in a brief way undertake to tell you of them.

The early history of the Hawaiian Islands is involved in great obscurity. The people had no written language, no records, no ideas of literature, and so far as appears, no tradition that their ancestors possessed any. In the place of history they had traditions, national songs, rude narratives of the succession of kings, wars etc. Each island was governed by a king and these kings were at war constantly with one another. Finally one, Kamehameha by name, prevailed and he assumed control of the group.[1] Up to his reign and through a greater part of it a system of rules, called the "Taber System," were in vogue. This system forbade women the pleasure of eating with their husbands. Various times, places and things were placed under "taber", or declared to be sacred. To enforce the taber highest penalty was annexed, and to punish women for jealousy was according to tradition, one of the objects of the taber. Claiming the right of soil throughout his realm, and using the privilege of a conqueror, Kamehameha wielded a despotism as absolute probably as the islands ever knew. To check the violence, which existed in a disturbed country he interdicted murder, theft and robbery.

It was deemed lawful and respectable for a chieftan to have as many wives as he could get, and to turn any of them off at pleasure, and supply their place by obtaining the wives and daughters of others. Kamehameha had not less than twenty, and his favorite was Kaahumanu.[2] She helped in the overthrow of the taber previously mentioned. She outlived the king and was Queen regent for nine years. She embraced Christianity and was much beloved by all. The missionaries arrived in 1820. The reign of Kamehameha was just previous to their arrival. In 1825 the ten commandments were adopted as a basis for a criminal code.

In 1827 a council of chiefs adopted a number of laws which were printed and promulgated, and these were the first regularly enacted laws. Penalties were imposed on theft, murder, adultery and bigamy. These laws were for the natives simply. In 1829 laws were adopted for foreigners as well as for natives.

From 1829 to 1838 no new laws were passed. The new constitution and Bill of Rights were adopted October 8th, 1840.

The Legislative Department of the kingdom is composed of the King, the House of Nobles and the House of Representatives. The

1. Kamehameha was the first king of the united Hawaiian Islands. He ruled by patronage and force until his death in 1819. Before his death he appointed his favorite wife, Kaahumanu, prime minister.

2. Kaahumanu was credited with the overthrow of the Kapu system of social laws sanctioned by the government and the gods. By eating at the same table as the new king, Kaahumanu publicly broke a social law that forbade women to dine at the same table with men. The downfall of these traditions symbolized the rejection of the entire Kapu system.

King appoints the members of the House of Nobles, who hold their seats during life, unless in case of resignation, subject, however, to punishment for disorderly behavior. The number of members does not exceed thirty. The House of Representatives is composed of not less then twenty-four, or more than forty members, and they are elected biennially and by the people. The English Common law forms the basis for our law. In 1856 a Resolution was passed by the Legislature to provide for the codification and revision of the then existing laws, (except the Penal Code of 1852) which were defective in many particulars, and inconvenient of reference on account of their being scattered through many separate volumes, and from the numerous alterations which had been made in them from time to time. In persuance of this resolution, the work of preparing the Civil Code was commenced, soon after the adjournment of the Legislature in 1856. The Code as now published, was finally passed by both houses on the second, and received the Royal assent on the seventeenth day of May 1859. In accordance with the Resolution certain men were appointed by the Minister of the Interior to compare the new Hawaiian Code with the English, assimilating the same as far as practicable. A perfect agreement was not effected; but the Code has been found satisfactory in all respects. "The judicial power of the kingdom is vested in one Supreme Court and in such inferior courts as the Legislature may from time to time establish. The kingdom is divided into four judicial circuits."

There are at present no women practicing law, but there are quite a number of practicing physicians. The popular feeling is for rather than against woman in the professions.

A few words in reference to the temperance question. Intemperance was prevalent from the first. The natives manufactured a drink of their own, called "Okolehao," which was very intoxicating. In 1831 a temperance society was formed among the natives. November 26, 1835 a temperance petition was presented to the king. It was in all probability the first written petition presented to an Hawaiian Monarch.

This petition was signed by Chiefs and Chiefesses of the highest rank, and the names of thousands were given in from the other islands. All united their influence to secure this important object, which was at length consummated, so far, at least, as to free the government almost entirely from the responsibility of the deleterious traffic. This law against the sale of liquor lasted until 1884. The Legislative session of that year annuled this law, and the liquor traffic has increased very rapidly since then.

Drunkenness has increased also, and matters in reference thereto look very dark and forbidding. The silver lining to the cloud is very narrow and dim. The W.C.T.U. are doing their best to abate this evil, but find it up hill work. The native women have formed a W.C.T.U. of their own and are working in unison with the American women.[3] They realize the peril that their families are in and are trying their best to avert it. The Blue Ribbon League is also trying its best to gain ground, and it is succeeding slowly.[4]

"Me ku Aloha mui,"
(With best wishes, etc.)
Alme E. Hitchcock

* * *

Dysart, Iowa

April 30, 1887

Dear Sisters of the Equity Club,

I highly approve of a legal or bar Association of women; and if I can make it convenient, when next in Chicago, would like to be presented for admission to the bar of Cook County.

I am now in the fifteenth year of my practice as a member of the bar of the Supreme Court of the District of Columbia and in the 8th year of my practice before the United States Supreme Court, and during that time, or until within the last three years, have been entirely absorbed, and my time wholly occupied with the exacting duties of my profession; with which from the first, I have been very much

3. In the 1880s, Frances Willard, president of the Woman's Christian Temperance Union, began to expand temperance reform beyond the continental United States. Temperance missionaries went to the Far East to address the problem of alcoholic and narcotic abuse. The formation of a chapter of the WCTU in Hawaii occurred within the context of this international expansion to the East.

4. The Blue Ribbon campaign was a popular temperance campaign of the late nineteenth century. Its followers signed a pledge of total abstinence and wore blue ribbons as a public symbol of their commitment to complete abstinence.

interested; each cause of litigation generally presenting some new phase of the law, and requiring special study and care to prepare it for the Court.

It is far from being a dry study, as many have supposed, but on the contrary, possesses a peculiar and fascinating attractiveness and especially when you have a case in hand to study up.

Since my admission to the bar in September, 1873 I have rarely read any book but a law book,—so completely and thoroughly has the law engrossed my time, until within the last three years; when circumstances beyond my control, have directed my attention to the moral, social, and political condition of the Country and the probable future of the Republic.

Since that time, I have at the earnest solicitations of friends, prepared a series of Lectures entitled as follows:

"The Women of To-day,"
"The Social and Political Life of Washington;"
"The Present or Political Aspect of the Temperance Question;" and
"Across the Continent or What I Saw."

So that my legal life has for three seasons past, been interrupted by seasons of Lectures lasting from six to seven months each year, and during which time I have now delivered about 500 Lectures; yet keeping up during the Lecture season, my law business at home with the aid of my two young women clerks, Lura M. Ormes[1] and Clara B. Harrison; and invariably returning to my law business again, as soon as the Lecture season is concluded; as I intend to do now in a few weeks; and to which end I am now gathering up and sending home as many claims against the Government as I can find; as this business is the most readily prosecuted when terms of absence from home are necessary; and in my experience have proved quite as lucrative, although special training, and a knowledge of the laws and rulings that govern them are requisite.

1. Lura M. Ormes was Belva Lockwood's daughter by her first husband. Lura Ormes married a pharmacist, Deforest Ormes, moved in with the Lockwoods, and took over housekeeping and care of her mother's young child, Jessie Belva, while Lockwood attended law classes at National University. After Lura Ormes went to law school, she became a clerk in her mother's law office.

In all large cities a lawyer may choose specialties, and find a practice lucrative enough to fully employ her time; but in the smaller towns it will be found necessary to enter into a general practice; and many of the male Attorneys even then, add to it a real estate business.

This latter business, like other branches of the law requires close application, much legal knowledge, the ability to read the Land Records of the County understandingly and with a clear knowledge of all their bearings, to draft a deed properly, and to have a description of the land conveyed accurate. And then the descent of property to heirs varies in the different States. But this collateral branch of the law is well-adapted to women; and a goodly number of women have already secured fortunes to themselves in buying and selling real estate. I opened an office of this sort with some success about 16 years ago, when I found difficulty in securing admission to the bar, and soon after joined with it a Claim Agency, for the practice of all sorts of Claims against the Government, which has now grown into a large and prosperous business, and in which I am considered an expert.

In this branch of the law, a Miss Gelston in Washington has made great success, and has earned for herself quite a fortune, but has never been admitted to the bar; while Miss Emma M. Gillett a member of the District Bar, has acquired a competence and some reputation, by devoting herself principally as an Examiner in Chancery and as a Notary Public, having in the latter capacity the business of two banks. She is very reliable and painstaking when given a job, and is always fully occupied with her profession.

As my admission to the bar was in the early days of such privileges to women, and at a time when the prejudice against women lawyers was so great that I was compelled to make a determined contest for such admission, I entered at once into the active and general practice of the law, taking up and entering earnestly into every case, no matter how difficult, occurring in civil, criminal, equitable and probate law. In the three last orders of cases, I have been markedly successful, and reasonably so in the first.

From the first beginning of my practice, until to-day I have had all and more good paying work than I could attend to without assistance. I would not like to-day to give up my knowledge of the law, or its practice. Aside from being a source of livelihood to myself and a large family, as it has been for years, it has given me strength in mind and body, and has enabled me to give valuable advice to my friends in the settlement of estates, and other important matters.

The drafting of Wills, Deeds, Leases and Bills of Sale forms a very pleasant specialty for a woman in a large city where she can draw from a large enough population to secure good custom.

In this day and age of the World, when so many avenues of trade, and so many professions are opening to women, the ground principles of the laws of each State (and they should be uniform) should be taught to the girls of the public schools. Women have always been the chief sufferers of bad legislation, and if being the weaker physically it is harder for them to acquire a fortune, the more need of the legal knowledge of how to keep it. There is plenty of room to-day for women who are willing to apply themselves in the law.

It is an old maxim in England that every gentleman's son should know the law. We ought to reverse that in our Country and expect every lady's daughter to be versed in the law, that she may be early schooled to a necessary protection of herself and children.

Belva A. Lockwood
Attorney and Solicitor
619 F. St. N.W.
Washington, D.C.

* * *

Omaha, Nebraska

April 27, 1887

To the Ladies of the Equity Club,

A short time ago, I received notice of your organization along with a friendly solicitation from the society to become a member. An organization like this, consisting wholly of ladies, the same being coworkers, without formality or ceremony meets my most hearty approval; to which I respond at once with a line. The motto of this Club implies much, and cannot fail to give it strength through which much good may be accomplished.

A kindly interchange of thought, where mind speaks freely and frankly, one to the other, discussing the many topics, from the various standpoints of life, seems essential to promote the great work of woman which our day, and generation demand. I shall hail the issue of your pamphlet with joy, and give it my most hearty support; for I well know, it will be a most delightful pastime for me, to read the letters, replete with interest, from true women of intelligence, whose objects and aims in life, are in unison with my own.

And now that this is to be a *family* affair, allow me to insert a little of my autobiography. I received my diploma in law in '81, also my license to the Michigan Bar. Just prior to this, during my law course at Ann Arbor I lost my nearest friend — This bereavement bore heavily upon me and so much so, that I was bodily and mentally disabled for active work. I soon married one of my classmates in law. We located in Omaha, he in his office at his profession, and I in "the home" to which I have become, almost a voluntary prisoner. The complicated and inexhaustible duties of housewife have interfered very materially with mental culture. I am much in need of correspondence with those who are more fearless than I; who are unwilling to stop by the wayside, lest some little difficulty arise.

I am now wife and mother, yet I do not regret the study of law; for I consider it an important step in the direction of confirming the theory, that true woman can think and act for herself independently, yet modestly; at the same time adorning the virtues of womanhood. Sometimes, when I am reading my little Edith of 4 years, comes to me and says, "mamma, won't you hold me?" When taking her up she seems so happy in her childish love and caresses, all of which has a responsive echo from my heart.

My experience and observation teaches me daily, that the theory is erroneous and inconsistent with the present age, that woman ________ in the professions or having power to express her opinions should detract from her maternal nature or interfere with any arrangement which The Creator may have planned—

Hoping to have the pleasure, of reading lengthy letters from many members ere long, I am yours most sincerely,

Leona T. Lounsbury

* * *

Ann Arbor, Michigan

May 1st, 1887

Dear Ladies of the Equity Club,

I write to hear and learn, not to suggest and give my experience. Certainly not the latter, for as yet I am but a student in the Law Department of the University of Michigan; nor have I fully decided to make any attempt to engage in actual practice. I believe that the mental discipline derived from a rigorous course in law, can not be other than beneficial to any one man or woman, and this,—in any walk of life. Yet I do not advocate giving every one, regardless of taste or talent therefore, even a limited course in the technicalities of practice; but this, that if one has a taste for the study of law and application sufficient to master the general principles of the same, such person's time will be much more profitably spent in this work than in the pursuit of many of the "ologies" and arts.

By far the greatest amount of time wasted in the study of any one of these, is that devoted to music. The idea that every daughter, and many sons must "take music lessons" is quite prevalent, and this, often irrespective of child's inability to master even the rudiments thereof. Not only is it a sinful waste of time, but may prove an actual permanent injury to the sufferer. Think of a little girl, eight or ten years of age, perched on a high stool, the little feet unable to reach the floor, the back without support, and the fingers vainly endeavoring to touch the proper key, in exact time and with due weight mumbling the monotonous "one-and," "two-and," etc.

What is the result of years of such torture? The limbs distorted, the back weakened, the temper spoiled; and the young girl grows into womanhood, feeling that nothing has been accomplished thus far, and with the idea,—though a mistaken one,—that too many years of her life have passed to warrant her in entering upon the study of any subject which requires long and close mental application. She will hesitate even though she be conscious of her ability, and will pass through life, feeling a lack of something—disappointed but failing to realize that her organization is such that mental stimulus and exertion are essential to her happiness and well-being. Give the child, the girl and the woman, food for thought. It is the surest safe-guard that can surround her. Select food adapted to her mental digestive apparatus. Should this be *law,* she need not thereby lose her "qualities" as often quoted. Far from it. She will be a better woman, will make a more companionable wife, a mother better able to understand and direct her children, a *more intelligent citizen;* and that our friends of the opposite sex may be reconciled, I add that she will be as good, nay, a better housekeeper, than if she be brought up on the hot-house theory.

But suppose she has not the opportunity (acceptable) to prove the above to be true. Her knowledge of the world and its practices will enable her the better to cope with its difficulties and changes whatever may be her chosen work. Should she choose the law,—may present success attend her efforts. Should she fail to realize the benefits of her labors,—they will yet bear fruit,—and coming generations will reap the benefit though of the sower they know not.

Prepare our women to be *intelligent citizens.* Let us not find ourselves in the condition of France with self-government thrust upon her by the zealous few, but the masses wholly unfit to exercise the same. I look forward to the time when I may read words of wisdom and experience, from those who know whereof they speak. Should the future give me a right of interest, a right that will be helpful to my Sisters and friends, it will be gladly contributed.

In the mean time permit me to sign my ________.

Your Sister-in-Law,
Rebecca May

Box 554
Ann Arbor, Michigan

* * *

Dear Equity Club,

To my mind there is something touching in this attempt to form acquaintance. Our need of sympathy and encouragement has led each one of us at some time—at many times, perhaps,—to wish to clasp the hand and look into the eyes of someone who could understand, without a word, that isolated *Ergo,* which express it as we will, cannot be fully comprehended by even the dearest friend who has not felt the same longings that have impelled us to choose new paths for ourselves. For what can be so refreshing to an aspiring soul, that has been stifled in a narrow conventionalism, as to be simply *understood*? Admiration, affection even, without that, is less than that. It is the breath of life.

And so as I have read your letters, and those from other women who have welcomed our plan and have promised to join us another year, I have rejoiced that we have formed this association although we are as yet but a feeble folk. By mutual endorsement and support each can feel the strength of all, and we may (even the most timid of us) reach a plane where we will be as calmly confident of the propriety of following the bent of our own natures as any man is. The time will come when no "double consciousness" will disturb a *woman* who wishes to be a *lawyer*.

May the Equity Club hasten that day.

Sincerely yours,
Martha K. Pearce
Corresponding Secretary of the Ann Arbor Society
Address during August and September: Ann Arbor, Michigan—after October 1—Beatrice, Nebraska

* * *

Calvert, Texas

April 9, 1887

My dear Miss Pearce,

Yours of the 26th all was forwarded after me and only received a few days ago. I wish it were possible for me to write a letter to the Club that would really say something, but I am overburdened physically and mentally. I see the object of the letters plainly and approve, but my contribution must be very short and may be too late for publication. Thanks for your kind words of sympathy and appreciation for my book.[1] They are very sweet to me, believe me. I know your Union Signal work and appreciate it.[2]

Yours sincerely—LJR

1. Robinson is referring here to her book, *Law Made Easy*, published in 1886.
2. The *Union Signal* was a popular temperance journal.

* * *

Dear Equity Club,

My contribution to the feast of good things which we have clubbed together to furnish for the mutual setting forth of our letter-ary table must be small and insignificant this year, for time and work presses me heavily—work not altogether congenial, being quite out of the line of the legal labor which I love. Yet its object justifies my temporary desertion of the office and bar, for it is certainly very desirable that some elementary knowledge of the law should be put into the hands of the masses of our people, and my present efforts are all devoted to aiding my publishers to establish my book "Law Made Easy" on the market in different parts of the country. I should not refer to the book, in this epistle, but that it is my text for the little sermon which, from my vantage-pulpit of five years' experience as an attorney, I may be allowed to preach to my younger sisters in the profession who are just about to take their degrees and enter upon their career.

For I must assume that all women who study law do so with the same purpose that their brother students have in view,—namely, that of being admitted to the bar and entering upon the practice of the profession which they have studied. If they hesitate at all, it is for lack of knowing just how to set about it and here I can sympathize with them indeed. When I graduated from the Boston University Law School six years ago with my degree as the result of a three years' consecutive course in the school, I was very much at a loss as to my next step. I had made my application for admission to the bar, and it was in the hands of the Supreme Court of Massachusetts awaiting a decision which I expected would be unfavorable. I had no special acquaintance with any lawyer, and all my efforts utterly failed to gain for me admission in any capacity into any law-office. So I took a trip into the country for the summer to recuperate, and in the fall returned to Boston, quietly hired a tiny office in a building full of lawyers, fitted it up, framed and hung my diploma, sent out cards, and, was ready for such business as I could do without going personally into the courts. Even this I might have done, for our statute permits a party to any legal action to authorize any person to represent him by giving him or her a power of attorney; but it was not my original intention to do court business at all. Six months later, the court had dismissed my application for admission to the bar, the Legislature had unanimously passed a law authorizing the admission of women to the bar on the same conditions as men, I had taken the examination and crossed the grand Rubicon which made me a full-fledged attorney.

Since that time, both in my Eastern and Western experience—for I grew impatient of the slow process of building up a clientage in our conservative "Hub of the Universe" and betook myself to the far West in search of a more rapid growth—I have found that two things were absolutely essential to the success of a lawyer young in the profession.

The first is the *patience* which I unhappily lacked. One must make up her mind with entire certainty that she will have to wait—wait—wearily wait. "'He commeth not,' she said," assumes a new significance when uttered by the woman lawyer waiting in her office for clients. It may well be worded in the feminine also, for *she* cometh not any more than does he. As a rule, women are more timid and reluctant to trust their affairs to the care of a woman lawyer than are men. The latter class are apt to say "Give her a chance," and to entrust small matters to her attention, which may be followed by better business if she proves herself trustworthy. But there is almost certain to be a great deal of the most discouraging kind of waiting for the young lawyer who has started in practice alone, whether male or female, and he or she must have both the patience and the funds to endure it.

The second essential,—though I scarcely know which of the two is first in importance—is that the young lawyer shall employ his waiting time in *study,* that he may be ready for the business when it does come. Now here is where my text comes in. I had little patience to wait, but great love for the study. Still with me, study must be for some particular object. To be prepared for an examination, or to work up the law for a brief, I could work day and night. So I cast about me for a specific object towards which I might work in study. I discovered the lack of any reliable treatise giving to the public at large those elementary principles of law which everyone must have in order to conduct the daily affairs of life intelligently. Then I said, this shall be my object. I will go to work at such a book, and if my manuscript never sees the light of day, it will at the least give me a grand review of the subjects which I shall treat and necessarily this review will be in most minute and careful detail. Thus the years of weary waiting were made endurable to me by the work which has grounded me more firmly in the faith and science of the law than any other could possibly have done, and at the last, just as success had awarded my efforts by giving me a "living practice," I find that the book has taken a deeper hold on my affections and my ambitions than the practice itself, and so it becomes, for a time at all events, first in its claims on my time and attention.

I have been told that the object of these letters is to give such aid to those of our sisters who are newly starting out in the profession, as may be possible from the experience of us who are older in it. Therefore I have given you my experiences in a word—my affirmative experience. My negative experience may be even more quickly summarized. I have had no "opposition" from anyone, either at home or abroad. If there has been a lack of sympathy on some sides, there has certainly been nothing pronounced about it. But neither have I had much help, except from my own people. And help is what we all sadly need in this life,—especially so in starting out in the practice of law. The graduate of law-school, either man or woman, who is obliged to open an office without having had preliminary training of a practical nature in an established office, is to be pitied. His embarrassments and difficulties are such as none but those who have experienced them can ever realize.

So, my sisters, have no fear of any difficulty in the way of opposition, ill-will or ill-treatment, because I truly believe you will experience nothing of the kind. Just go quietly on, getting a start in some established office if possible, and make practical lawyers of yourselves. If some little matters seem unpleasant, merely take them as matters of course, and pay no attention to them. *Do not take sex* into the practice. Don't be "lady lawyers." Simply be *lawyers,* and recognize no distinction—no existence of any distinction between yourselves and the other members of the bar. This will be your surest way to that forgetfulness of self which will give your mind freedom to achieve success. Let no one regard you as a curiosity or a rara avis. Compel recognition of your ability and respect for your industry from all. You can take this stand and yet in no wise cease to be ladies—true ladies in every sense of the word.

But above all things, have patience to wait for business to come, and patience to study continually for the business when it does come.

Your legal education can never be complete, work as hard as you may. As for "popular opinion"—pshaw! popular opinion will approve and applaud you when you have become a success! You must *create* popular opinion.

Yours sincerely,
Lelia J. Robinson
of Boston, Massachusetts

Calvert, Texas, April 9, 1887

* * *

To the Equity Club,
Dear Sisters in Law,

Those of you who conceived the idea of a "Correspondence Club," were certainly most generous to include in your invitation those graduates of Law Schools who are barred from the profession by choice or fate.

It gives me great pleasure to be recognized as belonging, in any sense, to the sisterhood; though I fear my "individual experience" will afford little help to the practitioners.

In order to make myself intelligible, it will be necessary to go back to the year 1873, when I was in charge of a department embracing Civil Government, in Howland School, which so far as my knowledge extends—was the first institution for girls that included such study in its course. Co-education was comparatively new at that time, and I was often consulted by parents as to the expediency of sending daughters to universities. It occurred to me that by going to Ann Arbor, and entering the Law School, three desirable objects might be attained: I should have personal knowledge of the workings of coeducation, gain a solid legal foundation for political and social science, and secure a few months for concentrated study, by breaking away for part of the year from distracting duties.

I entered upon the course just after the holidays, and was most fortunate in having Miss Mary Stockbridge for [a] classmate.[1] Her

1. Mary Stockbridge graduated from University of Michigan Law School in 1874. She moved to Fort Wayne, Indiana, where she settled down to a private life.

superior intellectuality, and rare womanliness had secured the reverence of faculty and students before my arrival, and she generously shared with me the favor which she had won. We were cordially invited to join the famous Webster Society,[2] to which women were not previously admitted; and every courtesy was ungrudgingly extended to us.

Three months after my entrance, the seniors, Miss Roper[3] and Miss Hubbard[4] graduated, and the following year there was an important addition of three ladies to the Law School—Miss Ellen A. Martin, Miss Fredrika Perry,[5] and Miss Matty Strickland.[6] The two first mentioned, came from law offices bringing with them a love and devotion for the profession of law not to be extinguished; and they soon gave evidence of the talents and power of labor that in a few years made them leaders in this new field for women.

Judge Cooley[7] was at that time the Eminent Dean of the legal department, and Judge Campbell's[8] scholarly and benignant face smiled upon us from the desk at regular intervals. The generous interest of these distinguished jurists will never be forgotten by the grateful women who were treated not only as students who were welcome there, but as friends whom they were glad to aid in their life work.

While in Ann Arbor I availed myself of the opportunity to review

2. The Webster Society was a student literary club at the University of Michigan.

3. Susannah Roper graduated from University of Michigan Law School in 1873, moved to Auburn, New York, and got involved in business.

4. Emma L. Hubbard graduated from University of Michigan Law School in 1873.

5. Mary Fredrika Perry graduated from the law department of the University of Michigan in 1875 and was admitted to the Michigan bar in 1875. She was Ellen Martin's law partner, and together they ran the law firm of Perry and Martin in Chicago. Perry practiced until her death on June 3, 1883.

6. Martha Strickland graduated from the University of Michigan Law School in 1881, was admitted to the bar, and then practiced law in Detroit. She was the author of an article on women lawyers entitled "Woman and the Forum," 5 *Green Bag* 240–43 (1891).

7. On Cooley, see Benneson letter, 1887, n. 1.

8. James Valentine Campbell was one of the first three professors appointed to the law faculty of the University of Michigan as well as the first dean of the law school at its founding in 1859.

Civil Government with Prof. Chas. K. Adams,[9] and Political Economy with President Angell.[10]

Altogether the ends which I had proposed in studying law were satisfactorily attained. I did not apply for admission to the bar after taking my degree in 1874 but returned at once to my chosen profession. I had long cherished the idea that social science is preeminently the study for women. I reasoned that if girls who have wealth and influence in prospect, and are ambitious for social success, can be made to see that "queens of society" are largely responsible for public opinion and the public weal, if they can be made to feel that it is their duty to understand thoroughly the true interests of society, in the broadest meaning of the word, there is large hope for the future. With a view to the better working of my ideal, I transferred my department to Granger Place School in 1876. This private institution is untrammeled by regents and trustees, and free to work for best interests of individual students. But the time that parents are willing to allow their daughters in boarding school is too limited to admit of a course in Social Science. The most that can be done is to open the door into this broad field, and stimulate interest in future investigation, by such glimpses as are afforded in the study of Political Economy and Civil Government, with the history of their growth, and the application of their principles to social interests. But, at least, opportunity is afforded for revealing woman's part in the great scheme, the part she has taken in the work of the past and her high privileges and great responsibilities in the present.

The immortal Wendell Phillips saw with prophetic eye the three great problems of our day—"The Temperance Question, the Woman Question, the Labor Question."

You, my sisters, are solving by your own success two of the riddles of the remorseless sphinx. The teacher, less fortunate, must labor ever with invisible beginnings, content to hope that somewhere beyond her ken, they will take tangible form, and bring forth results in

9. Charles Kendall Adams, professor of history, was the first dean of the School of Political Science at the University of Michigan. In 1878, the law faculty requested that Adams, the chair of the history department, lecture to the law students on constitutional history, but the regents rejected the request on policy grounds.

10. James Angell was president of the University of Michigan from 1871 through 1909.

the destruction of evil and the establishment of good, to the well being of mankind, and the glory of God.

Jane M. Slocum

Granger Place,
Canandaigua, New York

* * *

Ann Arbor, Michigan

May 2, 1887

To the members of the Equity Club,
Dear Ladies,

May a mere student in a law-school be permitted to apologize for daring to write to you before she is a dignified member of the bar? Most eager have I been to hear from you all, especially the pioneers in the profession; but my return for such a favor is necessarily meager.

It has been suggested that surely each of us, having lived a life more or less eventful, can furnish a few items of personal history. Your humble correspondent can with great confidence claim to have existed, however uneventful such existence may have been.

Imagine a little country girl, one of four daughters, left fatherless at the age of ten. With her mother's help, and by attending the district school in winter, this little daughter of Eve succeeded in winning the much coveted teacher's certificate. At fourteen, she became the "school-marm" of a neighboring district.

By hard work, teaching and studying, and close economy of time and means, she obtained a diploma from the Wisconsin State Normal School at Whitewater. Immediately after, she was called to take a position in the Milwaukee schools. But the idea of a higher education and its importance haunted her. Why should women be satisfied with just enough scholarship to earn a livelihood? Daily observation in the schools of a large city convinced her that politics ruled the public schools, so that it behooved women, especially teachers, to study public affairs. Right here, perhaps, is the germ which afterwards developed into the plan of studying law.

At this point, her marriage with a teacher occurred. After teaching two years together, both husband and wife resolved to enter upon a course of study in Michigan University. After three years' study, in 1885, they took their degree in the Literary Department. The notion of studying law became strong. The past two years have been spent in the Law Department. They expect to graduate next June.

Very pleasant have these five years of study been to me. The study of law has been a pleasure beyond my expectations. I wonder that more women do not take up the study of it for culture. Whether they have qualities of mind which would assure success in the practice of law will be revealed by such a course. Never can we hope for Mansfields[1] and Marshalls[2] among women till a greater number test their powers in the study of law. Who knows but the very young woman capable of great achievements in our profession is now all unconscious of her gifts, and awaits but an encouraging word from one of us. There had to be a host of disappointed women artists to give us a Rosa Bonheur; a myriad of less than mediocre female poets and novelists before a Mrs. Browning or a George Eliot appeared.

Not a few but many women must take up the law as a profession. An excellent law school is to be found here in Michigan University, where all the departments are open to women. A young woman can make no mistake in taking the law course; for its discipline will be valuable in any position in life. Some of us might have been here sooner had we known its advantages. The measuring of woman's mental ability with that of young men who seek prominence in the legal profession, is not the least of its advantages, since it inspires her with more confidence in herself.

Since taking up the study of law, I have been agreeably disappointed by receiving the greatest encouragement from women in society, whom I had been led to believe would frown on my presumption. My impression now is that non-professional women are looking to those pursuing a profession with an anxious interest. Most unwise is it for us to isolate ourselves in any way. Socially we should meet women as before. Men devoted to their profession have never refused or ignored the aid of society. Why should we? And yet I have

1. Sir William Murray, Lord Mansfield, was eighteenth-century England's greatest commercial lawyer and chief justice of the King's Bench from 1757 to 1788.

2. John Marshall, the fourth chief justice of the Supreme Court, believed in a strong judiciary and established the Supreme Court's power to review legislative acts.

noticed it done by women of great mental power who were so unfortunate as to be acutely sensitive to any remarks concerning their chosen profession. Men seem more philosophical in such matters. All your letters will be read with pleasure by

Yours Truly,
Margaret Lyons Wilcox

Letters from 1888

Martha Kellum Pearce, Report of Corresponding Secretary, the *Equity Club Annual,* 1888, n.d., n.p.

Addie Melvina Stephenson Billings, April 28, 1888, Geneva, Nebraska

Ada Matilda Cole Bittenbender, April 27, 1888, Washington, D.C.

Letitia Lavilla A. Burlingame, May 17, 1888, Joliet, Illinois

Florence Cronise, May 23, 1888, Tiffin, Ohio

Emma Millinda Gillett, April 18, 1888, Washington, D.C.

Mary Anne Greene, April 5, 1888, Jamaica Plain, Massachusetts

Mary Emily Humphrey Haddock, May 12, 1888, Iowa City, Iowa

Almeda Eliza Hitchcock [Moore], April 30, 1888, Ann Arbor, Michigan

Emilie Kempin, April 10, 1888, Zurich, Switzerland

Ada Harriet Miser Kepley, July 3, 1888, Effingham, Illinois

Laura A. Woodin LeValley, April 20, 1888, East Saginaw, Michigan

Ce Dora Lieuellen, May 4, 1888, Danville, Indiana

Ellen Annette Martin, May 25, 1888, Chicago, Illinois

Eliza Orme, June 18, 1888, Sheffield, England

Lelia Josephine Robinson [Sawtelle], April 7, 1888, Boston, Massachusetts

Marion Marsh Todd, April 4, 1888, Albion, Michigan

Catharine Van Valkenburg Waite, May 4, 1888, Chicago, Illinois

Catharine Gouger Waugh [McCulloch], May 2, 1888, Rockford, Illinois

Sarah Killgore Wertman, May 7, 1888, Ashland, Ohio

Margaret Lyons Wilcox, April 20, 1888, Milwaukee, Wisconsin

Jessie Elvira Wright [Whitcomb], April 23, 1888, London, England

The Equity Club Annual,

1888

Report of Corresponding Secretary.
My Beloved Equity Club,

As I have watched over your cradle, fearful sometimes that the breath of life would leave you in some of the trying moments through which we have passed, you have grown very dear to me. And now that you have attained a vigorous growth and are "like to live" and thrive, my satisfaction is too deep for expression.

I imagine that all will turn at once to the letters, which are arranged in alphabetical order for convenience. There you will find a rare treat. As they have come in one by one, I have felt a little sorry for all people who did not enjoy the advantages of a corresponding secretary of the Equity Club, but now I can believe that it would be even more delightful to read them all at once as you will. Having read them you will, I hope, give attention to the business details that I shall bring before you in this communication.

I should like to imitate the beautiful frankness with which so many of you have responded to the request for personal experiences, and if the greater privilege of giving the history of the Equity Club had not fallen to me I would have done so. It seems to me that if we are to receive the fullest possible benefit from our correspondence we must have a free interchange of confidence. Under the protection of our copyright and our limited issue, we can safely write on matters which under ordinary circumstances would not look well in print.

The history of our society is simply an account of a practical attempt to secure something of which every woman lawyer or student in a law school has at some time, perhaps at many times, felt the need—the sympathy and fellowship of other women of similar tastes and experiences. It so happened that there were seven women attending lectures in the Law Department of Michigan University in the fall of 1886. Mrs. Margaret Lyons Wilcox, Miss Rebecca May, and Mrs. Mary Whiting[1] had attended the previous year and were continuing the regular course as seniors. Four others had just entered, Miss Alme E. Hitchcock, Mrs. Corinne Douglas, Mrs. Bates, who was obliged to leave Ann Arbor on account of ill health, and another young woman, who did not appreciate her opportunities and soon left the school to pursue one of the more popular courses of study given in the University. Miss Burlingame, of the class of '86, had not yet returned to her home in Joliet, and I (a graduate of '83) was also living in Ann Arbor and devoting my time to my chosen work of literature.

One morning during the first week of that semester, Mrs. Wilcox came to my rooms with the announcement that there were four new "Lady Laws," and proposed that we, graduates and seniors, should give them a banquet. In the literary department it had for years been an established rule that the ladies of the older classes should invite the lady "Freshies" to what is known in the Ann Arbor *patois* as a "co-ed spread." These receptions have always ranked among the leading events of the year. The lady "Medics" had adopted the custom as soon as their numbers permitted, but there had so seldom been more than one or two at a time in the law school that I think it had never been observed there before. I heartily seconded Mrs. Wilcox's proposition and after discussing ways and means, we called on Miss Burlingame. Here, too, the project was approved, and Miss May having been consulted also, invitations were issued to the unknown ladies whose acquaintance we wished to make. Mrs. Whiting would not join in extending the invitations. On the evening of October 6, Miss Hitchcock, Mrs. Douglas, and Mrs. Bates, (the other stranger had declined) were escorted by Mrs. Wilcox, Miss May, and myself to Miss Burlingame's home with all due formalities. I shall not

1. See Burlingame letter, 1887, for identification of Mary Whiting.

attempt to tell you what a nice time we had, dear Equity Club. You will have to imagine that. The occasion is of general interest only because it was on that evening that we took the first steps toward forming a society through which women students and practitioners all over the world might become acquainted. We had often talked of it before. Some of us had written letters to one and another of whom we had heard, as doubtless the rest of you have done at some time, and we had, some of us, been written to by strangers with whom common interests made friendship easy. Miss Waugh had written to the ladies in the Michigan school during the winter of '85–6, and although her letter was never answered, that incident had its influence in shaping our vague longing into definite intentions. On that memorable October evening we felt strong enough for anything, of course, and if we had not in our calmer moments emphatically rejected the idea of calling a general meeting until it would be possible to have one that would be a credit to women, I think we would have decided to call one. According to previous agreement Miss Burlingame brought the matter formally before the company in an after dinner speech and before we parted we had agreed to form a local society which would afford its members an opportunity to discuss questions arising out of their legal studies and which should issue invitations to all women law students, graduates of law schools and practitioners whose names were known to us, to join us in forming a correspondence club. We could foresee that in time this club would become a power—an organized force which would be ready for some active work, but it was thought best to allow its future to be shaped in the light of the future, and, without placing the projected society under bonds to bring about all the reforms that we could think of, we devoted our thought to securing a friendly union among our isolated workers. If need arises we will be ready for united effort, if it does not, it is enough for us that we should have the comfort and the inspiration that our association secures to us.

The local society held meetings throughout the year. At first the time was devoted to plans for the general society, but later the discussions took a wide range and were of great interest.

As soon as our plans were matured the corresponding secretary was instructed to issue invitations. Sixty-two were sent out before May 1, 1887. Although many of the ladies addressed answered expressing approval of the club and its purposes only sixteen letters were received for circulation.[2] Nine ladies who failed to write, sent fees, but as we quickly realized that we could never succeed as a correspondence club if the letters of those who took the trouble to write could be obtained upon payment of the ordinary fee by those who did not, these ladies were informed that they could not receive the letters and their fees were either returned to them or credited on this year's payment.

These results were not quite what we had looked for. They did not discourage us, however, for we had already discovered that the foundations of our great expectations were lacking. We had taken too sanguine a view of the progress made by women in the legal profession and as we came to see the real state of affairs we were comforted with the thought that our society with that beautiful motto which places us shoulder to shoulder in all endeavor had been formed none too soon.

We did not print the letters in '87. Our fee—twenty-five cents—was entirely too small and did not even cover the expense of correspondence and of circulating them in the ordinary way. By-the-way they have not yet completed their round. I presume that some members have kept them long enough to take copies of them.

As soon as the letters for '87 were all in and the membership determined, an election was projected. As it seemed difficult to ballot through the post-office, we reduced the wants of the organization to the simplest terms and in accordance with the constitution, a copy of which follows this report, the only officers chosen were a corresponding secretary and an executive committee. The latter has authority to audit the accounts of the club in addition to the ordinary powers of an executive committee. The balloting resulted in the election of the officers named in the list on page 14. The corresponding secretary was, by action of the executive committee, given a vote on all matters of administration coming before that body.

Our name caused much discussion. We did not want one that would suggest the idea of a bar association, for several reasons. Chief among them were these two;— 1. We wanted to include as members many women who being non-practitioners would hardly be eligible to membership in a bar association. Some most desirable members

2. Fourteen of the sixteen letters for 1887 are in the collection of Equity Club letters at the Schlesinger Library.

have withdrawn from practice or are only just preparing for it, while none of our foreign sisters are full-fledged practitioners. Besides, not one of the founders had begun to practice. 2. We did not wish to even appear to place ourselves in antagonism to the bar associations already formed by men. We had received a hearty welcome from our brothers in law to their moot courts and debating clubs and had found that they forgot all troublesome distinctions just to the degree that we ourselves ignored them. Believing that it was to the advantage of women lawyers to cultivate a spirit of comradeship with men in the profession we tried to avoid using any name which could raise a suspicion of opposition or rivalry.

The name finally adopted, was suggested by Prof. Hutchins'[3] remark, "Equity has been the saviour of woman."

Our history is, you see, an uneventful one, and except for the results that have come from our quiet work, it would not be worth repeating.

A number of important matters are to be decided by the club this year, as will be seen on reading the questions following the constitution. First in importance is that of retaining our present form of organization. Of course, it will be understood that when we can have a meeting (and it may be possible at the time of the next International Council)[4] we will have need of officers who would now be superfluous, but the question is Shall we elect the officers now?

As those members that have not given any thought to the subject may not readily see the pros and cons, I will suggest a few thoughts *on both sides* as they have come up in our discussions in the executive committee.

If our officers are limited to a corresponding secretary and an executive committee we will be free from the worst curse of most societies—the place-hunting of people who want to advertise themselves. No one covets these modest titles, as I have discovered in

3. Harry B. Hutchins was then Jay Professor of Law at the University of Michigan, a position he had held since 1884. In 1895, Hutchins became dean of the law department after serving as professor of law in the law school of Cornell University for several years. He served as dean of the law department at the University of Michigan until 1910 when he was appointed president of the university.

4. Founded in 1888, the International Council of Women was a federation of established women's organizations united by the broad goal of public activity. The council focused on issues including women's legal status, women in the professions, and women's community standing.

trying to find some one who would like to be corresponding secretary next year. But to establish honorary offices will offer a direct temptation to some who would seek them simply because, while there is no work attached to them, they convey all the honor that the work of the other officers brings to the society. I earnestly hope that the Equity Club will never become a medium for advertising anybody. Of course it is customary for societies to have a president and they are necessary to carrying on the work of many organizations, but we are so thoroughly unique that by reason of our inborn originality we might be allowed to deviate from the beaten paths if we choose to do so.

Again, a superfluity of officers in a correspondence club increases the amount of letter writing more than one would think at first glance. This brings with it delays and an added expense. An executive committee of five is too large when its members are scattered as ours are, and if we had had other officers, rightfully jealous of their prerogatives, the mere work of setting our machinery in motion would have been trying.

On the other hand there are those among us whom we would delight to honor. I think of one who would never seek the office of president, but whom I should like to nominate if we are to have one. She has, next to her sister[5] *practiced* longer than any other woman in the world, refusing to go upon the lecture platform or to take up any side issue whatever, consistently demonstrating during all these fifteen years that a woman can practice law just as a man does. I am not a practitioner, but if I were ever to be one I should stick to business just as Miss Cronise has. Then it would be a graceful thing to show our esteem for our foreign sisters by giving them places of greater honor than that of associate corresponding secretary. If we should change we might organize after the plan of the World's W.C.T.U.,[6] letting each country where the club has a representative hold the presidency one year, the head in each being a vice-president between times. For instance, the president of our society in the

5. Martha Pearce is referring to Florence Cronise's sister, Nettie Cronise Lutes, who was the first woman admitted to the bar of Ohio in 1873. She practiced with her sister, Florence, until 1880 when Nettie went into practice with her husband whom she met when they were both reading law in the same office. The following year her husband became deaf. She continued to practice with him, taking on much of the work. Along with her active legal career, Nettie Cronise Lutes was the mother of three daughters.

6. Woman's Christian Temperance Union.

United States would serve the first year and all our foreign representatives would be vice-presidents. Then as Hawaii has a representative who is a "charter member," she would be entitled to the presidency and our head would, like the others, be a vice-president. Switzerland joined next, so the third year would see Mme. Kempin our president and during the fourth Miss Orme, whose cablegram has arrived just in time to make her a member, would be our liege lady. As the club receives accessions from other countries (and of course we will wait until people actually join us before we count them in as members) their representatives would take the presidency in the order of time of joining. When the office had been the rounds it would come back and start over again.

Now you don't know how I am going to vote on this question and I did not intend you should; I simply present these thoughts for what they are worth because there is so little chance for discussion before voting. It would be well for any one who votes for a change to express approval or disapproval of the above plan so that the executive committee will know whether or not to follow it in formulating the amendment if the club wants one.

All letters concerning the election, the change in the constitution, etc., should be addressed to Mrs. Margaret Lyons Wilcox, Union, McHenry County, Illinois. She will be our acting chairman of executive committee, as Miss Hitchcock will soon leave the country and Miss Burlingame thinks that she cannot undertake the work. I am glad that you are to come into closer acquaintance with Mrs. Wilcox. It will do you all good to know her. She is one of the "real folks" and if they are as rare where you live as they are in some other places, you will appreciate her. A woman lawyer who had been most cruelly wronged by slanderous tongues once said to me, "There may be other women besides Margaret Lyons who will stand by old friends through thick and thin; there *may be others* I say, but I have never found one." I hope that we can all together persuade her to accept in her own right the place which she fills temporarily this summer, so that we may have the full benefit of her shrewd, practical common sense which has done so much already to make our club a success.

Our fee will nearly, if not quite, cover the cost of postage, stationery, copyright, printing, etc. My correspondence has been very heavy during the past year. The work of tracing up eligible persons, and of explaining to interested parties the objects and methods of the society has been considerable. It can hardly be necessary to do so much of this again. Not including the cost of printing for which I have contracted at the rate of $1.25 per thousand words, the expenditures approved by the executive committee amount to $12.65. More than half this sum was spent before any fees for the current year were received. Twenty members have paid $2.00 each. One, who paid twenty-six cents last year but did not write a club letter and consequently had none of the privileges of membership, paid $1.74 this year, making a total of $41.74 received from members. Mrs. M. Ricker, San Jose, California,[7] and Mrs. Mary Geigus Coulter, Freeport, Illinois,[8] each sent $2.00 this year, but though thereunto urgently requested have not sent letters. Both these ladies are now traveling on the Pacific Coast. Mrs. Coulter takes a lively interest in the club and would write if it were not for her ill health. I think we may hope to have in our next Annual a letter giving the result of her studies on the status of woman in South America and the West Indies, where she has traveled much in late years. These two fees must be returned to the senders, in accordance with a rule of ours which I am convinced is a most important one, unless the ladies wish to have them credited on next year's dues or on honorary memberships. Mme. Kempin misunderstood, doubtless, for she did not remit her fee. But we are so glad to hear from her that the executive committee decided that in this instance the less important of the two requirements for membership should not be insisted upon.

A word as to honorary memberships. There can be no objection to granting a limited number at $5 each. They would enable us to make our little Annual more attractive without additional cost to the writers, whose fees should be as low as possible. The fee for honorary membership should not be kept so low that it would encourage those who might write to refrain from doing so, neither should it be so high

7. Marilla M. Ricker was admitted to the bar of the District of Columbia in 1882. She had an active practice, specialized in criminal law, gaining a reputation as "the prisoner's friend," and was appointed commissioner and examiner in chancery by the Supreme Court of the District of Columbia. In 1890, she became the first woman admitted to the bar of New Hampshire.

8. Mary Geigus Coulter graduated from the law department of the University of Michigan in 1885. At Martha Pearce's suggestion, she sought legal work with Ellen Martin in Chicago, but she married soon after and moved to Los Angeles.

that no one would be willing to pay it for the privileges that it would bring.

Next year all letters intended for the Annual must be in the hands of the corresponding secretary by the first day of May. We felt justified in extending the time this year and when you note the dates of several of the most interesting letters you will think we were right. If we were to wait a month longer, I think we would have six other members whose acquaintance would give us pleasure. But we are all getting impatient to see the Annual—I am for one—and I close the list hoping we shall hear next year *on time* from those friends who are just becoming anxious to join the Equity Club. In this connection I may state that we are already beginning to reap the reward of the work done. Instead of merely receiving answers to invitations sent out, we now have applications, as well, from those who were before unknown to me. These are considered very carefully of course and where there is any doubt of the eligibility of the writers I have referred them to the executive committee.

The copyright was taken out in my name because as an unincorporated society we would find it inconvenient, to say the least, to prosecute in case of infringement.

The request of our sister, Mme. Kempin, for an opportunity to teach in our schools while she is familiarizing herself with our language and laws, gives us a chance to prove that our motto is no "vain repetition" of words. I have suggested that she might do more good by remaining in her own country and fighting out her hard battle. But she thinks not. In a letter just received, whose strong, nervous, idiomatic phrases must be rendered by a master of both English and German to do them full justice, she says that if God gives her light and mental power, she will return to her home after a time and make use of her accumulated experience. She is sure that she can thus help her oppressed countrywomen most effectually. This idea is a reasonable one. These battles against prejudice must be fought mainly by individuals on the ground. We cannot, on this side of the water, do anything to help her directly, but if she should come here for a time and gain a standing in our courts, even our highest, she could return to her own land with new weapons for her now hopeless contest. If any of you know of a suitable position that can be obtained, please write to her at once giving her all the particulars necessary for her application. Or, you could send any suggestions to me. I shall interest myself practically in the matter, and by communicating with each other we might work to better advantage.

Miss Robinson's suggestion of a photo exchange will please, I feel sure. I will join it, for one. I propose that we bring the matter into practical shape by stating whether or not we will join, when we send in our votes on amending the constitution to Mrs. Wilcox. You will then each receive a list of those who are willing to exchange, and you can communicate directly as you please. I hope that no suits for "specific performance" will arise out of this.[9]

The present officers of the Equity Club are actuated, one and all, by a wish to execute thoroughly and promptly the will of the majority of the members. Many emergencies have arisen, in which we have been obliged to act in accordance with our own judgment, in matters which, if meetings were possible, would have been laid before the whole society. Working as we do under the disadvantages of a widely separated membership, we have decided to appoint committees on certain important questions with which the club must deal. As opportunity comes for us to help in any reform, it will be wise to get the best thought of the club in this way, and where action is determined upon, we will gain much in definiteness and unity of aim, by talking it over beforehand. Realizing that the question of *the relations of women attorneys to the existing Bar Associations, local, state and national,* is of vital importance to those members who are in active practice, we have appointed five *practitioners* to consider the subject in all its bearings, and report in the next issue of the Annual. This special committee consists of Miss Ellen A. Martin, Chairman, Miss Florence Cronise, Miss Emma Gillett, Miss Catharine G. Waugh, and Mrs. Laura Woodin LeValley. Of any other committees that it may be found desirable to form during the year, you will all be promptly notified by the corresponding secretary.

One sentence in Miss Martin's letter will occasion much discussion among us, and I am not sorry that she wrote it down, for when there is any evil abroad it is better to talk about it and find out why it exists, and how it can be overcome, than to leave it alone. It is her quotation of the statement that the physical organs pertaining to womanhood

9. Pearce is referring to the legal term, "specific performance," which is one in which a party uses an action in equity to force someone to perform a specific act; in this case, to force the Equity Club members to send in their photographs.

seem "made to get out of order."[10] It cannot be that the maker of this universe, so full of marvelous adaptations, has blundered in the construction of woman—that she alone of all His creatures has not a fair chance. We cannot give countenance to such an idea. Let us (if we must mention them) put the blame for woman's diseases where it belongs—on the blind errors of our ancestors who in ages past abused the powers that nature designed for the holiest uses. The mothers of our race have suffered a perversion of their functions which is so unnatural that we find no analogy to it in any other created being. The results have been visited upon their daughters in weaknesses that have no parallel throughout the animal kingdom. But the physical sufferings entailed are not all. They have their counterpart in some natures, in mental and moral blemishes which are even greater hindrances to woman's progress. Sometimes I feel that there is no question so sacredly important to woman as this, and that the ballot even will be worth but little to her until every married woman realizes the dignity and honor of womanhood, and (for her children's sake as well as her own) teaches man to realize it. This feeling was emphasized in my mind a few weeks ago, when I read a letter sent in answer to an invitation to join our club. It was so full of suggestion on the fundamental truths of life that I asked permission to give it to you. But the writer said, "No, it was intended for your eyes only, and you must never use my name in connection with it. I have often felt that some one of my own sex should know the truth, since if I should drop off, the few who know of me would wisely nod their heads and quote the old story of 'over study.'" Hers, sisters, is a case of a gifted girl who spent the years of early womanhood in unremitting efforts to prepare herself for the legal profession. Her course in a noted law school was marked by brilliant success, in spite of difficulties, financial and other, which would have daunted a less heroic soul. When she married a young man of fine character and high standing in the business world, who seemed as ambitious for her as for himself, I rejoiced that for her the rough places would be made smooth, and that her indomitable will would not be spent in battling with side

10. One of the central debates in the late nineteenth century was the question of whether women's health could sustain the rigors of education and professional activity. With an eye toward airing the issue of women's health in the Equity Club, Pearce invited its members to discuss the matter in their letters for the following year.

issues, nor her high purposes be weakened and dissipated through the need of caring for the things that perish. But, she moans, "with all my study, I did not study woman in the marriage relation." And now, her health wrecked at the very entrance into the opportunities for wide usefulness for which she was preparing, it is her keenest pain that her ills are attributed by everyone to any cause but the true one. "Usually," she says, "I listen in silence. And thus it has always been with woman. She has never been bold enough to help her sex by truthful lessons from her own experience. She has too long borne the most excruciating wrongs, suffered them in silent resignation, smiling through her pain. Often I think it were better she had been termed impatient and unwomanly, just so she had had the courage to speak at times for the enlightenment of her own sex."

Friends, let us take this matter to heart. Have you all read Ward's Dynamic Sociology?[11] If you have not, do, I beg of you, especially the last few chapters of the first volume. There is more literature on this subject, but not half enough, and what there is of it is not adapted to popular reading, but we should inform ourselves as to the truth, and quietly, as we have opportunity, interpret it to others. Then, if we must confess that women are handicapped by peculiar troubles, it will not be as they that have no hope. Such acknowledgements now give occasion to the enemy to boast, but if the causes were pointed out it would do good rather than harm to let the facts be known, because our people would thereby be frightened into obedience to nature's laws, and so our race come back to health.

I have received many letters that I would like to lay before you. Not all of our women who have entered the profession have found success, and more than one has declined to join, although heartily approving our object, because she has "accomplished nothing that is worth telling about." Others have attained success, but in their isolation their sympathies have become crusted over. They meet my advances cordially enough, but do not seem to care to make an effort

11. Lester Ward's *Dynamic Sociology* (1881) rejected the theory of Social Darwinism and argued instead that society had an obligation to reshape the environment to counteract the destructive and competitive forces of nature. Ward also argued against natural evolution because it differentiated between the sexes, inhibited women's inherent mental and physical abilities, reduced them to an artificial position of inferiority, and prevented them from taking what he believed was their natural position as the stabilizers of society.

to secure new friends. It has caused me a little heartache to give these up this year, for as I have reached out into the dark to find you, I have met so many warm, hearty hand-clasps that I long to have these, who need affection so much, come into our circle, too. Then there are many others who write most friendly words, who think that they have not time to write you a stately, elaborate letter, when if they would only "chat" with you instead of me, you would be as much in love with them as I am.

But patience must have her perfect work. We will all understand each other better some day, and in the blessed work of bringing about that happy time the Equity Club will share.

Martha Pearce,
Corresponding Secretary.

Address during the summer, Bridgewater, Adair County, Iowa

* * *

Constitution.

1. This organization shall be known as the Equity Club, and its motto shall be, "All the Allies of Each."

2. Its object shall be to promote acquaintance among women of the United States and other countries who are pursuing law as a study or as a profession, and to take such steps as may seem advisable to secure the success and usefulness of women in the profession.

3. All women practitioners and all who have pursued or are pursuing a regular course of legal study, whether in a school or an office, are eligible to membership.

4. Membership is conditioned upon the payment of an annual fee of two dollars and the writing of a letter giving personal experiences, or any matter which may be deemed of interest and profit to the club, for publication in the Club Annual.

5. The officers of this association shall be a Corresponding Secretary and an Executive Committee of five members.

6. The Corresponding Secretary shall be elected by the members of the club at large, but for the year 1887 the Ann Arbor branch will

act as Executive Committee. After this the Executive Committee also shall be elected by all the members.

7. Blank ballots shall be sent by September first of each year, by the Chairman of the Executive Committee, to each member, and shall be accompanied by a list of officers to be voted for. These shall be returned, filled out, by October first, and the persons receiving the highest number of votes shall be declared elected.

8. Amendments shall be presented to the Executive Committee, and, if approved and submitted by them, shall become a part of the constitution, when ratified by two-thirds of the members of the club.

9. The Executive Committee shall act as an advisory board in all matters which may arise, and may make such minor provisions as may be necessary to render the work effective.

10. The Corresponding Secretary shall receive all applications for membership and membership fees, all letters of inquiry, and all letters for the Annual, to the publication of which she shall attend prior to June first of each year. She shall also communicate with similar organizations through such officers as they may appoint.

11. Each member shall be entitled to receive one copy of the Annual free.

* * *

Officers for 1887.

Corresponding Secretary—Martha K. Pearce.
Executive Committee—Almeda E. Hitchcock, Chairman, Lettie L. Burlingame, Margaret L. Wilcox, Corinne W. Douglas, Rebecca May.

The Executive Committee suggest the following changes in the constitution. They are such as have sprung from the desires of members as expressed in their correspondence, and such as we may successfully make. We think the simplest organization the best for a correspondence club and would not recommend a full list of officers. However, we submit to the club the questions:

1. Shall we elect a full list of officers?
2. Shall we elect officers only once in three years?
3. Shall we have honorary memberships at five dollars each, obtainable by those eligible to full membership only; but not entitling to vote?

4. Shall the Annual be copyrighted?
5. Shall we attempt to have meetings?
6. Shall the Executive Committee fill vacancies arising until another election?

It is requested that each member write these questions on a sheet of paper, and after them put yes or no as they wish to vote, and return the same as soon as possible to the Acting Chairman of the Executive Committee, Mrs. Margaret L. Wilcox, Union, McHenry County, Illinois. Any question answered in the affirmative by two-thirds majority shall be formulated by the Executive Committee as a part of the constitution.

* * *

Correspondence

Geneva, Nebraska

April 28, 1888

To the Members of the Equity Club,

An invitation has been extended to me by the secretary of this club, Miss M. K. Pearce, to unite with you. And in compliancc thcrcwith I send this note of greeting to my sisters.

On the nineteenth day of last November I took the oath required by law and assumed my place as a member of the bar in the Fifth Judicial District of Nebraska. My welcome was most hearty and earnest and from every brother I have received words of good will and kindly encouragement. If over indulgence and great kindness can ruin I am certainly on the highway to disaster. Yet I can but think that if the same spirit of kindness and equality was extended to the women in all professions, it would rebound to the credit and upbuilding of the professions and the progress of humanity.

I look upon the law as the greatest of all professions, embracing and comprehending all others. With the Golden Rule the corner stone in its foundation, Justice and Humanity its crowning precepts, and progressive education its great requisite it can not but stand at the head.

I honor the bar everywhere and am proud to be admitted as one of its members, to be able to add my quota toward the development of better law, better government, better society and better people.

I am glad that the women of our land are arousing themselves to an appreciation of their God given powers and taking the positions for which they are so eminently fitted. To my sisters in the law I would extend the right hand of fellowship and ask to be accepted as one of your number and permitted to add my labor to yours for the upbuilding of our profession and the encouragement of all women who are seeking places on professional highways.

Yours truly,
Addie M. Billings

* * *

Washington, D.C.

April 27, 1888

Dear Equity Club,

I began the study of law on the solicitation of my husband in the spring of 1880. I read in his office and under his instruction. I continued the course for two years (the time prescribed by the statutes), passed a creditable examination in open court and was admitted to the bar April 17, 1882. I practiced some in the county court before admission. The day of my admission husband and I became law partners, which relation is still sustained. We removed to Lincoln, Nebraska, in December, 1882.

I enjoy court practice more than office work and have handled successfully some noted cases in different parts of the state. Was admitted to practice in the supreme court of my state August 19, 1883. I have won three original cases in this highest state court which I prepared and handled alone. Have been admitted to the United States district and circuit courts in Nebraska.

I find my sex no hindrance in securing clients, and feel it no drawback in the prosecution of cases. Apparently, I am as acceptably received before court and jury as are male lawyers. My brothers in the profession always treat me with cordiality and courtesy.

In the trial of cases I make it a point to keep good-natured and to be especially courteous in my bearing towards opposing counsel. In preparation of cases my rule is to brief for the supreme court before instituting action in the lower court, the evidence of leading witnesses having been first noted in writing and fixed in my memory.

The works most helpful to me in studying correct advocacy are:—"Reed's Practical Suggestions,"[1] "Donovan on Trial Practice,"[2] and "Hints on Advocacy,"[3] and "Illustrations in Advocacy"[4] by Harris.

A loving greeting to each and every member of the club.

Ada M. Bittenbender
Lincoln, Nebraska

* * *

Joliet, Illinois

May 17, 1888

To the Equity Club,

Dear Ladies:—Now that I have each one of you stowed away in her own special niche in the gallery of pleasant memories, it is delightful to sit down for a little chat with you all.

First, I want to speak a word for dear Miss May, who was one of our charter members and wrote for us last year, but who is now at the bedside of a dying sister, and whose voice will be silent in our Annual this year. Miss May opened an office in Topeka, Kansas, last September, and was winning friends and a fast increasing practice, by her energy and ability, when she was suddenly summoned at the call of love and duty, to leave her profession and take up the cares of the sick room. We shall all hope that her trial may be as light as possible, and that she may yet attain success in her chosen calling. She bids me express her hearty good wishes for the prosperity of the legal sisterhood.

I opened my office on the first Monday in May, and the first week I took three cases, besides having a number of collections given me

1. John C. Reed, *Practical Suggestions for the Management of Law-Suits and Conduct of Litigation* (New York, 1875).

2. Joseph Wesley Donovan, *Trial Practice and Trial Lawyers* (St. Louis, Missouri, 1883).

3. Richard Harris, *Hints on Advocacy,* 4th ed. (London, 1880).

4. Richard Harris, *Illustrations in Advocacy* (St. Louis, Missouri, 1885).

to make. I don't expect to fare as well as that every week; still I feel very hopeful. I received my commission as notary public this morning, so I shall expect a few pennies from that source, and every little helps. There is practically no opposition here to a woman's practicing law, or doing anything else she chooses, if she conducts herself properly. Mrs. Gougar[1] held a suffrage convention here a few weeks ago and it was a very great success. She is a charming woman, and her gracious presence aids the cause almost as much as her eloquence. I feel dreadfully (?) about Prof. H. W. Rogers'[2] letter to Mrs. Bittenbender, in which he hinted that women were unfit for the contentions of the forum, because I am just wicked enough to prefer courtroom work. Skillful questioning and honest logic have charms for me that filling in prescribed forms with parrot like precision never could have. I think women ought to go into the court room. Where are they needed more? If your heart, O woman versed in the law, fails you at the threshold of the forum, what of her whose all, and often more than all, is there at stake? Shall not your courageous dignity sustain her in her hour of trial?

Miss Robinson raises the question as to whether we shall wear our bonnets in the court room. Why, yes, if one prefers. I do not like to keep my head covered, and feel sure that I shall never wear my hat when conducting a case, but if I were just going to make a motion or something of that sort, then I would.

The laws of Illinois are on the whole quite favorable to women, and present few inequalities. Most of the cases of hardship which have come to my notice arose from the perfect ignorance of women as to the laws and their rights under them, and to men's taking advantage of their lack of information in this respect, not from the injustice of the law itself, and I confess I have little sympathy for many of them, especially for those who ought to be well informed, but who almost boast of their wrongs, seeming to consider them an evidence of their own beautiful womanly meekness and simplicity. Their sweet,

1. Mrs. Helen Gougar was a suffrage leader and an advocate of temperance in Illinois. She supported the spread of suffrage activity within the WCTU and viewed women's suffrage as a means of achieving temperance.

2. Henry Wade Rogers joined the faculty of the law department of the University of Michigan in 1883. He was the first full-time professor of law at Michigan. He served as dean of the University of Michigan Law School from 1887–91.

trusting natures seem to have two missions, to furnish French novelists with heroines, and make men commit crimes and abuse trusts which would have no temptation were these women only truly womanly and strong.

Miss Robinson, Miss Pearce, Mrs. Waite and others who wield their pens, have considerable to do in reforming the literature of jurisprudence. As long as in many text books on the "Domestic Relations," and in many a volume of reports, is set up a double standard of morality, sanctioned by custom, just so long will hydra-headed divorce despoil the home, degrade manhood and womanhood, and multiply the wards of court. License for man means degradation for woman. Nature knows no sharp lines, and it is impossible that one-half of the race should be wholly angelic if the other be sunk in the depths of iniquity.

My chief trial, so far as my office is concerned, just at present, is agents, agents big and agents little, with everything from needles and pins to cast iron safes. The chief contributions so far have been in the shape of blotters and calendars from neighboring insurance offices. They seem to be under the impression that I am going to use ink and time freely.

I received a cute little card last November. It read:

Date, Nov. 11th, 1887. Weight, 9 Pounds.
Donald Douglas, Lawyer,
Announces
His Arrival.
61 Peach Street. Atlanta, Ga.

It is probably the care of this dear little cherub that has caused Mrs. Douglas to forget her Equity Club letter this year. I have no doubt that her knowledge of the law is now more precious to her than ever, as it renders her motherly protection more perfect.

Blessings on the Equity Club, and health and wealth to all its members.

Sincerely,
Lettie L. Burlingame

* * *

Tiffin, Ohio

May 23, 1888

Dear Sisters of the Equity Club,

I suppose it is really equitable that only she, who writes, may read, or become a member of the club. So, though, on looking back over the last fifteen years, it seems to me an uninteresting and very every day view; yet, possibly by relating some things that have happened I can earn my place in your number. Fifteen years ago the coming September, I opened my office in Tiffin, Ohio, in partnership with a sister, Nettie Cronise, now Nettie Cronise Lutes, of the law firm of Lutes & Lutes. We rented an office, furnished it with a desk or two, a few chairs, a carpet (long since disappeared), and bought all the books we could afford. Then swinging our sign, "N. & F. Cronise, Attorneys at Law," we sat waiting for business, taking up all extra time in answering invitations to enter the lists of various lecture lyceums scattered through the country, promising to introduce us as the "Woman Lawyers," "Something New," etc., etc. Putting all such ambitions aside, we sat and waited, and it wasn't long ere an occasional shadow passed over the threshold and entered. Business came gradually, by no means in a rush, and slowly we worked our way up. Our brothers extended the hand in welcome, so far as to put no visible obstacle in our way—neither did they make an effort to remove any. We began on the same footing as any of the young men, and have kept on to the present. The following year my partner left me and entered into the new firm, while I continued to paddle my canoe alone. In the early days our work came chiefly from men, women having but little confidence in the ability of women. All this, however, has changed, and my clients are as frequently one as the other. I am as liable to be employed on the side of the man as of the woman. My practice covers all classes of cases, and I have never hesitated to undertake and conduct a cause by reason of its character, thinking where a woman is a party or a witness there it is proper for another woman to be—and never yet have I been made to feel that I was in any way indelicate by reason of so doing. My experience has taught me that a woman can go along by the side of men in the same profession, receiving from all the same professional courtesy that they extend to the brotherhood, and we must ask for no more. One of my earliest experiences was a suit brought against a liquor dealer. Our success was such that, in addition to a fair fee from our clients, the defendant, being overjoyed with the settlement, presented each of us with a little plaster image. Mine still adorns the home mantel. The last case I tried, a few days since, was in defending a young man in a breach of promise suit, brought for $5,000. The result, $1,200, verdict against my poor fellow. Of course, while I regretted losing my case even to that extent, I could but have an appreciation of the fact that chivalry was still extant, and Don Quixotes could be counted in Seneca County, Ohio, by the *twelves.* Along the line of these fifteen years I find scattered an innumerable lot of cases, railroad suits, insurance, land, divorce and alimony (one, both or either,) bastardy cases, labor claims, libel suits, suits of all classes against corporations, settlement of estates, etc., etc., far too varied to recall.

My business frequently calls me out of my own state. Two glorious summers I distinctly remember being passed in Northern Michigan, on Little Traverse Bay, clearing up land titles and drinking in the delicious lake breezes. (This, by the way, doesn't often happen, and 'tis well not to expect many such oases in the desert).

It has been made a rule of my professional life to go quietly on, remaining very closely at my business, seldom doing anything of a public character outside my law business, and the result I believe to be better than had I answered some of the many calls to appear before the people in behalf of woman's rights. But I don't want you to think that my professional life has been one of unceasing pleasures and successes, for it has not. It has its ups and downs, to-day, as it had years ago. Sometimes I have thought that the downs prevailed, but then everything would brighten again, and the result is a comfortable income and a success comparing favorably with that of the young men entering the profession at the same time.

Yours very truly,
Florence Cronise

* * *

802 F Street, N. W.,
Washington, D.C.

April 18, 1888

Dear Equity Club,

I taught school ten years and found myself growing tired, nervous and unhappy, and moreover earning but a mere pittance, never over $500 a year. The outlook was discouraging and I resolved to carry out an idea that had existed *in nubibus* in my mind for years and to study law.

In 1880 I came here and for a short time was under the instruction of Mrs. Lockwood, to whom I shall always feel grateful for assistance and encouragement. Then I entered the Law Department of Howard University[1] and was graduated in 1882–3. In June of 1883 I passed the bar examination and was admitted to practice in the supreme court of the District of Columbia.

As our lectures were all in the evening I had the good fortune, during my term of study, to secure a place in an attorney's office and found my experience there of very great advantage to me. I have continued in the same office since my admission to the bar. I do principally office work—preparing or superintending the preparation of pleadings, conveyances, wills, etc., taking testimony in equity cases, notarial work and supervision of accounts and correspondence. My active court work has been limited to the probate court.

I should like answers to two questions from all women attorneys:

1. Do you like the legal profession?
2. Do you make it pay?

For myself I am perfectly satisfied with my work. I can conceive of no sphere of life where I would be as contented as I am at present. As to the financial part, I either directly from my profession—or from opportunities thrown in my way by its means, made from three to four times as much as I ever made as a teacher.

I have endeavored to do thoroughly and conscientiously whatever I have had to do, to stick to my profession and not be lured into any

1. Howard University, a product of the reconstruction era's commitment to educating newly freed black Americans, was also open to women. It was the first law school in the country to accept applicants regardless of either race or sex.

class of philanthropic or other work, knowing the law to be a jealous mistress and believing that I could do no better work than to prove what a woman could by persistent application earn a competency at the law as one of the many who are doing it, and to avoid notoriety.

To a faithful adherence to these rules, I owe the modicum of success I have attained.

Very truly,
Emma M. Gillett

* * *

1 Warren Square,
Jamaica Plain, Massachusetts

April 5, 1888

My Dear Sisters,

What an inspiration it was in our Ann Arbor friends to plan this club, and invite us all to the feast of good things! It has been a great pleasure to me to make the acquaintance of so many enthusiastic fellow-laborers, and a benefit as well.

I found, in reading the package of letters last year, that, although every one was interesting and helpful, those which told the story of personal experiences were particularly so. In consequence, at the risk of appearing egotistic in the relation of my own work, I venture to write "in the first person singular," though my experiences are very tame and uninteresting, in comparison with those of my sisters in the club, which gave me so much pleasure.

I have passed a very uneventful year in the law school, the only woman in it this year. Uniform kindness and courtesy have characterized the behavior of my fellow students. Nothing at all unpleasant or disagreeable to me ever occurs. Of course delicate subjects are necessarily discussed, but we all feel, I think, that those are necessary parts of our legal course, and so view the matter in a business light, putting all false modesty aside. And in any case, a woman's position in a law school can never expose her to the unpleasant features of a course of *medical* study in a mixed school, which so many hundreds of women are now pursuing.

Since the first of January I have been doing the work of the middle year as well as of the senior year, in order to make up what I lost last year during my long illness and still graduate with my class this coming June.

One thing I am very grateful for, that is, for the kindness of Mr. Hemenway[1] in permitting me to go into his office and learn what I could of office work. When I think of the trials of Miss Waugh, so pathetically and humorously related to the club, and of others who have tried in vain to find such a helping hand, I really do not know which to be most grateful for, my patron's kindness or my own good fortune. Miss Wright enjoyed the same privilege last year, in the same office. So you see that conservative Boston is not entirely indifferent to the demands of the spirit of the age.

Not long ago an amusing incident occurred. I was asked by one of the gentlemen in the office to assist his colleague, who had come from a country town in the interior of the state, in preparing a brief. We worked busily for several hours, he looking up cases and marking extracts from the opinions, which I copied. Evidently he supposed me to be a correspondence clerk, or something similar. Finally it came out that I was a law student. He looked at me in a state of stupefaction, and remarked in a pathetic, despairing and regretful tone, as if he had been cruelly defrauded of the sight of such a *rara avis,* "Why-I-never-saw a woman law student before!" The discovery proved an aid to our work, however, for after that, the volumes of reports were, as soon as found, turned over to me with the remark, "You know what we want. Make your own extracts."

I shall probably open an office in the fall, in Boston, and take whatever business presents itself. Miss Robinson's friendship, sympathy and counsel are of great value to me, and I think it is helpful to both of us to feel that neither is "the only woman lawyer in Massachusetts." Conveyancing is the special branch of the law to which I desire to devote myself, but I shall take whatever business comes, until I can afford to select—if that happy time ever arrives.

Knowing that

> "A little nonsense now and then,
> Is relished by"—our wise women,

1. Alfred Hemenway was a prominent Boston lawyer. His support of Mary Greene was significant given his prestige in the Boston legal community.

I venture to append some specimens of legal deductions culled from the fly leaves of my note books. They are actual productions of the masculine mind, taken *verbatim,* on the spot, in our class room:

No. 1. *Mr. A, (instructor)* "Does anyone know what, in law, is the shortest distance between two given points?"

Mr. B.—"Should think 'twould depend on circumstances."

Mr. A., severely—"Mr. B., is it possible to have *two* shortest distances between the same two given points?"

Mr. B., stiffly—"Yes sir, I think it is, 'twould depend entirely on circumstances."

No. 2. *Mr. C.,* a student of Hibernian extraction—"Don't you have to prove malice sometimes in a suit for slander when an indictable offense has been charged?"

Instructor—"I don't understand it so, Mr. C."

Mr. C.—"Well, I read a case where the plaintiff was accused of *having been hung,* and the court non-suited him for lack of malice."

No. 3. The power of circumstantial evidence was illustrated by the lecturer by stating the fact that the finding of Dr. Parkman's false teeth in the crucible at the laboratory, was the main link in the chain of evidence convicting Dr. Webster.

Instructor, some days later—"Mr. D, what is circumstantial evidence."

Mr. D, hesitating—"Well-um-well-false teeth in a furnace."

And yet there are a few people left in the world who think it is impossible for the feminine mind to compete in the professions with the vastly superior masculine brain!

Success and long life to the club and to each member of it.

Cordially yours,
Mary A. Greene,
Class of '88, Law School of
Boston University.

* * *

Iowa City, Iowa

May 12, 1888

To the Equity Club,

Are the times out of joint? Surely our fathers of the old time might think so could they but read of and listen to the tales of woman's progress to-day. In those old times the baby girl was raised that she might keep within her proper "sphere." But now, oh halcyon days! That limiting phrase, "woman's sphere," has dropped out of good English, thanks to the pioneer workers for woman's advancement, and the earnest, intelligent, noble women who to-day stand in the front ranks.

Fifty years ago we might write with propriety letters, poetry or stories, if we had wit enough. Now we may write what we please, and make ourselves known in every profession. Lectures are written and delivered from college chairs by women occupants. Sermons are written not for a dull husband's dull delivery, but to fit the gentle voice and persuasive manner of the writer. Oh! shade of the great apostle, what thinkest thou of that? With all the assumed wisdom that usually accompanies the title of Doctor, woman's hands may and do write those mystic slips from which are concocted as vile compounds as any man dare lay claim to. And we of the law may write pleadings, prepare briefs and arguments, shape wills, contracts, and deeds, and have a hand in defending right or upholding wrong; depending upon which side of a case we have the good or bad fortune to be retained in.

And I may write to you, my sisters in the law, and tell you without egotism of myself! Well, I must say I would prefer a different subject, but the corresponding secretary of this club has developed one of the requisites for a successful attorney, that is, she does not readily yield a point. So I now proceed to introduce myself. "How did I come to study law?" I had been ten years a married woman; my husband was steadily working his way in his profession; and I was doing what usually falls to the lot of women—*home work,* after two years of teaching in our public schools. I do not now remember how the thought came to me, on the tenth anniversary of our wedding day that I was really growing rusty in the little I knew, while my life companion was taking great strides in advance of me. I thought out the subject seriously and concluded that I must do something—not alone with my hands—but my head, though purely feminine, must go to work, too.

These thoughts came to me perhaps from the fact that "no children played around our door." I put the case and question to my husband, what shall I do? He said at once, enter the law school and prepare yourself for office work. I immediately acted upon the advice, and was welcomed by the professors and students of the law department of the state university with the greatest courtesy.[1] No year of my life is more full of pleasant memories than that first year in the study of the law. My health failed one month before the close of the year. Not, as many thought, from the mental effort, but from the fact that I, like all women who attempt to do anything outside of homework, did really the work of two people, that of a student as well as that of a housekeeper. However I graduated with my class of nearly a hundred young men and was one of ten chosen to represent the class at Commencement. After a year of rest I took what was then termed the advanced law course of one year and received at its close a certificate of special proficiency in the law, and was again chosen as the single representative to speak for the class. My subject was "Homesteads," in which I tried to bring out the great good to women as well as men that had grown out of these laws.

Well, I have no trials to relate. My second year in the study was pleasant as well as profitable.

I was then prepared for office work, of which in the years that have passed I have done not a little. There has been no occasion for me at any time to take public part in the practice, as I was in my husband's office, and I preferred the preparation of a case to its argument.

While I have not in any public manner made use of my knowledge of law, it has been of inestimable value to me. The mental discipline that is required in mastering the common law, with its intricacies, its niceties, its refinements, is far superior to any study of mental philosophy.

As you all know these are times when women are generally aroused to think on all topics, literature, science, art, and I am glad to say on business topics. A few years ago by request I prepared and read a

1. The University of Iowa admitted women law students as early as 1869.

paper before the Des Moines Women's Club, on "The Property Rights of Women in Iowa," and I have since read the paper before several other similar clubs, and I have been shocked in this state in which general intelligence is very great, to be asked the most surprising questions, and to learn how little women know, as a rule, of the very laws of most interest to themselves. I have felt since that in a quiet way it was one of my missions to help all women who cared for help to a better understanding of their legal status.

In October, 1886, I read a paper before the women's congress in Louisville, Kentucky, on the subject of "Women as Land-holders in the West." After I was through reading a woman, a stranger to me, came to me. Her face haunts me yet, there was such a helpless, longing, anxious, careworn, look in it, and it was draped about with heavy folds of that dreadful evidence of mourning, crape. Said she, "Oh, Mrs. Haddock, you can never know the loss and trouble, and indeed in many cases great suffering which comes to us women who have no idea of business. We are so helpless, and with many of us the loss of husband means the loss of all property, and we are thrown without means, and without knowledge, upon our own resources." I looked at her and knew she was telling me her own heart secrets, though she made it general, and I felt pity and disgust for that social order of things, which from the very cradle trains a *boy* to know the value of money and the road to its attainment, and builds walls about girls to insure their ignorance and inefficiency in the smallest details of business life.

I had almost forgotten to tell you that for three successive years I had the honor of being appointed by the supreme court of Iowa as one of the examining committee to examine law applicants for graduation in my Alma Mater.

Hoping soon to know you all through the letters published, I am happy to subscribe myself as one of you.

Emma Haddock

* * *

Ann Arbor, Michigan

April 30, 1888

Dear Sisters in Equity,

This brief history is written by request. My early life was a very uneventful, but an exceedingly happy one. Out door life tends to make one happy, and, as that was my early life I, consequently, was happy as the day was long. Playing with dolls did not afford me any amusement, save so far as to have them die and be buried. After the funeral I would run off with my brothers and cousins and climb trees or chase the calves around the pasture.

School life was very hum-drum on my part, but not so on the part of my teachers, for they had a hard time from beginning to end, to keep me quiet. My lessons were learned in no time at all, and consequently time hung heavily on my hands. I can well say that the familiar saying, "Satan finds some mischief still for idle hands to do," is a very true one, for mischief seemed to be the order of the day.

After finishing at the home school, my sister and I went to the Oahu College, at Honolulu.[1] Want of health would not let me finish the course.

After the summer vacation of '81, I took a country school and tried teaching for a year. That occupation proved very trying, and so it was given up for more congenial work, in father's law office. The idea of studying for the profession, had not then entered my thoughts. My highest aim was to know enough to help father. He would take me on the court circuits with him, until I began to wish for more knowledge of the law; but still the thought of entering a law school had not entered my mind. They came soon, however, for I had the pleasure of meeting one of the graduates of this college, on her way around the world. She knew that I was in a law office, and of my liking for the law. While out riding one day, we commenced talking of the profession, when all of a sudden, there flashed across my mind, the idea of going to a law school, and taking a full legal course. The matter was broached to father, and his consent was immediately gained. Catalogues of different schools were sent for, and much dis-

1. Hitchcock's grandfather founded Oahu College as a missionary school. It was later renamed Punahou.

cussed. There was some hesitation between the University of California and that of Michigan. The latter was finally decided upon, and preparations were commenced for the two years' life away from home.

The first year here was very hard—hard in the sense that I was a "stranger in a strange land." My legal sisters, in their senior year, took me into their circle of friendship and their kindness will never be forgotten. The life here at college has been all that one could ask for. My classmates have treated me with respect and kindness. Not an unpleasant thing has occurred in my college life. Whenever help was needed on knotty matters it was freely given.

Admission to the bar was gained December 27, '87. The finale is drawing near when we, as a class will say farewell to our Alma Mater. A feeling of sadness, as well as joy, comes over me whenever I think of the end that is near. Joy that the terrible quizzes are nearly over, and sadness that college life is so nearly at an end. Your sister in law and equity,

Hilo, Hawaii Almeda E. Hitchcock

* * *

Zurich, Switzerland

April 10, 1888

To the Equity Club, U.S.A.,

Miss Martha K. Pearce, Corresponding Secretary:—I thank you for your letter of March 20, which was cordially welcomed, with all the members of the club, my sisters struggling for justice and truth! I am rejoiced that such harmony prevails in the body of American ladies at law—they will in this manner attain greatness. Concerning your invitation that I should join the club I am the more overjoyed because I stand all alone upon the continent. There is to my knowledge only one other lady-lawyer upon the continent; this one is reported to live in Turin, and beyond this I know nothing of her. In Brussels there is studying at present a young Belgian lady, and in England it is said that several have taken the examinations. What these are doing is also unknown to me.

Of my experience there is little to say. I began to study in my 32d year, being then the mother of three children, and took the examination for Doctor's degree in the summer of 1887. Immediately thereafter I became established in the office of our leading jurist, Herr Professor Dr. Meili,[1] where I have since offered my services for practice. I cannot go before the court. Twice have I sought recognition before the highest court, but without success. No one can be admitted except such person be in possession of active citizenship, and this has in view, throughout the land, only the masculine citizen; while every gin for catching birds may be an advocate, and make game of the law, a woman, no matter what her qualifications, even though all that are requisite, has not this right. I attempted to prove that women in deed and truth, possessed the active right of citizenship; but that the statute law interposed with the regulation that the possession of civil rights, or standing in law, was requisite; and not other qualifications. But the judge rejected my arguments upon the narrow ground that this was in opposition to what had hither to been the custom. With this naturally all was at an end. So my activity is very limited. This is very discouraging and disadvantageous, and accordingly most important in an economical sense. Any improvement is not to be expected in the next ten or twenty years, because of the interposition of both bench and bar, and the character of those who furnish most of the business. The people go ten times to a disreputable pettifogger, where they go once to seek an honest counsellor. Prejudice is stronger and more general here against woman's advancement than could possibly be held in a Republic. In Switzerland, women are permitted to go on in their studies quietly, so long as most are foreign women; but in actual life here a woman must study only to be patient and faithful. That I should study law was deemed not only wonderful, but a half demented idea; but when I began to turn my knowledge to practical account, then they cried out that it was impossible for a frail woman to reason logically. Of course, there were some right worthy exceptions to this rule, and foremost my employer. Besides helping me as his secretary, he placed my trifling merit in the most auspicious light, whenever possible; and reproved others, who would have frowned; and in the most important cases he had only me for a partner. Such a faithful friend as my employer has been have I also

1. Professor Meili, the foremost advocate in Zurich, was one of the best-known lawyers in Switzerland.

among my former teachers in the college; and they have lightened my pathway that would otherwise have been dark with difficulty and mortification.

I am filled with enthusiasm for our noble profession, and came into it by no means to become notorious, but to win employment, with the thought that after a while I would journey to North America. There, of course, I would encounter the difficulties of unknown laws and language, but I could follow the profession of an attorney in your free land better. I can read the language and write a little but cannot speak it. I might, perhaps, teach German and spend the hours after school time in an office. Here I have done well with drawing up wills, deeds, and other documents, and with collections, but in all most serious and important cases I must send my clients to a man attorney, who can conduct the case before the court. I delight in scientific research, and would persuade my pupils to drink deep of the well springs of Roman and German law, whence all the inspiration of their own laws and language are drawn.

Could any of you assist me in obtaining such a position as I have mentioned, I would be most grateful.

With most cordial greeting and shake of the hand,

Dr. Jur. Emile Kempin

[Translated from the German by Lettie L. Burlingame.]

* * *

Effingham, Illinois

July 3, 1888

Dear Sisters of the Equity Club,

I had a bid to join your ranks last year, but not having a full understanding of what was proposed, I was left to wait a year before being able to enter your charmed circle.

I was one of the early women who studied the law and asked for admission into the ranks of the legal fraternity. I was a student in the law office of my husband, Henry B. Kepley, in 1868–9, and took a nine months' course in the University of Chicago[1] (Ill.) in 1869–70,

1. The University of Chicago Kepley referred to had no connection with the present University of Chicago. It was the antecedent of Northwestern University.

under the Dean-ship of Judge Henry Booth,[2] who has always been an ardent advocate of the rights of women. I received my certificate of graduation June 30, 1870, and the degree of *Bachelor of Laws* was declared duly conferred upon me. I made application for admission to the bar, with my male fraters, to the state's attorney of Cook County, but though he granted their request he refused mine, on the ground that the law of Illinois conferred no right upon him to do so.

Perhaps it might be well for me to say here, that I, like many another woman, received my impulse to enter this, one of the noblest professions, from a good man, and in this case it was my husband. I was willing enough and desired to help my kind and the world, but like many others the usages and customs of sex so bound me that I needed an impelling force, and I gratefully record this as due my "partner" in law and life.

In the winter of '71, when our legislature met, Mr. Kepley prepared a bill looking to the giving women, married and single, the same rights as men to enter the *learned* professions. This was sent to the Honorable Edward Harlan, of Marshall, Clark County, then our Senator, and was by him introduced and read in the Senate, and it was, so far as I know, the first bill of the kind introduced. Other bills similar were introduced and worked for by other parties during the winter, but the substance of Mr. Kepley's bill was finally incorporated into the body of our laws.

I did not make application for admission to the bar until January, 1881, on the 13th day of which I was admitted to full attorneyship. I have been twice commissioned as notary public.

I have appeared in cases, though I have not followed the regular practice of the law. In such cases as I have handled I have usually had success. In one case in our Circuit Court I raised a point that was entirely new that I was sustained in by the Court, and that was of value to clients in such cases.

My study of the law and attending law school created a large agitation of the "Woman Question" where I was known, and elsewhere among our people I can see signs of that agitation to-day.

I have been twice elected to serve as school officer, and as such have sat a number of times as judge of election, and though qualified

2. Judge Henry Booth was the first dean of the law school of Northwestern University. In the years of the Equity Club, Northwestern was known as the Union College of Law.

to attend to that, I was the only judge who acted on these occasions that was refused a vote. I have been a candidate for state's attorney on a County Prohibition ticket, and received more votes than any other candidate thereon. Had I been elected I proposed to test the question whether or not a woman could act as states attorney, as the right was disputed.

It is but right to say that the lawyers of Illinois are just, as a rule, to women. Our State Bar Association admits us to membership, and I believe four of our women lawyers, myself included, are members of that body.

For nearly ten years I have been engaged in W.C.T.U. work, and my knowledge of the law has been of great use to me in many ways, both as an educational force and as a means of securing enforcement of the laws.

I believe a study of the law, and a knowledge of it, strengthens, dignifies, elevates and broadens the thought, and is calculated to elevate the character. To sit amid the bulwarks of civilization and study their principles and mechanism must be uplifting to any human being, and I am glad and proud that I belong to a profession which numbers Moses, Deborah, Jonathan, Daniel, Joseph of Arimathea, Ezra, Gamaliel, Paul and Zenas in its ranks—for they were all lawyers, in a broad as well as in the narrow sense in which men are accustomed to regard that honorable profession.

I think, dear women of the Equity Club, we may all congratulate ourselves on being so happy as to belong to a profession which more than any other has helped the world to "Sweeter manners—purer laws."

For our *lawyers* have largely been the framers of our laws "since the time whereof the memory of man runneth not to the contrary."

Yours fraternally,
Ada H. Kepley

* * *

East Saginaw, Michigan

April 20, 1888

To the Equity Club,

Dear Sisters—I desire to assure you that it is for no lack of interest in women in the legal profession that I failed to manifest my hearty approval of the plan of the Equity Club a year ago. I did not forget my invitation to join you, but my life is a busy one, and, while I often wished that the letters might find their way to me, I found it easy to defer writing one of my own.

We have recently organized a society here called the University Club, which is for the mutual advantage of lady graduates from the various departments of the University of Michigan. We hold a meeting once a month, at which one member reads a paper on a topic assigned at a previous meeting. This is followed by a discussion in which every member is obliged to take part or pay a fine of twenty-five cents. The subject for the next meeting is: "Is it desirable that the United States restrict immigration from Europe?" We have ten members, consisting of two physicians, one bookkeeper, six teachers (in the high schools of this city and of Saginaw City), and one lawyer. It promises to be very helpful.

I trust that all members of the Equity Club have learned by experience that a large part of any calling consists of drudgery, and I take it for granted that for persons thus experienced there is little consolation in ideals, and that nothing that I might say in few words would be of so much interest as a brief outline of my work. I was of the law class of '82, U. of M., and my husband of the class of '81. He "swung his shingle" here among strangers in September, '82, about four months before we were married, and we made our way through the "starvation period" together. And while we have not grown rich, our office is a busy place and business is increasing. I have never made an effort to take an active part in court. In fact I never intended to do so, but have been assisting my husband in the office, and have given much time to stenography and office work, and to the prosecution of U.S. claims. I have a large pension business, which requires a great deal of attention, so that I have not found time to read law as much as I had planned to do; but still I cling to the resolution to carry out the plans in the future. Hope lures us on, you know. We have done considerable general reading, and prior to 1885 made a specialty of English History, during the preparation of Mr. LeValley's publication, entitled "The Royal Family of England,"[1] and among other things we are in the third year of the C.L.S.C. work.

Sincerely yours,
Laura A. W. LeValley

* * *

Danville, Indiana

May 4, 1888

Ladies of the Equity Club,

As a stranger, a place in a quiet corner would be far more desirable until the aims of the organization are more familiar to me; but the fiat has gone forth that "She who will not write may not read." May be you will care to know who I am?

The story of my life is very simple, and may be outlined as follows. The Goffs of Tuckahoe, N.J., and the Lieuellens of the Old Dominion were my father's ancestors. The Taylors, who, before Penn's colony was a score of years old, settled on the Brandywine, were my mother's. My parents were married in Athens County, Ohio, and after a few years moved into Meigs, where I, the youngest of a family of six children, was born, June 9, 1854. Before I was two years old they sought a new home in Clinton county of the same state, where they spent the remainder of their days. This was my home until 1876, when my business called me to this state, and later to this pleasant little city, where I now claim the cosiest little cottage home that can anywhere be found.

My mother's ill health and my father's lack of a son in his later years, made my duties heavier than usually fall to the lot of the farmer's daughter, as I must needs be "boy" on the farm as well as housekeeper. Childhood I only know from books, and from having observed other children, rather than from experience. Dropping corn, picking berries, milking cows, running errands, attending school, and after the age of twelve the undiminished duties of house-

---

1. Written by Laura LeValley's husband, *The Royal Family of England* was a history and chart of the royal family of England and was recognized as the standard work on the subject.

keeping, the care of my mother, and the nearly exclusive association of adults had made me think, feel and act like a woman. At the age of eighteen I was older than I have been since.

When but six my sisters took me to visit school. On my return in the evening my intention to become a teacher was announced, and the business at once begun, with my pet kittens for my pupils and the sitting-room chairs for their desks. My work for the public commenced when I was seventeen. Since then I have taught twelve months in country schools, received the degree of B.S., after a year's work at Lebanon, Ohio, held a principalship in a graded school for the same length of time, and with this year I expect to end my career as a teacher, and this one will make twelve years that I have held a professorship in this college. In all this time I have not lost one day on account of my own sickness, have cared for my parents, who are now no more to me than helpful, spiritual influences-fond memories; have taken but one vacation, have made many short journeys and two longer ones, have collected an excellent library, furnished myself and others a good home, lived busily and happily and have many good friends. Within the last six years more than a hundred ladies and gentlemen have graduated from my special class, and in the general school it has been my pleasure to guide many hundreds in their study of history and literature.

All these years I have been a student in special lines at different times. Comparative theology occupied my Sunday afternoons for five years. Philosophy, with Plato's Dialogues as the basis, five more, and this last year I have been studying Robert Browning. My poets are Shakespeare, Mrs. Browning and Lowell. My novelists, Hawthorn, Winthrop, Dickens and George Elliot. Emerson seems to me to embody the wisdom of all the sages. Herbert Spencer, great as seen through his Sociology and Data of Ethics. Humorous literature contributes much to my happiness. Channing and Savage are my most helpful spiritual teachers. I like politics.

My reading in law has been at the expense of my social life and has extended over seven years, much the better part of it having been done in the last three. Pomeroy's Equity Jurisprudence[1] for the present occupies my best time. My odd minutes are being used in a careful

1. Lieuellen refers here to J. Pomeroy, *A Treatise on Equity Jurisprudence, as Administered in the United States of America,* 2d ed. (San Francisco, 1892).

review of constitutional history, with Cooley's limitations as a text.[2] So much about myself.

Every step that woman takes interests me. If backward, she arouses my fear for her safety; if aside, she has my sympathy in her sorrow; if forward, she inspires in me hopes for better times, when man and woman will venerate truth and justice more than they now do custom.

With a strong desire to help and be helped,

Very truly yours,
Ce Dora Lieuellen

* * *

Room 70, 143 La Salle Street
Chicago, Illinois

May 25, 1888

My Dear Miss Pearce,

Secretary of the Equity Club,

Your letter, suggesting that I give the club some account of the hindrances and difficulties likely to be experienced in the first years of practice, has been received. As I have said before, I wish the members of the club well, and if I can aid those engaged in a sober-minded way in the work of the profession, I shall be glad to do so.

I became a law clerk on a small salary nearly seventeen years ago, and, excepting two years spent in law school, have been continuously in the work of the profession since. During that time I have learned considerable of lawyers and law practice as a matter of course, but it is difficult to write for those whose needs are quite unknown to me. But I will strike out at random, without regard to what anybody wants, and write of that which is most usually inquired about and most important.

I presume it is understood that no one should enter the legal profession who is not fond of the profession for its own sake. Other avocations furnish a better field if money making is the object. Of course lawyers when once established may expect to make a comfort-

2. Lieuellen is referring to Thomas M. Cooley's *A Treatise on the Constitutional Limitations Which Rest Upon the Legislative Powers of the State of the American Union* (Boston, 1868).

able living, and something over. They sometimes become wealthy, but generally that is from a careful investment of their small surplus. Probably the majority of incomes are within the range of $1,000 to $3,000. The larger incomes are enjoyed by comparatively few.

It is considered that if a man lawyer pays office rent the first year and in addition makes a living for himself the second year, he does well. It generally takes longer than this, unless there are unusually favorable circumstances. People will trust their physical and spiritual well being to faith, but not so their property matters. People with desirable business are slow to entrust it to attorneys without experience, and so it happens that experience must be acquired from poor paying business, and it takes a long time to get upon a self-sustaining basis. Many men get discouraged and give it up.

Unless attorneys have reserve capital they generally find it necessary to dovetail something else in with law for a few years—as fire insurance, posting books and the like.

Women have established a paying business in the shortest time calculated upon for men—two years—but generally it has taken them longer. Women have more difficulty than men in making an extensive acquaintance among business men in an easy, off-hand way, as men attorneys make it in clubs and business and public places. The greatest part of profitable law business comes from business people with important interest, and these are now mostly men.

Another difficulty women attorneys are apt to have is that they have not come in contact with the business world enough to have a good general knowledge of affairs, and do not seem to know how to get at the bottom of things. The freedom with which boys move about in public places enables them to gather up a great deal of practical information before they reach the business age. The increase of women in business improves the facilities for girls going about the same as boys.

I count as part of the most valuable of my preparation for practice that I studied law in an office where the principal enterprises of the vicinity were talked over in detail before entered upon. The office was open evenings and the leading business men of the place would drop in from time to time and talk over affairs generally—gossip, so to speak, about their own and other people's affairs. The office was also the office of Gov. Fenton when at home (I studied in Jamestown, New York), and in addition to the large clientage of the law firm, we had frequently there representative men from all parts of the country—men well versed in business, and whose conversation gave us an insight into matters public and private not otherwise easily obtained.

There were three students besides myself in the office, and we had a great deal of discussion on legal and business matters, which helped to bring out important points and fix things in mind. In addition, the young lawyers and law students of the town had a club that met once a week and discussed the law applicable to a given state of facts. After that was over we discussed everything that was going on in the community, and between us all we knew pretty much everything of importance.

Another help to me from childhood was that my father prepared for the bar and was always a great deal among lawyers and in court, and took pains to tell at home what was going on and explain the legal points involved.

In addition to the difficulty of acquiring an acquaintance among business people and a general knowledge of affairs, women have to contend, unless very robust and healthy, with a physical condition that is very trying. I refer to the close relation between the brain and the organs peculiar to women, and to the fact that any trouble with those organs (and a celebrated anatomist says they seem made to get out of order) seriously affects the brain and the nervous system.

The trial of causes is a severe strain upon the nervous system, and men who have proper interest in their cases suffer greatly. The peculiarity I have mentioned makes women liable to suffer more from this nervous strain than men. Hence, it becomes of prime importance that women attorneys have a first-class physical condition.

A word as to charity clients. Up to the time of Miss Perry's[1] sickness we did a great deal of work for women for little or nothing. Miss Perry's death was caused by overwork—in doing a great deal of work for women for nothing and then enough more to make a living. Had she not been overworked, the cold she took would not have been serious. Work for charity clients is more severe than that for business people, because as a rule they are incompetent to do anything for themselves and have no money for incidental outside expenses. When Miss Perry died I said, and have followed the rule since, when I have

1. On M. Fredrika Perry, see Slocum letter, 1887, n. 5.

anything to give away I will give it in money and not in legal services, except where I have a personal obligation.

I think women attorneys owe it to themselves to follow this rule as soon as they are through doing business for experience, and the physical disadvantage I have mentioned makes this all the more important.

Events have led me to think there are some matters not understood by all women attorneys.

One is that their best *practical legal education* must come from association with the best lawyers of one's own vicinity, whether men or women. Lawyers are almost universally ready to talk with a woman on legal matters if they find she has a practical mind and grasps the subject. This association is of incalculable value and indispensable to success. It is from an infinite variety of observation and experience in actual cases that lawyers get the skill and knowledge necessary for the proper application of principles to constantly varying circumstances.

Another matter that seems to be not understood by all is that the question whether women have ability to understand legal principles is not debatable by women nor in the presence of women. Women who understood legal principles went gray-headed to their graves long before any woman now living was born.

Another mistake is the assumption that it is a matter of great moment for a woman to study law. Women studied law before there were any women lawyers. Literary and intellectual women of the higher grade often read the leading text books. Women court reporters often read law and besides are pretty well versed in practical law matters.

Another matter misunderstood is that a lawyer cannot devote any great amount of energy to anything else and make headway in the profession. Law is a severe task master and demands undivided allegiance.

Another matter is that undergraduates are not authorized to speak for attorneys, either men or women. Young men do not attempt to do so, and herein they are properly modest. There are some things people only learn by experience, and this is the case in law more than in any other profession or business, probably—the field of knowledge, theoretical and practical, is so wide.

It was my good fortune to know personally, long ago, Miss Perry,

Miss Goodell[2] and Miss Hulett,[3] three of the best women practitioners—lawyers in fact—women who ranked with the men of the profession in judicial discrimination and practical sagacity; women who had the lawyer's instinct, so to speak.

I sincerely hope the members of the Equity Club will seek to emulate these women, and will follow the profession in a sober-minded, matter-of-fact way as they did, and as some women yet living do.

It would be easy for the Club to harm the cause of women in practice by ill-advised action; it could raise a presumption against their practical sagacity. A considerable number of thoughtful and substantial men and women who are friendly to women in any avocation they chance to take up and conduct honorably, are getting disgusted with the froth and pretense of some of the women attorneys. The two classes whose good opinion is of most value to women lawyers, and all lawyers, are the solid men of the profession who do the bulk of the law business, and the solid people in general business who furnish the greater part of the paying law practice. These people are not affected by any variety of moonshine nor dazzled by glitter and glow.

I shall be glad to see at my office any member of the Club who comes to Chicago.

Yours, with best wishes,
Ellen A. Martin

* * *

2. Lavinia Goodell was a pioneer woman lawyer in Wisconsin. In 1876, she was denied admission to practice law before the Supreme Court of Wisconsin. This rejection led to the passage of legislation providing that no person should be denied admission to the Wisconsin bar on account of sex.

3. Alta Hulett was denied admission to the Illinois bar in 1871. In 1872, she drafted a bill that was passed by the Illinois legislature that provided that no person could be barred from any occupation on account of sex. In 1872, she became the first woman admitted to the bar of Illinois.

[CABLE MESSAGE]

Sheffield, England

June 18, 1888

Martha Pearce:

Cordial greetings. Will write letter next year.

Orme

* * *

5 Pemberton Square, Room 25,
Boston, Massachusetts

April 7, 1888

Dear Equity Club,

A year ago I wrote you from Texas, while travelling. Happily now I am back in Boston, settled once more in the dear old home nest, and spending business hours in my office in the same building where I was located for three years before going to Washington Territory four years ago. When I wrote you before it was with a hampered pen, for the one thing I wanted to say was that now women had proven themselves entirely capable of studying law, it was all essential for them to prove themselves capable of *practicing* law, and that it was the duty of every woman who had been admitted to the bar to get into active practice as quickly as possible, and to stay there, working her way, rapidly or slowly, as other lawyers work theirs. I wanted to say this, for I believe it to be the all-important thing. But how could I, with any emphasis, when I myself was travelling in the south, far from home, engaged in the business interests of my book, with neither office nor practice of my own?

My only excuse for this was that my book was strictly a legal one, and that it would aid in establishing the reputation of women lawyers if it could be made a recognized success. Still, even that excuse was a poor one. The business of the book should have been in other hands altogether, and I should not have indulged myself in a winter south, but should have been in my office increasing my clientage. Anything whatever that lures the woman attorney away from her office should be put aside—must be put aside—if women are ever to establish themselves as a recognized element of the bar of this country, as women physicians have become recognized in the medical fraternities.

If a woman who has studied law or been admitted to the bar abandons practice, even temporarily, for the lecture field—whether her subject be temperance, suffrage or any other great stirring question of the day, and whether her object be philanthropy, money, fame, or all three—she may be the more successful lecturer for her legal training, doubtless, but the world will say that she lectures because she cannot succeed in practice. And so of any other path, aside from that of the law itself, which she may choose.

A woman may justifiably abandon her legal practice, as she may her dressmaking, or her dishwashing, or any other employment of her single life, if she marries and such employment proves incompatible with the new duties which she has assumed, because they are woman's highest duties and must be paramount; but the happiest thing, surely, for the woman lawyer who marries is to marry into law rather than out of it. Was there ever a more delightful romance than that of the husband and wife, who, having studied together in college and law school, graduated together to start—as I suppose Mr. and Mrs. Wilcox have ere now done—in practice together?

It was only yesterday that I received last year's Equity Club letters, and I sat up until nearly midnight reading them. (It is now several days since the date at the head of this letter, for I have been continually interrupted.) So at last I feel really acquainted with you, and can place you each one in her own little niche of my thoughts, and if we were to meet I feel quite as if we might recognize each other. By-the-way, I have a suggestion to make. Next best to a personal meeting (which looks very difficult of achievement at present), is letters and photographs. The letters we have. Now I propose the photographs. If we could all agree to a mutual exchange, each picture to be endorsed with the autograph of its original, would it not be charming to have such a gallery in each of our homes?

There are advantages of a practical nature to be derived from real familiarity with each other, which perhaps those of our number who are not yet inducted into the mysteries of practice, may not fully realize. Lawyers frequently have matters brought to their attention which must be sued upon, or defended, or otherwise cared for in other states, and which must be sent to some lawyer in such state for attention. Yesterday I received a letter from a Chicago attorney, a friend of mine, asking for certain information relative to a matter on which testimony is to be taken in Boston on a commission from the court of Illinois, and stating that the commission would probably be issued to me. (This acting as a commissioner to take evidence is good paying work and particularly suited to a woman. So is referee work and auditor's. I had considerable experience in Washington Territory as referee, and all my findings were sustained by the court.) And a few days ago a lady called to consult me regarding an application for divorce which her husband had just filed against her in California. I told her she must fight it and file a cross-libel. But to do this it was necessary to employ a reliable attorney there without loss of time, and as she depended entirely on me in the matter, I felt the responsibility of selecting just the right party very keenly. Fortunately I knew exactly the man for the business, a law-school classmate of my own, who is in good practice in the city where the matter will come up, and whom I can trust absolutely. So I telegraphed the case to him, following it with a letter containing instructions and retainer, and the matter is off my mind. In this way lawyers in different parts of the country profit by being well known to each other, and it is especially desirable that we women should be as familiar as possible with each other's professional standing and experience, that we may be able to render mutual aid and support.

For the encouragement of our younger sisters just coming into the arena of practice, I will say that I notice a decided difference between the general opinion which seemed to obtain concerning women attorneys half a dozen years ago when I was first admitted to the bar in Massachusetts and now, when I return here after four year's absence. My experience in trying to get a clerkship or a foothold as student in any Boston law office, when I graduated from the law school seven years ago, was so similar to that of our bright little Kittie Waugh[1] that I repeated my own disappointments in reading her very amusing account of hers. It was because of this failure to get into an office that I opened my own, even before the law had been passed allowing my admission to the bar, for I could do office business without admission, and I never expected to do court work at all, the sound of my own voice in public being quite unknown to me. I reasoned in theory

1. Robinson refers here to Equity Club member Catharine G. Waugh McCulloch.

as Mrs. Corinne Douglas argues in her club letter, that "the law business that will fall most naturally into her hands, is that not less honorable and more remunerative if less public class known as 'office work.'" "Surely," thought I, just as Mrs. Douglas thinks, "it is better to make a deed over which there can be no litigation than to twist a meaning favorable to one's client out of one unskillfully drawn." But I have found in experience that the public, from whom business must come if at all, judges a woman lawyer as it does a man, largely by his success or non-success in court, and if one is never seen or heard there, one's abilities are matter of serious doubt.

Of course if a woman lawyer has a large circle of friends who have legal business and will entrust it to her, she may gather up a good office practice without going through the usual test of public work in court; and if she is lucky enough to be associated in any way with an established office that is full of business, she may have work of this sort turned over to her. But even in the latter case, the most fortunate of all chances which can come to a young lawyer in starting, it is apt to be the salaried clerk who draws the papers, and the older lawyers who have to give advice (clients being unwilling to be turned over to a young practitioner when they have gone to an old one), and it is the small matters coming up for trial in the inferior courts which are most likely to be given to a young lawyer to take care of. And further, I think that when Mrs. Douglas becomes interested in her clients' rights, and feels the responsibility of the duty which devolves on her to protect them, she will realize that it includes not only the drawing of a sound deed, but quite as imperatively the saving him or her from the loss which threatens through an imperfect deed formerly drawn by an ill-trained or careless party. The one duty is quite as strong as the other, and the work as honorable.

So our pioneer, Mrs. Lockwood, tells us that "in all large cities a lawyer may choose specialties and find a practice lucrative enough to fully employ her time." She admits that she herself "entered at once into the active and general practice of the law, taking up and entering earnestly into every case;" but she attributes the necessity for her doing so to the fact that prejudice was so strong against women lawyers in the early days of her beginning. But I have found it to be the case, both east and west, that young lawyers of the other sex, unless they step into a place ready made for them in a specialist's office, must take whatever business comes during all their earlier years of practice, and that it is only when circumstances have developed them in some particular direction that a specialty chooses them, rather than they the specialty. And I see no reason why the rule should work differently with a woman. In my own case, I very emphatically chose office practice, but it didn't choose me in any encouraging degree. Business came in very slowly during the three and a half years that I had my office here before going west (about one year of the time being the period of delay that elapsed between my graduation from the law school and my admission to the bar under the new law), and consisted mostly of small and rather hopeless claims for collection. In the rare cases of my bringing suit on them, I engaged another lawyer to take them into court; thus, of course, reducing my own profits very considerably. At last, shortly before going west, I did go into the probate court in person to claim separate maintenance and custody of children for a deserted wife, and, though the case was hard fought, I won it. Then, just four years ago, circumstances combined to influence me to go west, chief among them being the accounts which I heard of the liberality of western views on the "woman question," and other live issues of the day. So I settled in Seattle, Washington Territory, expecting to remain permanently and to be joined there by my parents and sister. I stayed nearly a year, was delighted with the place, climate, people, and the bright, new civilization; succeeded well professionally, because though I had very few matters entrusted to my care, and had a great deal of uncomfortably leisure time, three or four of my cases paid excellent fees, and the referee work which Judge Greene[2] gave me was sure pay and good pay. There, too, the advice of my friends in the profession was not contradictory, as it had been here, concerning the advisability of my doing court work. All united in urging me to undertake it, and the judge started me in earnest by appointing me as counsel for a prisoner at the opening of the first term after my arrival. So I made the attempt, with fear and trembling, and shall always be glad, for besides finding I could do the work, I had the invaluable experience of going

2. Judge Roger S. Greene of the Washington Territory was an advocate of women's rights. He contributed articles to the *Woman's Journal* in support of women's suffrage.

more than once before a mixed jury of men and women—something that I suppose no other woman attorney has ever done.[3]

But it proved impracticable for my family to join me, and I became exceedingly heart-sick for lack of them; then too, my book was ready for publication and needed my personal attention while going through the press, so I came home, fully expecting to return. A few month's illness at home followed, then six months in Chicago, while my book[4] was coming out, then nearly a year of co-operation with my publishers in superintending the work of agents who were putting it on the market, then—at last back home last fall. And after so much absence I could not leave home again. As they from whom I could not bear separation could not go west with me, I must stay in Boston with them. And in that case I must resume practice here for I have never for a moment given up my plan formed ten years ago of *practicing law*. But from my former experience here, I dreaded the prospect; besides I had forgotten much of the little I had known of the methods of practice in this state. So I sought again for a clerkship, and by the aid of stenography, which I had learned in Seattle, for its value in reference work, I soon found a chance which paid me enough to live on, and gave me three months of experience, which is worth a couple of years in many offices, for I was general law clerk to an old lawyer who has a tremendous business (for one man) that extends from the supreme court to the municipal criminal; so I got a little of everything. And right here, I advise every woman who studies law to study stenography also, for it will be invaluable in getting her clerkship opportunities, and if she practices west, it will give her the chance of filling in empty hours by reporting testimony in court, and in many other ways will be useful. There is a great lack of good stenographers in the far west, and a demand for them, especially when they combine such a knowledge of law as enables them to act intelligently. If I had been a fairly good stenographer when I went to Seattle, I should have been kept constantly busy with excellently paying work directly in the line of my profession. And but for my

3. Robinson's experience speaking before a mixed jury of men and women was unusual for her day because nineteenth-century courts did not call on women for jury duty. After women won the vote in 1920, they increasingly demanded the right to sit on juries based on their new status as citizens.

4. The book Robinson refers to here is *Law Made Easy: A Book for the People* (Chicago, 1886).

knowledge of the art, I could not have obtained the clerkship last fall which was of so much help to me. I intended to retain it for a year, but it proved a little uncomfortable. The work was extremely hard, and my employer was entirely unaccustomed to having a woman about the office, and could not get used to it; while I, though full of admiration for the man's energy and fighting qualities, and for his sterling good heart, could not get used to his gruff, short ways of speech and manner; and at last—you will laugh, dear Equity Club—when I went into court with him to take the testimony in a hotly contested case, one of the court officials who knew me (as of course they all do) put my name on the list as one of the counsel, and so it came out in all the papers next day, to my intense surprise. This was too much for good Col. H.,[5] so he told me that he really thought I was wasting my abilities in his office, and that in justice to myself and all women, I ought to be in practice for myself.

Well, there was some truth in that, and especially as I did not find another clerical opportunity which seemed to promise well, I made arrangements the first of January for this little office, from whose window I see the daily growth of our magnificent new court house just across the square, sent out some cards, put a card in the *Woman's Journal*,[6] and sat down to wait for business, determined to wait till business came, however long that might be, and whatever discouragements might intervene. In fact, I was so tired that I rather welcomed the idea of a good rest. But I didn't take an office alone, for it is very bad to have to lock up when one goes out. If a client comes the whole day long, he is sure to come while you are gone to luncheon, or on some necessary errand, and to be disgusted if he cannot get in to wait for you, and the chances are that he goes off to somebody else. I was very lucky in getting a little room opening from the large offices used by two attorneys who do a trust and conveyancing business, and who let me have it, rent free, on consideration of my rendering some little services for them occasionally. By that means I have the chance of getting a splendid training in the practical work of abstracting titles, and the inestimable benefit of their advice and help in many ways, and the use of their large library, which you will all appreciate. I have not fitted up as I did in my first little office, by any means. I have

5. Robinson refers here to Thomas Wentworth Higginson.
6. The *Woman's Journal* was the main nineteenth-century suffragist journal.

come to the conclusion that too much luxury in a lawyer's office doesn't look business like. So an oil cloth carpet—because the floor is a very poor one—a desk, office chair and a couple of common chairs are all I have put in, and I don't worry about dust, or spots on the windows any more than other lawyers do.

And now I come to what I started to tell you: "The sun do move!" Somehow or other there seems a great difference in the general public feeling concerning women attorneys now from that which prevailed when I first started in here. Half a dozen years seems to have cleared away the fogs of doubt and hesitation through which I was viewed, and the idea of a woman in the law is no longer an uncomfortable novelty. Last June Miss Jessie Wright graduated from our law school, so that I am no longer the only alumna of that institution, and though she is not a Boston girl and does not intend to practice here, she will practice somewhere, as we may hear in her club letter this year. Better yet, Miss Mary A. Greene, who belongs here and will practice here, will graduate this June and be admitted at once to Suffolk Bar. Her you know already, for she is one of the first year's members. She has had the advantage of a position as student in one of the leading offices of the city during the past year, Miss Wright having held the same position the year before, and is a woman whom I shall be most glad to welcome into the ranks of the profession, for when there are two of us we can march on with a firmer and stronger tread. These ladies have helped to accustom our good old conservative Boston to the thought of women in the legal profession, and I have two women students who are doing fine work, although studying mostly at home, who will increase our number in two or three years. Truly enough does our Mrs. Strickland[7] say, that "once the novelty is worn away, the fitness of women appearing in our courts—not as frightened witnesses, or oppressed and anxious litigants, but as intelligent and self-poised officers of those courts—will be recognized." And that is the grand object to be achieved now. More women must come into the actual field of practice, and the eyes of all must become accustomed to the site, then will the path grow easier to tread. Was it not the dean of the Michigan University Law School who said last summer that there was no longer any question as to women's ability to study law, but it yet remained to be proven whether they could

7. On Strickland see Slocum letter, 1887, n. 6.

succeed in its practice? A true saying, indeed, and the burden of proof rests in large measure on us, my sisters.

I have said that the strangeness of a woman's appearance at the bar in Massachusetts—or in Boston at all events—seems to have worn away in great degree during the past half dozen years. It may be partly that I myself became so broadened and liberalized by my experience in the far and middle West that I look out from more comforted eyes, and that my own greater self-confidence helps people more readily to place confidence in me. At all events, it is certain that present prospects look most promising for my speedy success, which they scarcely did four years ago. Opening here last January was exactly equivalent to opening in a new place, so far as actual business went, for I have not received as much as a call from any client whose business I formerly had. They have died, gone away, secured other legal advisers, or have had no necessity for my aid since my return. All that has come in has been new business, and almost all from strangers. During the first month, January, my cards were going out and people were only beginning to find out that I was here, so I did not take a dollar, although I gave some gratis advice; but since then my receipts have steadily increased, and so rapidly that my average weekly income since the first of January has been just equal to what I was paid by Col. H. as a clerk last fall. During these first two weeks of April I have taken fifty dollars, the bulk of which comes from two cases which I tried, unaided, the first of this week and won. I have a fortunate record thus far, having never lost a case. I give you these particulars for the possible encouragement of "new beginners" amongst us, for I used to long to know just what others in the profession were doing, and when I was taking very little money and having very little business (for business and money are not always synonymous, and either one would have been welcomed), it was a real consolation to me to learn by comparing notes with some of my classmates whom I knew to be bright fellows and able lawyers, that they had even less business and money than I. In these large old Eastern cities, it is exceedingly difficult for a young lawyer to gain a foothold in the active ranks of the profession. Our people are very reluctant to trust any but gray hairs. In the West all this is very different. Both the ladies who are studying with me are over forty years of age; one is teaching in one of our public schools, the other keeps house for husband and one unmarried child, but is blessed with good "help," and both ladies have beautiful gray hair, on which I congratulate them.

One thing to which I have already referred has done much to familarize lawyers and clients with the presence of women in office and court, and that is stenography and the type-writer. Women have been engaged in very many offices of these capacities, though not so generally in Boston yet as in New York and other large cities; and women who are expert stenographers go into court to take the evidence so frequently now that it is no longer a novelty, though it has come into vogue entirely during the last half-dozen years. One of our official superior court stenographers is a young lady, who is thus an officer of the court, and earns more money than probably one-half of our lawyers do.

Practical questions, which though small, are yet important—and sometimes those that are not small—frequently arise before the woman lawyer, which she must solve for herself, unless she can consult with others, hence the real value of our association and its plan of correspondence. For instance, being the only woman in law school, I had to decide, with nothing to guide me, what social attitude I should take towards the hundred and fifty men in school. I knew none of the students, and the dean, to whom I introduced myself, did not give me any introductions to students or professors. I was not even told where to sit at lectures, further than to "sit anywhere." So at the first lecture I attended I took a back seat, but could not hear well, and was uncomfortably conscious that the men with difficulty restrained themselves from turning round to look at me. So the next day I resolved to take a front seat, and seeing a gray haired student of elderly appearance, I sat down between him and an exceedingly young man. (I didn't learn till weeks later that they were seated in alphabetical order, and that I had unconsciously ousted one of the C's from his seat, and when I did learn this, the generous C would not resume it, but left me in possession.) Next, I thought it would be absurd not to speak to these men whom I was to meet daily, for lack of an introduction, so I began to bow and speak to all whose faces I could remember, wherever I met them, in school or out. Long afterward I found that this had made it very easy for me, for it seemed that a lady from the west,[8] who had taken part of the course the

8. Robinson is probably referring to Mary Dinan Sturgess of Mansfield, Ohio, who attended but did not graduate from Boston University Law School.

previous year, had never spoken with any students except one or two with whom she was specially acquainted; that she came a little late to lectures, took a back seat and left a little early, and did not attend recitations at all, thus seeming to feel herself out of place and consequently causing the men to think her so, while the general opinion seemed to be favorable to my attendance, and they paid me the great compliment of calling me a "good fellow." But in settling these and many other small points while in school and after beginning to practice, I was often in great doubt and perplexity.

One problem is not yet settled entirely to my satisfaction, and that is: Shall the woman attorney wear her hat when arguing a case or making a motion in court, or shall she remove it? I decided the point for myself, temporarily at least, when I went into court with my first case. I had always been accustomed, like the majority of women, to wear my hat or bonnet in public places, and as my chief idea was to feel as much at ease as I could, I determined to wear a small hat which set back from the face, knowing that if I should uncover my head there would be an added sense of unaccustomedness besides that which the place and the business must create. The same feeling has led me to wear hat or bonnet ever since on similar occasions. And it seems to me well that when our object is to accustom judge, jury, clients and the public to the presence of women attorneys in court, there should be as few minor variations from the usual customs and appearance of women in public places as may be. Women who go on the witness stand do not remove their hats; why, then, should women attorneys? And it is surely no mark of disrespect to the court for a woman to appear at the bar in her bonnet, which it is customary for her to wear in church. Yet one of my valued students criticized me the other day for wearing my hat when trying the cases of which I have spoken, so I determined to bring the matter up before our club for discussion. Is there any good reason why a woman who is trying a case should bare her head—and with no chance to look in a mirror to see if her hair is straight, or rather to see if it is still in curl?

With this question I will close this long letter, which has been written at intervals through two weeks, with so many interruptions that it is a thing of shreds and patches, hoping at a very early day to hear from you all through the happily-bethought medium of our club letters.

Most sincerely yours,
Lelia Josephine Robinson

* * *

Albion, Michigan

April 4, 1888

To the Equity Club,

I am going to steal time enough to write you a short and probably an uninteresting letter, but don't know that I should have thought I could have stolen the moments had not the total depravity in womankind first manifesting itself in the Garden of Eden been excited over the recent execrable act committed against all women by the ruling spirits of Harvard College, that institution which has been and is held up as the great light and civilizer of this country, in the matter of Bowdoin prizes.

The Bowdoin prizes[1] are the highest to be obtained in Harvard for English dissertations and they range from $100 downwards. The judges for the historical essays were Professors Torrey[2] and Young.[3] An essay entitled "The Roman Senate Under the Empire," was awarded the prize of $100, but when the judges discovered that the author, E.B. Pearson,[4] was a woman, a student in the annex, the prize was entirely cut off, and that of $75 awarded to a young man. How proud he must have felt!

I have sometimes thought it was a misfortune to have been born a woman of brains.

We flatter ourselves that we have but little sex prejudice now to overcome. It is a mistake. Woman has achieved many successes, when we take into consideration the almost insurmountable obstacles she has had to grapple with, and no greater success than in the department of the law.

I well remember the discouragements which greeted me in this field. I came in contact with gentlemen in college who, while profess-

1. The Bowdoin prizes were awarded annually to undergraduate and graduate students of Harvard University for original dissertations in English, Latin, or Greek.

2. This was probably Henry Warren Torrey, McLean Professor of Ancient and Modern History 1856–1886; McLean Professor Emeritus 1886–1893.

3. This was probably Ernest Young, professor of history, 1887–1888.

4. E. B. Pearson was Eleanor B. Pearson, a graduate of the Harvard Annex in 1890.

ing great regard for me personally, were very anxious lest I should commit the terrible breach of propriety of putting into practice what I was learning. One young man in particular did not believe that woman was "built right" for practicing law. When I referred him to Mrs. Gordon[5] and Mrs. Foltz,[6] who were practicing and with whom we came in contact daily, he responded that they were turning themselves into men.

I had the satisfaction of sitting beside this gentleman in a class of 19 who went before the supreme court of the State of California, for examination. I was the only woman in the class, and I fancy he had a sort of pity for me; but I passed the ordeal and he was rejected.

I do not wish to be understood that I received satisfaction over his defeat, but over my success. You see it turned out that I was "built right" and he wasn't, after all.

Mistakes will occur, even among the *elect.*

In the practice of law I met with better success than I had expected, by far, and can say with pleasure that two important cases have been decided in my favor during this winter which were left in the hands of other attorneys during my absence. One of them, that of Galloway vs. Jones,[7] went before the supreme court on appeal before I left my home, and judgment affirmed since of $635; the other during the last month gave me judgment in the case of Noble vs. The Seal Rock Tobacco Co. of $1,480.

I practiced over three years, and in the meantime did not turn into a man, and am perfectly satisfied that I shall retain my sex the rest of my life, unless the discussion of politics metamorphoses me. During the last four years I have been lecturing on that vulgar topic, with no perceptible change as yet.

I well recollect speaking in Iowa upon one particular occasion, and when returning to the hotel I overheard these words: "Mrs. Todd is a very bright woman, no mistaking that. I cannot deny the facts she

5. Here Todd is referring to Equity Club member Laura de Force Gordon.

6. Clara Shortridge Foltz became the first woman admitted to the bar of California in 1878. With Laura de Force Gordon, she successfully filed suit to prohibit the Hastings College of Law in San Francisco from barring women from enrolling. She had a successful legal career in San Francisco and was an active suffragist as well.

7. Galloway vs. Jones, 13 Cal. 712 (1887).

states exist—the mal-administration for years past; but she had better be home taking care of her husband than talking politics."

Now, I have tried to impress upon these sympathetic creatures that I have no husband to neglect, and cannot afford to get married these terrible hard times—it's too great a responsibility. Still there is an occasional uninformed masculine who feels for my supposed husband.

While women have achieved many victories, there is a greater victory yet to be achieved. Woman is *doubly* enslaved while man is but singly enslaved. There is a bondage which is tightening every day about the limbs of the producers of this country which must enslave woman though she stood man's equal. If woman would rise man must rise also.

Before this can be accomplished the labor problem must be solved, and woman must help to solve it. It is the one great pressing demand. Our country can boast of its declaration of rights, its constitution, its goddess of liberty, its star-spangled banner, but these are merely subterfuges to blind the eyes of the credulous, for slavery exists in its worst form.

When Patrick Henry said "The Constitution is a sleeping potion prepared for and administered to the people for the purpose of quieting their fears, relaxing their vigilance, and obscuring their vision," he was wiser than many thought.

We do not object to the panoply of freedom unless it ends in mere parade alone.

What I ask our women to do is to investigate the great wrongs of our country. Men have been voting slavery upon themselves for years, intoxicated with that national anthem, the song of the ballot, which it is claimed belongs to the free alone. It would make our women no freer under our present systems. The man or woman who replies to such injunctions with "crank or crazy," is either an ignoramus or a hypocrite. The time has gone by to be mealy-mouthed in regard to facts. There are burning questions to be solved.

Nothing establishes a better discipline than the study of the law. Its fundamental principles should be taught in our public schools. I think it better fits us to lay siege to the stronghold of this iniquity, and to this end we should bend our energies.

There is something besides law to be studied. It is human justice.

When I realize the women and children in our factories and work shops, half fed, poorly clad, who have displaced strong men because of cheaper wages—women who should be at their hearthstones and children who should either be in the nursery or school room—when I realize that 10,000 children starve to death in the city of New York every year, according to the report of the board of health of that city in 1884, or in the exact words, "die for lack of proper nourishment," I feel that woman has yet her greatest victory to achieve in helping to solve this terrible problem of "millionaires and mendicants—gorged indolence and famished industry."

In the language of the Rev. Hugh O. Pentecost,[8] "Look at this earth. You have but to tickle it and it laughs into harvests in every field. You have but to stab it and it bleeds with fountains of oil that are fountains of gladness for the uses of men. You have but to rip open its sides and everywhere myriads of tons of ore and coal, more than enough for all the wants of man, appear. You have but to search upon its surface and into its depths and you cannot name a human want that might not be fully supplied by the great treasures that the Creator has stored up against the wants of his people, just as much as against the wants of the birds of the air and the lilies of the field." And yet with all these natural bounties we have to face the terrible fact that among the 350 millions in what constitutes christendom, there are 200 millions who do not have enough to eat from one year's end to another.

We have many recipes for the suffering of the country. Edward Atkinson[9] has lately diagnosed the malady afflicting the people. He says the distress of the masses arises from the fact that it takes a thousand bushels of corn to produce two hundred pounds of pork, that there is a great loss of starch and protein in the process, and that it is a great waste of wealth to eat pork instead of corn. Therefore, eat corn. He lays it all to the hog, you see. I think he is correct here, only the hog that's to blame hasn't got four legs. Perhaps nature made a mistake, however, in the anatomy of the animal.

8. Rev. Hugh O. Pentecost was known in New York City for his concerns about urban poverty and his advocacy of social reform.

9. Edward Atkinson was a well-known economist and anti-imperialist. He was a founder of the Massachusetts Institute of Technology and the New England Immigrant Aid Society in Boston.

But my intended short letter has grown altogether too long, for which I beg pardon.

Mrs. Marion Todd

* * *

96 Ashland Block, Chicago, [Illinois]

May 4, 1888

Dear Sisters of the Equity Club,

I have been so hurried since my return from Washington that I do not feel equal to writing anything that can entertain, interest or instruct the Equity Club.

I desire to be a member of the club and hope to become better acquainted with the women who like the law. As for myself, I have studied law more or less for many years. I have always had a taste for it and enjoyed reading Blackstone[1] and Kent[2] when most women would have read novels. It was not until 1885 and '86 that I took the regular course of reading at the Union College of Law in Chicago.

Soon after graduation I commenced the publication of the *Chicago Law Times,*[3] a quarterly magazine devoted to legal literature. The success of the magazine thus far has been greater than I had reason to expect.

While in Washington attending the Inter-National Council the women lawyers there assembled organized a Woman's Inter-National Bar Association,[4] the object of said association being—

1. To open law schools to women.
2. To remove all disabilities to admission of women to the bar, and to secure their eligibility to the bench.

1. Sir William Blackstone, *Commentaries on the Laws of England,* 4 vols. (1765–69).

2. James Kent, *Commentaries on American Law,* 1st ed., 4 vols. (1826–30).

3. The *Chicago Law Times* was a quarterly legal journal. Under Waite's direction, it included articles on a range of reform topics such as the progress of women lawyers, the legal rights of women, and the legal aspects of insanity, abortion, and divorce.

4. The Woman's Inter-National Bar Association was organized in 1888 in Washington, D.C., under the auspices of the International Council of Women. Waite was elected the association's first president.

3. To disseminate knowledge concerning woman's legal *status*.
4. To secure better legal conditions for women.

We did not mean to cover the ground of your club which, as we understood, is social and for mutual pleasure and profit.

We all desire to become members of the Equity, and wish you all to become members of the "Inter-National."

We learned that there were many women in the old world who were anxious to become acquainted with us, and to have our sympathy and assistance in their struggle for recognition in the law.

Wishing the Equity Club great success, I am

Very truly yours,
Catharine V. Waite

* * *

310 West State Street, Rockford, Illinois

May 2, 1888

Fellow Citizens (for I believe we are even if debarred from voting):

This year when I humbly besought Miss Pearce in the words of Scripture, "I pray thee have me excused," she heartlessly informed me that letters were as much a criterion of membership as fees. She also said that in default of anything else, I could tell of my great treat at the International Council. As you have all, no doubt, read full reports, I will refer to some points not so often referred to.

If any of you have ever taken such a trip at a day's notice, you can imagine the rush we two young women were in. "We," includes my companion, Miss Carrie Ashton, of this city; also dark eyed and dark haired and equally enthusiastic in behalf of women, total abstinence and anti-tobacco, a not incongruous trio. 'Tho two days late we read reports of the meeting all the way along, went directly from the train to the opera house, so as not to lose a moment of the addresses, leaving such immaterial things as baggage and boarding place till the close at 10 P.M. Once there were attended every single solitary session and special called meetings during intermission, so that several days found us so absorbed in meetings that the hour for luncheon had come and gone unheeded, and we were only pulled down to earth again when the terrible gnawing of hunger suggested the need of material sustenance.

It was the most magnificent meeting we ever attended, or any one else, for that matter. All the good women, the brilliant, the philanthropic, the noted that we had ever heard of seemed to be there, except those that were dead, and as for them, I do believe those dear old saints who worked so hard, long years ago, were present in spirit, looking down on us with great joy, that their daughters had so nearly approached their long hoped for goal.

Suffrage, philanthropic and other advance work must be a sure preventative of old age, for there were women claiming to be from fifty to eighty years old, who looked fully twenty years younger. Hosts of grandmothers, whom the cares of wifehood and motherhood had not made into broken down old ladies, were as fresh and vigorous, as quick of wit, as clear of intelligence, as clear cut in expression, as we would expect women of half their years. Some who over thirty years ago had been rotten-egged for lecturing or studying medicine, looked now as if their unsavory bath had rather been a shower from the waters of eternal youth. There was such a determined content and calm peace about their faces. What a difficult thing to preserve the freshness of enthusiasm, without the rasping of fanaticism, or succumbing to restless discontent, when success is wanting. To peacefully labor on with zeal, but not worry, with determination steady but not fitful, to count present failure but a step to future success, this is what these women exhibited in their faces, and words, and actions. Yet the ridicule, vile names and insults these consecrated women have had to endure many times, brought heart-ache and bitter tears, but they have labored, and we have entered into their labors.

There were several lawyers present whom Mrs. Bittenbender represented during the profession evening. That was decidedly a kid glove affair, for nearly all the speakers of the evening were gloved. You all know that gestures made with arms and fingers tightly bandaged are not much better than those made by Mr. Burdette's boy, whose false arm only worked at the hinges. Some speakers kept on their wraps, and others their bonnets, but when our legal representative appeared it was evident her rubbers, gossamer, bonnet, veil and gloves had been left at the door, and to my mind she was much more in speaking trim. What would we think of a he-orator lecturing in his overcoat, stovepipe hat and mittens? But some seem to think that a bonnet is absolutely necessary on a woman's head to redeem her from the curse deserved for lifting up her voice on the rostrum. Of course the bonnet of to-day don't cover up much of a woman's head, but I object on principle as much as though it were a hood or sun-bonnet. Mrs. Bittenbender referred to us of the Equity Club and announced the organization of the Woman's Inter-National Bar Association, which one paper reported as Beneficial Association, which tho' quite right was also decidedly wrong. I chased up that Bar Association for quite a while, anxious to ally myself with that high-sounding organization, and when I found it, must confess that it was large and magnificent only in quality and purpose, for it then consisted only of its president, general secretary and treasurer. Others wanted to join it, but couldn't find it, but at its second annual meeting a year ahead in Chicago there should be a crowd. Mrs. C. V. Waite, from our own Union College of Law in Chicago, and now editor of the *Chicago Law Times,* was chosen president, and if she puts into it any fraction of the push she always has given her own individual business concerns it will prosper, for she is a very successful woman of business.

We met Mrs. Belva Lockwood at a reception where she was resplendent in pink satin covered with black lace and embroidered in front with white pearly beads. I scarcely recognized the woman whom I once met on her travels, clad in modest grey. But 'tis plain she can be a butterfly of fashion as well as a leader in reform work. She was very friendly and nice.

Miss Emma Gillett was most cordial and would make a good member for our club. Her partner, or the man in whose office she studied and still continues to practice, seemed proud of his pupil, rattling off her praises and the number of appointments she had received very glibly.

Mrs. Somers, also of Washington, is a plump, motherly creature with a head stocked full of information about different persons and things, and I'll not forget how she crowded us into her pew Easter Sabbath at St. John's while many others stood up or were turned away. Their collection was the quietest I ever heard, for the usual noisy clatter of nickels and dimes was replaced by the dignified rustle of bank notes. The colored woman attorney of Washington I did not see.[1]

1. Catharine Waugh is referring here to Charlotte Ray, a graduate of Howard University, who was admitted to the bar of the District of Columbia in 1872. She was

Miss Mary Hull, of Hartford,[2] is the only woman lawyer in Connecticut. She don't look mannish either. She wears her hair in long curls. We met many times and had quite a visit going to Mt. Vernon. She says she confines herself strictly to office work, as public sentiment would be much against a woman's speaking in court. Some bristling aggressive woman lawyer ought to stir up those slow going people or Miss Hall had better come to Illinois, where it is just as honorable for a woman to talk to men publicly as in private.

Mrs. J. Ellen Foster, of Iowa,[3] spoke on the program for ten minutes. She was appointed treasurer of the W.I.B.A. Miss Phoebe Cousins,[4] of St. Louis, was sick and so did not appear on the program at all.

Miss Cora A. Bennison was not at all like I had imagined her. A woman who had had such thorough preparation for work, who had traveled so extensively and lectured so much must be very grand and imposing in appearance, with a touch of hauteur, I thought. But her honors did not seem to inflate her a bit and she was just as chatty and companionable as common folks, and a very little woman into the bargain. It seems a special dispensation that most of the women lawyers, at lease those I have met, are unusually feminine in all that goes to make up true womanliness. Providence favored them in that way, making it a much easier struggle.

At the receptions given by notables we were not only dazzled by the brilliancy of attire, but shocked at the scarcity of it. These women in full (un)dress looked disgraceful. They were not the suffragists, you can be sure. And yet those are the kind of women who would dub us unwomanly for addressing a judge and jury or speaking with our heads uncovered.

---

the first woman of any race to gain admission to the Washington, D.C. bar and the first African-American woman lawyer in the United States.

2. The reference to Mary Hull is a typographical error in the *Equity Club Annual*. Waugh is referring to Mary Hall, the first woman lawyer admitted to the Connecticut bar in 1882.

3. Ellen J. Foster was admitted to the bar of Iowa in 1874 after studying law with her husband, an avid supporter of women's rights. In addition to her law practice, Foster was an active temperance advocate. In 1900, she represented the United States at the International Red Cross Conference in St Petersburg. In 1906, President Roosevelt chose her to investigate the condition of women and children workers in the United States.

4. Phoebe Wilson Cousins graduated from the law department of Washington University in St. Louis in 1871, the first woman to receive a law degree from the school.

We were disappointed at Helen Gougar's[5] absence, for she would have been a brilliant addition. You have probably all read of the successful suffrage campaign she is now conducting in Illinois. If we don't have municipal suffrage it won't be for lack of a perfect leader.

One thing which amazed me during the council was that those scores of women working in so many widely different organizations, each aiming at some particular right to be gained or wrong to be crushed should so unanimously insist on certain foundation principles. The main ones were that there should be but one standard of right and wrong for both sexes, that intemperance and impurity were the great evils threatening the world, and that woman's political influence was needed to down these evils and secure her own rights. These were not distinctively suffrage organizations with two exceptions, but they saw, as no woman who is truly interested in her sex and the race, or who has spent years of service in such reform work can help seeing, that woman's ballot is not only just, but a necessity.

I think the two favorites of the council whom we were always glad to hear were Susan B. Anthony and Frances Willard. The latter never seemed so brave as that afternoon during the Religious Symposium. Some of the speakers soared away talking of polar opposites, spirit manifestations and rhythmic atoms, advocating the supposedly simple liberal beliefs now so much in vogue, while she stated the plain Gospel faith which never seemed so natural and easy to be believed as when in contrast to those complicated, unintelligible creeds or lack of creeds broached by some others.

It was a grand meeting throughout, and I shall be always glad I went even if I must go in calico, and barefoot for the coming summer. Yes, I had just started a bank account, but it has run down pretty low now. But if I have little in the bank, I have more in my head than before.

Best wishes to you all,

Catharine G. Waugh

* * *

5. Helen Gougar was a leading suffragist in Illinois. See Burlingame letter, 1888, n. 1.

Ashland, Ohio

May 7, 1888

To the Members of the Equity Club,

You asked me to join your society, and write a letter—"Personal experience preferred." The former I will gladly do—the latter, partially decline.

I could not reveal the secrets of my life, even to the Equity Club, and the ordinary routine is too tame for interest. The touch of the Master can alone awaken the truest melodies of our nature, and only this ear is attuned to understand its refrain, His will be done.

Woman's place in the practice of the law, as elsewhere, is not such much to bring to it wisdom and justice, as the purifying graces,—lifting the profession to higher and nobler purposes than the selfish aggrandisement that now characterizes so much litigation.

The wrecks of manhood strewn all along the shoals of this occupation tell plainly how much *principle* has been sacrificed for success.

Ours the part to give to the profession the love-lit hues of Christ's teaching so beautifully set forth in the "Golden Rule," a development of faith and trust in an over-ruling Providence in the practical affairs of life,—to which the practice of the law is so opportune.

Daily living, loyal to humanity, to the truth, to the right, and to God.

Mrs. Sara K. Wertman,
Graduate of the Law Class of Michigan University of 1871.

* * *

423 18th Avenue,
Milwaukee, Wisconsin

April 20, 1888

Dear Friends,

The past year has brought me no experience in matters of human law. The Divine Lawgiver, however, has deemed it best for me to watch a dear mother go slowly down into the Valley of Death. Just now, in my loneliness, I am realizing that a patient submission to Divine decrees is essential to the performance of earthly duties.

Whenever, during the year, I have given a thought to the profession in which we have a common interest, I have reviewed my reasons for entering on so arduous a toil as it will exact. Laying aside the private reasons each one of us has, surely there are reasons why we, being women, do claim the right to practice a profession which men have exclusively practiced for centuries. Women especially have asked me my motives for such a step. Has not each of you heard the question?

Not long since a Chicago paper prefaced an article on "Lady Lawyers" with the remark that while all could see the need of women in the profession of medicine, it was not so evident that woman's work was needed in the courts of law. Absurd as this remark may seem to you and me, dear friends, it is one that we shall often hear from persons who are fairly intelligent on other questions. Of this fact I became convinced during a five years' residence at a large university.

It is of little use to remind them that not long ago the idea of a woman's studying medicine was ridiculed as unnecessary and preposterous. At times human reason is illogical, as human nature ever is.

Our American people are naturally utilitarians. They require every suggested change in the order of things to be of some manifest benefit to the world. If to such persons we can readily suggest how a woman, as a lawyer, may prove a useful member of society and the body politic, we have gained for the subject a respectful consideration in the minds of those who are honestly in doubt. For however firmly *we* may be convinced that every woman has an inherent right to "life, liberty and the pursuit of happiness," by practicing this profession which some states have pronounced lawful for her, there is a large majority of our fellow-citizens who need educating in this fundamental principle of Anglo-Saxon liberty. Until this is done, clients and cases will not reward us with such liberal fees as fall to our brother lawyers. And by the struggling young lawyer a fee is not to be despised, however lofty may be her ideal of professional devotion.

In this education of the public are we not justified in using, as a lever, the feeling of self interest which every member of society possesses and which he or she feels is subserved by every benefit accruing to society? Surely there is need of woman's presence in the criminal courts during the judicial investigation of crimes closely affecting woman's welfare. What more fitting than that a woman, trained in legal reasoning, a member of the local bar, should be there to study the needs and rights of members of her own sex in law. What a comfort and encouragement such a state of affairs would have been to the brave women of the W.C.T.U. of Milwaukee, who felt it their duty (and did it nobly) to enter a police court and listen to a trial so as to compel lawyers and witnesses to show due regard for the feelings of the young girl plaintiff, who otherwise, after having suffered nameless tortures at the hands of her brutal assaulter, would have been compelled to face judge, jury, lawyers, witnesses, and a crowd of spectators, *alone*—with none of her own sex even present.

But it is hard to show the need of women as lawyers without insisting also on the need of women as jurors. A woman's right to be represented in court by those of her own sex cannot be denied, if the swaying of human sympathy has aught to do with jury trials. The more clearly we can make this lack of justice appear to the mind of the average man and woman, the more readily shall each of us be allowed to do our chosen work, quietly and earnestly (as men lawyers are now privileged to do) which, I believe, is all any of us would ask. Try to imagine how great an amount of nervous energy would be saved, and directed to useful study of the law, if the young woman who enters on the profession of the law could do so without meeting and fighting down the prejudice which now meets her both in and out of court.

Lack of space forbids my mentioning the several branches of the law where I see the needs of woman's work; for example, divorce courts. And how much I should like to have some one convince our temperance women that every branch of this vast organization ought to have among its members a woman familiar with technical law. A woman who has studied the law of real estate could make herself very useful to the property holders of that society, in directing and advising investments in and transfers of real estate. Would not such a woman, with her keen moral intuition, point out the culpable carelessness of allowing liquor and beer companies to secure the handsomest corner lots for palatial saloons, as has been done all over the city of Milwaukee?

But enough of my reasons. I should like to hear from some of you, my sisters, on the usefulness of the woman lawyer to society. Can we not by common consent bring our arguments together and weigh them carefully before presenting them to the unconverted? Or, indeed, should we try to convince by any means other than a close and faithful attention to our professional duties?

Most truly do we beginners feel that by following in the footsteps of those women, the pioneers in law, who have so bravely and so grandly proved their fitness for their work, and convinced the world that a profound knowledge of the law is not beyond a woman's mental grasp, that by devoting our best energies to the study of our profession we shall make our most convincing argument.

Nevertheless, we are growing in numbers, and in united effort there is strength. Why not try to mould public opinion in this reform by persuasion, as men lawyers have always done in the leading of every great reform, and of which they are never weary of telling, with a pardonable pride in their profession?

Yours ever,
Margaret L. Wilcox

* * *

London, England

April 23, 1888

To the Equity Club,

Before beginning my heading I meditated very seriously on the question as to what I should say. I have not had any legal experiences or trials that would properly entitle me to write a letter to this club.

As I have taken a lengthy vacation just at the worst time for me, immediately after graduation from a law school, instead of beginning work, I am afraid that I shall be regarded with some show of reason as a deserter. But the law is my chosen profession, and my profession it shall remain; and simply to ease my own mind, though I cannot suppose it will be a matter of interest to anyone else, I must most stoutly declare that I shall make a beginning in the course of time, by next fall, I hope, and shall stick to my business like a little lady.

The dean of our school, Judge Bennett, of the Boston University Law School,[1] used to smile on me benignantly about three times a term during the three years I was in the school, and ask me how I liked the law. I could very truthfully avow my devotion, interest,

1. Judge Edmund H. Bennett, a member of the original faculty of the Boston University Law School, and instructor of contracts and wills, was dean of the law school from 1874 to 1898.

admiration, and enthusiasm. I did always take pains to draw it a little strong, and he would assent in a musing, suggestive way, adding that I would find the practice a very different thing from the study of the law. I hope I shall, though I have enjoyed what studying I have done in that line immensely.

As this is my first letter to the club I may introduce myself, I suppose. That is what the writers of last year's letters did, and to my mind it made them vastly more lifelike and interesting.

I graduated from the Boston University Law School last spring—'87.

I went there immediately after graduating from the University of Vermont.

I had not a single really high-toned creditable motive for studying law, such as I find others have had. I am now cultivating some.

I learned a great deal from the last Equity Club letters. I had not thought that women were peculiarly needed in the law, as I thought they were in medicine. I did not think that it was an odd thing for a woman to want to study law, or that few women had done it, or that it had ever been hard work, or that it would make things easier for some one else. I knew nothing, as a matter of fact, about women in the law.

I was, as I see now, in a state of frightful ignorance. I wanted to study law personally, selfishly, determinedly, and that was all there was to it.

Now I know more about it, and have acquired quite a stock of other ideas on the subject—much more commendable.

We came over to England last fall. I had the opportunity to come, and though it did seem to me a little unwise to leave just at this time, when I was practically fresh for work and ought to be getting a good start somewhere, I was anxious to take the trip again, and did not know when I should so well be able to leave for some years if I let this slide.

And I have had a fine time, have enjoyed every minute. Here in London, as a matter of course, I have been much interested in the law courts, and have had an excellent chance to see something of the way things are done. Only last week I was making the tour of some of the courts with a barrister, and staring with all my eyes— I might say that I have only the usual number—at the different judges named and pointed out to me, judges with whose names I was already quite familiar from the late English reports—"Coleridge, Chitty, Kekewich, Kay, Cave," Baron Pollock, and so on.

But the pleasantest experience in anything approaching a legal line was my meeting Miss Orme.

A short time ago I received a letter from Miss Pearce, very kindly giving me an address I was wishing for, the address of Miss Orme.

Miss Orme and Miss Richardson I had been told were doing some kind of law business in London, though they were not yet admitted to the bar. 27 Southampton Building was the address, and though I had looked in a late directory, and had found a great variety of names put down as belonging to 27, the names I most wished to see were not among them. I concluded that the omission was due to the irony of fate, or of the directory perpetrators, and decided to make an advance on the place.

I felt quite excited about it. I had never seen but two women lawyers in my life, Mrs. Foster and Miss Robinson, and now I was to see a third and fourth. I have not yet gotten over a sort of feeling of loyalty and hero worship for a woman, a live woman, who has practiced law, and I gazed at myself in a pier glass for quite a while before I sallied forth, hoping that my hat was all right and that my umbrella was rolled up in exactly the correct way, and that my gloves were what the occasion demanded, and that my shoes did not look conspicuously degenerate.

"E. Orme, M. E. Richardson," on a brass door plate, delighted my soul when I reached 27.

I went up two flights of stairs and imagined increasingly horrible things on the way. Suppose she should be out; suppose she should not be pleasant; suppose that was an old sign, unaccountably left among the other signs, and that Miss Orme had moved or had given up the business; suppose she shouldn't like me. I began to feel quite dispirited, and if Miss Orme had lived three flights up I dread to think of the consequences.

I knocked on the door with the little brass knocker hanging above the sign "Orme and Richardson," and was ushered in.

Miss Orme was busy in another office with a client, and I waited. I had a good chance to look around, and I looked diligently.

The floors were carpeted, a blazing soft coal fire burned in the open grate, two large windows were lowered from the top, a book case stocked with reports was behind me. On the walls I noticed a couple of good autotypes, one of the St. Helena of Paolo Veronese, and the other Millet's Angelus, both favorite pictures of mine, and I liked Miss Orme immediately in consequence. A good-sized office table stood in the centre of the room; it was loaded with papers, pamphlets, books—a fine chaos. A revolving chair stood on each side. In one of the chairs sat a very pretty girl, with short, dark, curly hair, and she was scrawling away in the most business-like manner. She was Miss Lawrence, one of the firm. Near her, waiting for an order, stood a black-eyed little office boy, in a gray suit. He was as stiff as a ramrod, for the time being, and only looked at me by rolling his eyes, without moving his head.

On the whole, I do not think I am likely to soon forget my first impressions of a woman's law office in London.

Miss Orme is fine; a first-rate kind of a woman, and nobody could have been more kind and cordial than she has been to me.

She tells me that she has never applied for admission to the bar, but that when four or five women are ready to ask for admission they will do so. She says she thinks things look more hopeful now than ever, and that several of the benches are already in favor of their being admitted—not as solicitors, for which an act of parliament would have to be changed, as I now understand it, but as barristers.

She now has a good business, working for barristers and solicitors, but getting their work as they do, she says, they only get half fees; though, of course, when they do what work they are qualified to do—drawing of wills, for instance—for private parties, it is different.

But as, perhaps, Miss Orme herself will have a letter in this edition of the club's letters, I will say no more about it.

As for myself, I can only say that I have enjoyed the study of the law so far, and hope to enjoy the practice and future study still more. I was in a law office of one of the best firms in Boston during my senior year in the law school, and so gained a few little ideas about practice that I prized highly, and that I am sadly afraid I do not half remember.

I have not yet taken my bar examination, not having decided where I shall practice. I can go where I please, and so far that has proved too much liberty to facilitate choice. I am very anxious to begin, and it does seem as though if I could actually get to work I should feel perfectly happy. Rather rash, I suppose. Yet next fall, "somewhere, somehow," I sincerely hope I shall be launched. Any suggestions thankfully received.

Jessie E. Wright
Hyannis Port, Massachusetts

Letters from 1889

Martha Kellum Pearce, Report of the Corresponding Secretary, n.d., Chicago, Illinois

Ada Matilda Cole Bittenbender, May 10, 1889, Washington, D.C.

Letitia Lavilla A. Burlingame, April 22, 1889, Joliet, Illinois

Florence Cronise, n.d., n.p.

Emma Millinda Gillett, April 27, 1889, Washington, D.C.

Mary Anne Greene, May 22, 1889, Boston, Massachusetts

Almeda Eliza Hitchcock [Moore], May 8, 1889, Hilo, Hawaii

Ada Harriet Miser Kepley, May 28, 1889, Effingham, Illinois

Lelia Josephine Robinson [Sawtelle], May 22, 1889, Boston, Massachusetts

Marion Marsh Todd, n.d., n.p.

Catharine Gouger Waugh [McCulloch], April 26, 1889, Rockford, Illinois

Margaret Lyons Wilcox, June 1, 1889, Chicago, Illinois

The Equity Club

Annual

1889.

"All the Allies of Each."

* * *

Report of Corresponding Secretary

Dear Friends,

"The letters that she longed for never came." Perhaps you will think at first sight that this means you but it does not. It means your corresponding secretary, and the letters in question are from friends of ours who intended to write but didn't. The report of Miss Martin's Committee[1] has not been received either but I have been assured that it will be sent in before long and it can be forwarded to you when it comes, along with any other letters that may be on hand then.

It seems best to have our year end about the first of January. Accounts can be made up more satisfactorily then than now, for that time marks the natural division between the work of this year and that of next. So at the end of December I shall ask the Executive Committee to examine the accounts and to report thereon.

I must ask also to be excused from further service as corresponding secretary. I find it impossible to give the time and attention which the work seems to need. This year I've had more than one "bad quarter of an hour" over the delays which have come to the Annual because it was impossible for me to push it through myself. The lady who did the copying and "taking off" was in the highest degree faithful and pains-taking but she could not go ahead and right certain accidents which befell some manuscripts nor do any thing else which required judgement. As the Executive Committee has desires to fill vacancies it will not be necessary to hold an election, I suppose, and if another secretary can be appointed to assume the work in January she will have ample time to attend to the correspondence necessary as a preparation for the Annual for 1890.

There are several subjects now being discussed among thoughtful people, about which the women of this society should be peculiarly fitted to speak. I wish that we could take up such vexed questions as that which the case of Mrs. Sarah J. Whiteling has raised in Medico-

1. Pearce first mentioned Ellen Martin's committee in her report as corresponding secretary in the 1888 *Equity Club Annual.*

legal circles![2] Women physicians have come forward to give their thought as to the law which should govern such cases; women who have studied law should be heard also.

If we cannot arrange to have a meeting before 1892 we can I feel sure have one then which will be a success. Most of us will want to attend the World's Fair wherever it may be and it will only be necessary to so time our visits as to be there at the same time.

The photo exchange ought to be a success. Miss Robinson's face, strong and sweet, is an inspiration to me and I hope for the time when I shall see the pictures of all of you, since I can not see you in the flesh.

With best wishes for you all, individually and collectively, I remain,

Yours sincerely,
Martha K. Pearce
1 Central Music Hall
Chicago, Illinois

* * *

Washington D.C.

May 10, 1889

Dear Equity Club,

I wish I could express to you with how much pleasure and profit I read our Annual for 1888. Both were considerable I can say truthfully for which I return my grateful thanks to the "Lady Laws" who conceived the idea of forming the Club and to those who have so faithfully and well executed the trust. And to our dear Corresponding Secretary I return special thanks for her noble zeal and unremitting efforts which have so largely contributed to these happy results.

Yes, all unknown to the most of us, to all except the "chosen few," you, dear Equity Club, were called into being and tenderly nourished.

2. In 1888, Sarah Jane Whiteling, a poor woman of Philadelphia, poisoned her husband and two young children to collect the insurance money on their lives. At her trial, the defense lawyer argued that Whiteling was insane. The case created public debate over the legitimacy of the insanity defense. The jury ultimately found Whiteling guilty of first degree murder and she was hanged June 25, 1889.

And now, conjointly with the charter members, the rest of us are permitted to behold the "vigorous growth" attained, and with our Corresponding Secretary to feel satisfaction "too deep for expression" that you "are 'like to live' and thrive." Gladly will I do what I can to help along the living and thriving. So command me whenever you think I can be of service in any way. I am fearful, though, that you will not feel altogether like trusting me because of my tardiness in writing this letter. I really did mean to be on time but somehow had fixed in my mind a later date than the first of May for its reception. However, I venture to send it, with this apology, to show my good intentions. Should the verdict be "too late," I will say the punishment is deserved, and will try to profit by the lesson.

And I want to join the "photo exchange" too. Please let me in although I failed to ask in the stated way. Will you?

No, I have not read Ward's Dynamic Sociology,[1] but I mean to this summer. I can sympathize with our sister who unburdened her heart and said "with all my study, I did not study woman in the marriage relation." Neither did I, but soon after marriage I learned it was needful and began the lessons, and have been saved to follow fields of usefulness as inclination dictates with fairly good health which is growing better all the time. I talked the matter over frankly with my husband as I do all other interests of life, and since have received his hearty co-operation in this as in all other efforts I make. I gladly impart the knowledge which came to me to others as I have the opportunity. Of course I was delighted that Sister Pearce spoke out as she did in her report, and surely henceforth none of the legal sisterhood will suffer in "silent resignation."

Marital excesses, I, too, believe mainly cause the disarrangement of the "physical organs pertaining to womanhood." I also believe that they were not "made to get out of order" any more than those pertaining to manhood. The laws of nature must be obeyed in sexual intercourse by human beings as they are by dumb animals. Until they are married women generally will continue to "groan" while many of their God-given powers will remain unused. Besides mental and physical deformities will continue to curse offspring for generations and to burden society. I would recommend the occupying of separate

1. On Ward's *Dynamic Sociology*, see Pearce's Report of the Corresponding Secretary, 1888, n. 11.

beds, and also of bed-chambers when convenient, by married people.[2]

My heart went out in tender sympathy for dear Miss May as I read of her affliction. I, too, once stood by the bedside of a dying sister. She passed on to the next sphere of life in the early days of young womanhood. That was nearly sixteen years ago. But her loving spirit seems ever near to comfort and to help me. Again and again I thank the Author of our being for the blessed knowledge of immortality and that loved ones in spirit life may visit and commune with earth friends. These great truths, of which the Bible is so largely fraught, furnish much of the charm which the inspired Word has for me.

We who have taken up "side issues" receive many a rap in the Annual from you who have not, or who have ceased so to do. Well, well! The blows may be merited. I will not gainsay it. But as for myself I believe I am drawing nearer to a successful professional career than would have been the case had I stuck entirely to my office and the court practice which would have come to me through such sticking. The outside work I do is mainly of a legal character, and it has brought to me the position of attorney for the National W.C.T.U. at a yearly salary of $1,500. The most of the routine part of my department work as National Superintendent of Legislation and Petitions of the W.C.T.U. in the future I hope to have done by a regular office secretary. Some of it, in the past, has been done by a temporary clerk. I am also legal adviser of the National W.C.T.U. Department of White Cross and White Shield.[3] But the work of this office I presume our Club will call "regular." Generally I have time for three hours of law reading daily. When in Washington, a considerable part of this reading is done in the Congressional Law Library where I come in contact with many of the leading male lawyers of our country. While here I have the privilege, also, of occasionally attending a daily session of the U.S. Supreme Court. These privileges I value very highly, and they are available to me only through "dabbling in side issues."

History records that the lawyers who have stood at the head of the

2. Bittenbender is expressing the nineteenth-century notion of voluntary motherhood. This view supported the idea that sexual relations in marriage should occur exclusively at the wife's discretion, only when she felt physically and emotionally able.

3. The White Shield—White Cross program was the social purity department of the WCTU and was dedicated to saving women from prostitution.

bar of this and other countries at times went outside of the regular practice to benefit humanity by their legal skill in other ways. And were they not better lawyers for so doing?

To the questions of Miss Gillett, "Do you like the legal profession?" and "Do you make it pay?" I would answer: Indeed I love the profession dearly. None other could I love half so well. As to making it pay, how? In dollars and cents? Doubtless I would make more money by sticking closer to the profession. But would I do more good? Usefulness to others I consider the pearl of great price.

There is much more I feel like saying as I again read the entertaining history of our Club and your letters, dear sisters, each one teeming with interest and instruction. But I must forbear. Anxiously I shall await the coming of our next annual to hear from you all again, and to imbibe encouragement and zeal from an interchange of thoughts and experiences in this delightfully social way.

I almost forgot to say that on motion of Honorable Henry W. Blair[4] I was admitted to practice in the Supreme Court of the United States the 15th of October, 1888, becoming the third woman thus admitted.

With affectionate greetings, yours,
Ada M. Bittenbender,
Lincoln, Nebraska

* * *

Joliet, Illinois

April 22, 1889

Dear Equity Club,

As I write this letter my first year of legal practice draws towards its close; and rich has it been to me in new and delightful experiences, as well as in less comfortable ones. However, the woman who, in this day, attempts the practice of law, must expect to quaff the bitter with the sweet.

4. Henry W. Blair was senator from New Hampshire when he made the motion to admit Bittenbender to practice before the Supreme Court.

I opened my office alone, and wholly independent of others, borrowed the money with which I bought my books and furnished my office, and with no capital but courage and patience, faced the doubtful future. But fortune for once was kind. Eleven dollars, which ought to have been twenty-five, and would so have been, had I not foolishly underrated my services, were the fruits of my first month's labor, including the first case which I tried and won, in a justice court, and for which I charged only five dollars, the case involving sixty dollars; but my modesty in that regard soon fled.

More courtroom than office work falls to my share. The present month my receipts are one hundred and ten dollars, not one cent of which is from office practice, but all from two cases both of which I won, a divorce suit and assumpsit[1] upon a promissory note. While I have spent considerable valuable time in giving advice, and looking up questions pertaining thereto, I have never charged anything for it. The other lawyers say I ought to do so, but sometimes it seems awkward to begin now. Are any of my Equity Club sisters ever bothered with people who wish them to take cases upon contingent fees? Usually such cases are doubtful and the people themselves unwilling to run the risk necessary. I took one such case but hereafter my services are not at the disposal of fortune-hunters. I lost it; but the gentleman was so pleased with my efforts that he paid me twenty-five dollars, which did not half cover the work and worry. I have had the full conduct of only one jury trial; that resulted in a victory for my client to the full amount demanded, $1507.00. The defendant appealed, but has since backed down and paid over the full amount with damages for delay, so I have lost my chance to win a case in the Appellate Court. This was tried in Ottawa, Illinois, so I have had some pleasant trips on business, and was delighted with my treatment in this strange court, where kind Judge Blanchard and all the officers of the court, vied with each other in courtesy, and all whom I met gave me cordial greeting. While thus enjoying myself I thought of Miss Cronise's charming sojourns in the north, and wondered if such would ever fall to my share.

What has been my experience with members of the bar at home? Well, my brother lawyers, with one or two exceptions, though most

1. Assumpsit is a form of action at common law for pleading a case in which the claim is for damages for breach of a simple contract, that is, a contract not under seal.

of them disapprove of women entering the professions, gave me hearty welcome, as an individual I suppose. There was some restraint in their manner at first, but I never see it now. I think some of them are glad to have me there, and these are the best ones, the real lawyers; it is the hangers-on who dread to see me succeed where they have failed who show disquietude in my presence. But none of my practice has ever come from work given or secured to me by other lawyers; it has come solely through my own efforts and business reputation, and has been strictly professional. The borrowed money has been repaid from my own receipts, and I begin the new year hopefully. (Interruption)

Well now! I never expected to take the oath to any man's application for a saloon license, and I am pondering in my mind what ever he came to me for. Men come to me quite as often as women, but I'd thank the saloon crowd to keep their distance.

Last November was my dullest season. I took a prominent part in the campaign, speaking for the Republican Party.[2] I now think this was a mistake, not the color of my standard by any means, but the neglect of my office occasioned thereby, and consequent loss of business. Still I gained a wide acquaintance among business men, as I have in the equal suffrage work.

Miss Martin speaks of woman's delicate organization. Having been very subject to the peculiar difficulties of my sex, I think I ought to record that I am never in better health or spirits than when put to the spur and excitement of trying cases, nor does any hurtful reaction follow the glow. It remains, my ambition is satisfied, and I am now stronger and able to endure more than at any other period of my life. Indeed, I stand court room work better than many of the men.

Now I imagine some one is saying she wishes I would tell about some of the less comfortable experiences, but they are scarcely transferable to paper, and very often consist of little things, a snub here, a sneer there, sometimes the weight of a glance or a feeling that "something bears foul upon the wind." What matters it? Friction only fires progression, and the dullest flint when struck emits a spark.

I wish I had space to comment on all those nice letters of last year,

2. Burlingame is referring here to the presidential election of 1888 when Benjamin Harrison ran for the Republican Party.

but it may not be, so with kindest wishes for each and all, I send this my offering, and remain,

With love for law and lawyers,
Lettie L. Burlingame

* * *

Dear Equity Club,

I've been so busy for some time past, that I've had no time to write. It seems as though Court had been in session all the year round. At last it is fairly over for the summer, though new work keeps coming in and there is no rest for the weary, and I am actually weary, and just at present see no way to a summer's outing. I'm not complaining for I'm never happier than when crowded with work. My office hours from 9 A.M. to 12 M. ______ from ______ P.M. to 7—except when engaged at the trial table or before the Court. Only once in a while lock up and go for an hour attending to social duties. I don't know what I can write you this year that will be of any interest for it has followed its predecessors and seems as matter of fact as they. Last week our Circuit Court (one of our higher courts) was in session and we were fortunate enough to have set aside all former decisions in a libel case we were defending and sweep up the glory of a most complete victory. I say we, because I had connected with me in the case one of the old members of the Bar. It was a case in which so much was at stake, that we still congratulate each other whenever and where ever we chance to meet. Right here I want to assure my sisters that I'm not in the habit of having any assisting counsel, preferring to do the work and reap both honors and fees. This week I've begun a civil action for damages in the sum of $5000 for assault and battery. We do not anticipate getting quite that sum but feel that we ought to do well for who would have a broken nose irredeemably broken, his cracked ribs and a generally dilapidated condition for much less money? also an Injunction suit to prevent one farmer from shutting up a roadway and depriving another farmer from his right to an easement [on] his farm. Also been retained to defend a claim for $900 sought to be enforced by Armour & Co. on ground of partnership liability. Have looked after some criminal matters, spent one morning in Probate Court on exceptions to final accounts, besides innumerable other things which are constantly coming up. So you may know I've been busy—All these clients are men. So though I may be a woman lawyer, I don't have only women clients. When I look at my work, and know what I am really doing, and then read such articles as I glanced at the other day in the *North American Review,*[1] written by women, too, in which one writer, her name I don't just now remember, says that women have under taken men's work, and do it in an inferior manner, and are in short inferior men, then I feel too indignant for expression. If only men and women will give women a fair showing, giving her all the privileges of men, and expect no more of her than of men, I know she would hold her own successfully. In many cases she is doing it pretty thoroughly—What a libel such an assertion is on our many women physicians, saying nothing about our own profession. I cannot agree nor feel any sympathy with our sisters of Equity Club who think woman's mission into the profession is to purify. I am too matter of fact. My mission is to honestly, earnestly, and decently earn my living, doing it in the way I may seem most fitted for. When I entered the profession I did it with no other thought than that I could better earn a living practicing law than teaching at a thousand dollars a year. I have done better, and much better—No thought of being a public benefactor ever entered my head. I cannot accept any sentimental view of woman's mission—this world is plain, hard facts, sentiment may be beautiful to look at and indulge ones thoughts in occasionally, but it will earn no bread and butter, accomplish no genuine good, and should be set aside for holiday recreations and not allowed to show itself as our hard work days. But I am letting my letter run on at too great a length, though I seem to have so much to say. I wish I had the time and liberty to write you some of the experiences of my sister Nettie C. Lutes,[2] Ohio's first woman lawyer. I do not think any other can have had

1. See Rebecca Harding Davis, Rose Terry Cooke, Marion Harland, Catherine Owen, and Amelia E. Barr, "Are Women to Blame?" in 148 *North American Review* 622–42 (1889). Cronise is referring in particular to Amelia E. Barr's assertion that women who reject their traditional place in the home for participation in the public arena are not only unable to perform or compete as well as men, but are neglecting their womanly duties as well.

2. On Nettie Cronise Lutes, see Pearce, Report of the Corresponding Secretary, 1888, n. 5.

anything similar. However I have not her permission to speak. Maybe she will grant it when I write for the Annual next year. I've read last years letters so many times during the interval and have enjoyed them so much. I shall surely call and see Miss Ellen Martin when I go to Chicago, and she will go with me to find Miss Pearce and others. At least, so I hope. About two months ago I was looking forward to a short season in Boston and I arranged for a call at 5 Pemberton Square Room 25 on Lelia J. Robinson and anticipated seeing her. Every word of her letter found an echo in my heart. But as other bright anticipations, this too has vanished. With warm affection for you all

I am Yours,
Florence Cronise

* * *

Washington, D.C.

April 27, 1889

Dear Equity Club,

In reading the letters in the last Annual it seemed to me that, the ability of woman to become learned in the law having been conceded, the question now arising in the minds of many, even among her friends is her ability to endure the practice from a physical standpoint. Women practitioners must solve this problem and they are being observed with that end in view. I believe that physically and mentally woman is fitted for the work of the law, and have not myself found my work too hard. I have had to contend all my life with a constitution by no means robust but my health has steadily improved since I began the study and practice of my profession.

I have never gone into jury cases and have done very little court work, but I deliberately chose this course at the beginning as I knew by experience that my nervous organism would break under the strain. This lack of nervous endurance I do not count as a feminine failing as I have tested it more especially in caring for the sick or young children, the very place where as a rule, a woman endures beyond a man. Judging from analogy the average woman will endure a prolonged nervous strain better than the average man.

Knowledge of my limitations of endurance has made me extremely cautious for I started without the approval of my immediate circle of friends and prophecies of failure made me all the more determined to succeed. The second year of my student life when I was working hard, not only to stand well in my final examinations but also to earn as much as possible for my own support, I received a visit from a friend from my old home, one who had encouraged me in my undertaking. The moment our hands met in greeting he shook his head and told me I did not exercise enough, circulation was poor. A few days after, I received a letter from him, terse and pointed. I wish I could reproduce it here, but I can only give the substance: viz; A good circulation is essential to good health and good work. A test of circulation is placing the hand on the head; if the head feels cool all right, if warm all wrong. To secure a good circulation, one should exercise light gymnastics twice daily, use a flesh brush vigorously morning and night either with or without bathing and never go to bed with cold feet; if necessary use a hot iron. Exercise in the open air all that is possible.

The letter was a very helpful one to me and I have followed its precepts more or less faithfully as I felt the need or overcame disinclination to allow existing conditions, however wrong, to remain.

Lack of exercise is the bane of people who follow sedentary occupations. Women in their ordinary avocations have sufficient exercise and custom and tradition lead them to rest at every opportunity. Care of the household coupled as it generally is, with the work also is responsible for this state of things. The tired woman uses her moments of rest in picking up book or paper and this mental occupation she does not call work, but diversion. When all this is reversed and hard mental application is called for, it is a new gospel that she must exercise for rest and diversion. It is hard for her to understand how tired she is. Harder than for the man whose traditions include regular hours of work and recreation. Yet many a brilliant young man has failed in studies or profession by reason of too great mental application and too little exercise.

Work done when weary is usually below the standard, which we cannot afford. When I find I am not doing good work, unless the occasion is urgent I stop and take up something else, an out door errand if possible. When in school I deliberately sacrificed my lessons a number of times and I believe that ultimately I did the better for it.

In practice there are times when one must go on unless absolutely ill, but there are innumerable other times when the unwilling spirit is goaded on by the conscientious woman believing she must do the stint she has set for herself when there is no possible object to gratify except her own self will. Let her adapt her work whenever possible to her physical condition and ninety-nine chances out of a hundred when the strain comes her physical condition will adapt itself to the work.

Again, I have cultivated hardness of heart. I can listen to distressing things unmoved, visit the dying and sleep soundly after it and cut short a garrulous visitor without hesitation. Nothing is more wearing than sympathy and nothing unfits a lawyer more for the trial of a case than to have her sympathies actively interested as it blinds her to the true merits of the case from a legal standpoint. While we should right a wrong whenever it is in our power to do so, we should calmly view the matters presented to us and save ourselves from every strain in order to have strength to establish the right.

Charity clients should be shunned unless in extreme cases. They have no more right to a lawyer's services for nothing than a washerwoman's, and when one takes charity clients to any extent she lowers her professional tone besides using her capital of time and strength. If she uses all of her income for charity that is her matter but if she drives herself beyond her strength and fails in her work it concerns us all.

A further matter of importance is how we spend our leisure hours. If we have home work pressing on us during office hours and hurry home to assume cares of various kinds we cannot expect a fine nervous condition. Men go home to their dinner, evening paper, a stroll down town, or a chat over the fence with a neighbor. If we presume that we must work sixteen hours in the twenty-four, and go home to run a sewing machine in a hot close room, or take domestic cares from some one we love, and have a little brother or sister sleep in the same room, over whom we must keep a watchful eye when we should take uninterrupted sleep, and then fail, I do not think the blame should be laid on our profession. Self-sacrifice of this kind is absolutely wrong and unjust to what one sets herself out as capable of doing. If we take up work that has been monopolized by men we should study the manner in which they have accomplished the work and how they have spent the hours not occupied by their profession, and follow the general line of their experience. I allow myself to indulge in seeing out door sports if I can and in going to the woods when possible. Communion with nature is health giving. If too tired after dinner to be with people I shut myself in my room, close my eyes and rest for an hour or so absolutely. So far as possible I avoid outside cares and responsibilities.

As to the burdens of the wife suggested by Miss Pearce, I feel that I should say but little. A glance through the Annual would seem to indicate that the majority of the practitioners who are sticking to their work and plodding on in the only sure and safe way to win success are unmarried. The care of children must necessarily interfere with any thing so sensitive to interruptions as a law practice. I do not believe the relation of wife alone should do so. Nor do I sympathize very deeply if it does for no woman has any right to give up her health, happiness and future prospects in life for the mere gratification of her husband, but in the marital relation as in every other relation should insist on equal rights to self-gratification or restraint. I have found advice of this kind given to wives has almost invariably resulted in increased respect and happiness in the home and improved health on the part of the wife.

Mary Anderson's[1] nervous prostration has been ascribed by the *New York Sun* to her celibacy, which, it argues, is not compatible with hard brain work and heavy nervous strains. Should one attempt to illustrate that either the married or unmarried woman is capable of doing distinguished work she would not be at a loss for examples. Either state, rightly lived, should not handicap a woman in her attainments in any department of the world's work it is her deliberate choice to take up.

Emma M. Gillett
802 F St. NW

* * *

1. Mary Anderson was a popular actress in both New York and London. In 1888, she began to suffer the strain of overwork from her travels between the two cities. In 1889, the year of Gillett's letter, she suffered a nervous breakdown. Young, beautiful, and talented, her illness was attributed by some to her singlehood. In contrast, her physician, the eminent neurologist, Dr. S. Weir Mitchell, attributed her illness to overwork. On his advice, Anderson cancelled all her bookings for the remainder of the season. The following year she married and never resumed her professional acting career.

209 Washington Street
Boston, Massachusetts

May 22, 1889

Dear Equity Club,

Last year I addressed you as a student on the verge of graduation from the Boston University Law School. Now I am a full-fledged member of the Suffolk Bar. I was absent on a trip to the Pacific Coast when my brothers who took the bar examination were sworn before the Supreme Court. Consequently I had to be admitted on special motion, and this was done on September 28, 1888, the Supreme Court represented by Judge Field,[1] being convened especially for the purpose, and immediately adjourning, to allow the Court in Chambers to occupy the room. A week before, a report was circulated that I would take the oath upon a certain day, and all the newspapers had reporters there, and a crowd assembled only to be disappointed while I, quite ignorant of the whole thing, was quietly visiting friends in Rhode Island. So when the event did actually occur, no one was present beside the usual court officers, except my mother and the members of the bar who as my "sponsor" moved my admission.

I have been having the usual miscellaneous experiences of a young lawyer since then—Perhaps a little more than ordinarily miscellaneous, as there have been several interruptions in my work owing to the illness of myself and the sickness and death of some very dear relatives.

Miss Robinson and I have been doing a little legislative work together. Our Mass Act of 1883, ch 252, whereby women who are attorneys-at-law may be commissioned by the governor to administer oaths, and take depositions and the acknowledgement of deeds,—proved in practice to be so vague in terms as to render it doubtful what our powers were in scope and effect, so we asked for amendments which were granted, and we are given the powers of a justice of the peace as to the foregoing acts and also have the additional power granted to take affidavits, and to issue summonses for witnesses.

1. Walbridge Abner Field was appointed to the Supreme Judicial Court of Massachusetts in 1881. He served as Chief Justice of the Court from 1890 until his death in 1899.

Some of my time has been employed in translating for the *Chicago Law Times*, a French pamphlet by Dr. Louis Frank,[2] the champion of Mlle. Marie Popelin in her late unsuccessful attempt to gain admission to the bar of Brussels, Belgium.

This pamphlet is a very exhaustive historical and critical review of the subject of the *Woman Lawyer*, and I think the members of our Club will be much interested in its perusal. The first installment appeared in the January number of the *Law Times*.

I have appeared as a "stump speaker" at our School Suffrage meetings and have enjoyed it. Nature has blessed me with a rather large amount of self-possession, and I have never in my life known by experience what "stage-fright" is.

I agree with Miss Burlingame that a woman lawyer ought to go into court. Her beneficial influence is needed there quite as much as in the law schools and offices, and the less agreeable the moral atmosphere the more is her presence needed.

As to the question of wearing the bonnet in the court-room, that seems to be settled in Massachusetts in the affirmative. Miss Robinson and I always do so, and also the ladies who are at present studying law. It was really a question in my mind at first, but the matter settled itself naturally. Having become accustomed to wearing my bonnet from morning till night in lecture hall, library and court-room during my student days, nothing would have made me feel more conspicuous and awkward than to remove it before entering upon the trial of a case at the bar. So I kept it on, and felt quite civilized and fittingly attired, and I think the custom may perhaps now be sufficiently established in our State to have almost if not quite the force of a law to govern future women advocates in the matter, here. I may add that I tried that my first case, in company with a young gentleman friend and we won it. It was a mechanic's ____, and we were for the plaintiff mechanic.

I should like to comment upon all the questions raised in the club letters of last year, but fear I should thereby make my letter too long.

In answer to Miss Gillett's two questions I can say that I *do* like the legal profession, but of course I cannot tell as yet whether I shall make it pay in money.

2. Dr. Louis Frank, "The Woman Lawyer," 3 *Chicago Law Times* 74–86 (January 1889), 1201–41 (April 1889), 253–68 (July 1889), 382–411 (October 1889).

My experiences lead me to feel very strongly the necessity of which Mrs. Haddock speaks,—the necessity of instructing women in the conduct of business affairs, as well as in business law. It *must* be done by special instruction, under our present social system—for the girls who have means do not go into the business circles and breathe in with the atmosphere those laws and rules which their brothers learn as a matter of course as soon as they are old enough to comprehend them.

And right here comes in a partial answer to Mrs. Wilcox's suggestion about the usefulness of the woman lawyer in society. She can by dropping legal information here and there in response to questions or voluntarily in the social circle, enlighten her lady friends upon these subjects. I have imparted a good deal of information in that way, which has been eagerly received.

Miss Martin speaks of charity clients. I, in common with others, have suffered from the ingratitude of that kind of people. I do not mind the ingratitude for favors conferred so much as I do the insinuation and probably the genuine belief of the charity client that I have not taken the pains in working up his case that I would have done if I had received money for it. But if it be our duty to take such a case, and we have really done our best "for the Love of Christ, and In His Name," we ought to leave results to Him for whom the word is done, and who understands and appreciates it fully. I try to realize this, but we know how much easier it is to preach than to practice.

I shall leave to Miss Robinson the pleasure of telling you about our new recruits in law study in Boston, and of our woman's law club and its monthly dinners. (Also, to Mrs. Jessie Wright Whitcomb the tale of her desertion of us Bostonians for a partner in law and matrimony in Topeka.)

Sincerely yours,
Mary A. Greene

* * *

Hilo, Hawaii

May 8, 1889

Dear Sisters-in-Law,

Wherever you are you cannot be further away in any direction, than I am from the busy active world. But, notwithstanding the distance and isolation of this little Kingdom, we have our dissensions and strifes as will larger nations.

Wherever man is there you will see some sort of Tribunal. The "Paradise of the Pacific" is not exempt, and it is of the workings here and more especially of my first experiences that I will talk to you.

After graduating, last June, ('88), mother and I went travelling in the East, and did not arrive at Honolulu until November. We had to wait there three days to make connections with the Inter Island Steamer, and so in that time, with father's help, I was admitted to the Hawaiian Bar. The Chief Justice of the Supreme Court admitted me on presentation of my license from the Michigan court. This was the first time the Court had been asked to admit a woman, and there was some controversy about letting me in, but finally a telephone message came for me to go to the Justice's office and get my license. The same day the office of Notary Public was given me.

The Third Judicial Circuit was about to sit at Waimea, Hawaii so instead of going directly to Hilo, we landed at Ka-wai-hae, and rode twelve miles to the above named place and attended court. My first motion was made there and gained.

The natives were all astonished to see a "Wa-hi-ne-lo-io" (woman lawyer), and the remarks as I passed by were often amusing. They did not realize that I understood their language.

The work here in Hilo has been very satisfactory so far. In a good many instances the party arrested has plead guilty, causing a good deal of merriment among the young men here, who say that I scare the poor fellows into the plea.

The Circuit Judges generally govern their circuit three times a year. The last circuit made by one was March, and as we, that is the firm of Hitchcock and Hitchcock, ________ a little work in the out districts, it was decided that would be the ________ to do it.

The only way to get around the Island is on horseback, and a journey of two hundred miles more or less was before me. I had three cases to try and hoped to pick up more on the way, but ere the journey was quarter ended a telephone message came from home, telling me to return as soon as my three cases were disposed of.

The Sheriff had to leave the town on urgent business, and I was called to take his place during his absence. The Sheriff is to our Island what the Governor is in one of your states, and so you can realize in a measure the position I held for five weeks. During the five weeks a bold burglary was committed, but as luck would have it we found the man and nearly all the money within four days.

At present the Circuit Court is here and the Chief Justice is presiding. This Court sits three times a year on this Island—in May, September and November. One of the four Justices of the Supreme Court presides at every Circuit. The calendar this term is heavy with criminal cases, some of which are murder, manslaughter and assault with a deadly weapon. A wave of crime seemed to pass over this Island some months ago, and murders to the number of five were committed.

"All work and no play makes Jack a dull boy." A very old but true saying, and in order not to be too "dull" or worn out in this debilitating climate we take little vacations now and then. I have just taken one of three days in visiting the Volcano. The ride of fifty miles is a very hard one, but one is well repaid when emerging from the beautiful tropical forests, the awful workings of nature bursts on one's vision. Stretching out at your feet lies the largest active volcano in the world, in a constant state of activity. One is awed into silence when the lake that "burneth with everlasting fire" bursts on one's view. The surging and dashing of the fiery mass against the walls of the Lake can only be likened to the waves of the Ocean in the fiercest storms.

One feels like exclaiming "How great and wonderful are Thy works, O God!"

Dante before writing his Inferno must have seen a volcano. You could not feel very much surprised if His Satanic Majesty should come forth from the seething mass and salute you.

In this beautiful land of sun, flowers and tropical fruit, I often think of my far away sisters, freezing part of the year and roasting the next, and wonder if they think of their Heathen acquaintance here.

Your sister in law and equity,
Alme E. Hitchcock

* * *

Effingham, Illinois

May 28, 1889

Dear Equity Club,

I think it would be well for us to make a study of our laws during the coming year and give our ideas fully concerning needed changes therein, and suggest ways and means whereby the changes suggested may be brought to pass.

Let this be the burden of our letters in the next Annual. Why may we not help to bring the day of

"Sweeter manners, purer laws!"

__________ __________,

Ada H. Kepley

* * *

5 Pemberton Square, Boston

May 22, 1889

Dear Equity Club,

Does it seem a year since we were last writing our club letters and looking eagerly for the Annual which should bring us all together? However a year it certainly is and an eventful one too, in Boston at all events from our own peculiar point of view as women lawyers and law-students. A year ago, there was but one woman member of the bar in Massachusetts; one other, Miss Jessie Wright, had taken her degree from the Boston University Law School, she being the second woman to do so; and a third, Miss Greene was about to graduate and intended to be admitted to the bar and to practice. But there are so many slips 'twixt the cup and lip, that who can wonder I feared we might lose her up to the last minute! Especially if you knew what a pretty girl she is! (By-the-way, what about my proposed exchange of photographs? I have two or three of the Equities already, and have had a couple of dozen copies made of my own especially for this purpose, and shall be very glad to send to all of you who wish to exchange. And I think it would be well if we were to make them all autograph pictures, signing on the margin below the picture where practicable. I suppose we all agree in keeping these pictures strictly private, and never allowing them to be published or used in any public way. For myself, I have always avoided this kind of publicity, and have never allowed my photograph to become general property, though probably my notion in the matter is all nonsense.)

Well, the year has passed, and where are we? It is Jessie Wright whom we have lost instead of Miss Greene. In the summer Miss Wright returned from Europe, and decided to settle in Boston for the practice of the profession she had studied. I introduced her to a lawyer who took her into his office as a student, and was very interested in her success and proud of her quick readiness. She was reading for our December bar examination, and all was going well, when presto!—almost as if touched by a magician's wand, so sudden was it, she was off to Kansas, and married to a law-school classmate. And so Boston lost her, but I hope that the Equities may keep her still.

But meantime Miss Greene returned from her summer in California, took the bar examination (ranking first in the entire number of some forty applicants, as she had ranked second in the large class with which she had graduated from the school) was admitted, opened her office and has been in the practice ever since.

A year ago there was no woman registered as a student at the law-school except Miss Greene who was just leaving it. *Now* there are *four* women studying there. One of these, Mrs. E.M. Campbell, was studying under my direction when I last wrote you. In the fall, she entered the school, and she will probably graduate a year from now, taking the course in two years. Another lady, Miss Colesworthy, entered at the same time.[1] She is a stenographer in a lawyer's office, and proposes to study only with a view to making herself more useful in clerical work, but I doubt her continuing in this mind after graduation. The other ladies entered the school this spring. One, Mrs.

1. Despite Lelia Robinson's expectations that both Mrs. E. M. Campbell and Lydia Colesworthy would complete their law studies at Boston University, neither woman graduated from the law school.

Fall,[2] is the wife of a very able young lawyer, and she has been studying with him for some time. The other is a lawyer's widow. When I entered the law-school ten years ago, she began to study with her husband, and continued to do so, though with many intermissions, till his death last fall, and now she is doing what she knows would be his wish for her. Young, bright and with practical knowledge of legal thought and methods, she will succeed.

My other student of whom I wrote you last year, is still going on, though slowly, and two other ladies are reading under my direction, and yet another is reading with Mr. Fall and she intends, I understand, to go into the school in the fall. Others still there may be, of whom I do not know, but there are a round half-score of whom I have told you, and is not this a goodly number for the conservative old city of Boston?

Last fall we organized ourselves in a club, and on the first Saturday afternoon of each month the Portia Club[3] has met in a private dining-room of one of our down-town hotels for dinner and discussion, and both have been of the best, I assure you, the sauce of mutual admiration having much to do with their palatableness. Our club, its name and its members are kept very quiet however, for we do not desire to "get into the papers," for various reasons. Another year, if not now, I hope more of our Portias will also be Equities.

I think there is no more news to tell you, except what Miss Greene has written. My business has been steadily on the increase and exceedingly promising for the future. It is taking a decided turn towards probate matters of late, which is very satisfactory to me. I have made a number of important wills, in most of which I have been named executrix or trustee or both. I had several cases on the jury

2. Anna Christy Fall graduated magna cum laude from Boston University Law School in 1891. She married George Howard Fall, a classmate in the College of Liberal Arts, and they shared a law practice in Malden, Massachusetts, for almost forty years. In addition to her legal career, Fall was also involved in the women's movement of her day. She served on the Malden School Board, was an active speaker on behalf of women's suffrage, and was an advocate of the reform of Massachusetts property laws for widows.

3. The Portia Club was an informal dinner club of women lawyers and law students in Boston. Lelia Robinson first proposed the idea of a women lawyers' club in the fall of 1888. On December 1, 1888, a group of women lawyers in Boston, including Anna C. Fall and Equity Club members Cora Agnes Benneson and Anna Greene, met. The Portia Club flourished for several years.

list during the season, but am not likely to try any of them myself. I have done a little court-work, one criminal case among the number, but my business has been mostly in the office. My office expenses are rather heavy this year, but I am able to meet all demands for money with a degree of ease which would have seemed highly improbable half a dozen years ago. I sincerely believe that the chances and the prospects for us women in the law are as good, and a little better, than for men who start under the same circumstances. This was more quickly proved by the pioneer women in the West, but it is proving itself also in the East.

I do not know that I believe there is anything in the physical condition of woman that need hinder her in the practice of the profession, that is, of woman per se,—but I do think the great problem is that of the married woman. *Is* it practicable for a woman to successfully fulfill the duties of wife, mother and lawyer at one and the same time? Especially a young married woman? I wish some of our members would discuss this question in its pros and cons.

Always sincerely yours,
Lelia J. Robinson

* * *

Dear Equity Club,

I have no experiences in the practice of law to relate this year and may not have for many years to come. Most of my time has been spent in the lecture field discussing bad law and worse precedent, but as a letter is made the condition upon which the privilege of receiving the Equity Club Annual depends, I am willing to "pass under the rod."

I think it is not too much to say that the practice of the law leads one into the gloom of the middle ages.

Progress is made in almost every other profession but in this, lawyers chain themselves to a stake and are limited to the chain's length, however much justice may cry out.

Gen. I.N. Stiles,[1] a prominent lawyer, says, "As an old lawyer I say

1. General I. N. Stiles, a prominent lawyer in the West, died in 1895.

and say honestly that the last place to get justice is in a court of justice. There is more sticking in the bark, as they say down South—I mean a failure to get down to the essence, the right and wrong of a question—in the legal profession than in any other equally intelligent body of men under the sun.

"Charlatanism is scarcely the word by which to designate this practice, for it is as often policy as otherwise and it is poor policy too."

That which defeats justice, save it be accident, is unrelenting precedent.

The law and interpretations of the ancients are not well calculated to meet the needs of a growing people. Law and order have not always accompanied each other in the past and we have reached a period when disorder follows in the wake of law. It is a condition which will continue until much of our law is swept away and the tyrant precedent abolished. The reverence paid to past decisions which seldom meet shifting conditions and circumstances amounts to idol worship. Each separate age is better qualified to pass judgement upon itself than any preceding one and many of our best lawyers are asking today for less veneration manifest toward this *fetish.*

Lawyers have been most instrumental in making our laws, and might become most instrumental in cleansing the statute books but this need not be looked for until honor in our legislative halls takes the place of a polluted ambition. Congress and legislatures are almost entirely composed of lawyers and the complex and contradictory nature of much of our law works into their hands supplying them with many a fat job.

No one class should legislate for the whole. We would object to all farmers or all mechanics legislating for us, lest selfishness might discriminate in favor of the farmer or the mechanic, still for years lawyers, the majority of whom have been the paid attorneys of corporate greed, have occupied this position. Protected by the power of consolidated capital many have stood ready to perform, for gold, any service regardless of decency or shame. These men are supposed to have been sent by a regular constituency and many times their positions have been so obtained, instead of by purchase, but the claims of their constituency are disregarded at the command of the corporate employer until robbery has supplanted justice, poverty has bred slavery, and revolution has been planted in the breasts of exasperated citizens.

As an illustration of that majority which has ruled for years the state of Maine affords a good one. Since Maine became a state she has been represented in the National House of Representatives by

1	Printer	1	Teacher
1	Stone-cutter	2	Contractors
2	Clergymen	3	Farmers
3	Editors	4	Manufacturers
19	Merchants	69	Lawyers

Last Congress had 307 lawyers in it and the present one has 316. Ohio had 21 lawyers in the last Congress and 20 this Congress. Other states have been as well represented usually. Our Presidents and Cabinet officers, Senators, Representatives, Ministers, Governors, Commissioners and members of committees are nearly all lawyers, and this is as it should be providing they do not work in the interests of lawyers exclusively. Class legislation has made a burlesque of free government. A knowledge of law is of great advantage to the honest legislator but it is an evil ally to the conscienceless.

Very Truly,
Mrs. Marion Todd

* * *

Rockford, Illinois

April 26, 1889

Dear Friends,

The Equity Club Annual has made me feel on speaking terms with all of you and has interested me as much as the modern novel does the society maiden. If it was not for missing the reading of yours, I would not send a letter this year for there is little to tell. My second year was much like the first only a little more so, for then, one good case on the Circuit Court docket each term satisfied me and now it comes up to two with smaller matters in between and more women coming in for consultation. My present office is much better than the first one and in a better location. The master-in-chancery and I have two good rooms together and though my share is six dollars a month and soon to be eight, I always have my rent money ready and never let myself run in debt for anything. Enough fees come in to allow me a new book occasionally and a new gown when necessity demands. So I know I am doing as well as any other young lawyer in the city and therefore keep up courage.

When I have no special business on hand, I study and congratulate myself on not being too much rushed with work to prevent my preparing myself thoroughly in the first principles and when work comes, it is so gratifying to practice what I do know. When a good fee comes in, the money is, of course, gratefully received and when the client is a poor woman who cannot afford to pay anything I call that a free dispensary case and rejoice that I had an opportunity to learn some new point there. This philosophy keeps me in good spirits and undismayed—generally.

Miss Cronise' advice about sticking to law business is excellent but it is difficult for me to resist outside pressure to help in church, temperance, and suffrage work. The good master-in-chancery gave me a fatherly lecture not long ago. He said, "It's about time you made up your mind whether you are going to be a lawyer or a temperance and suffrage evangelist. These good women who take up hours of your time visiting about these matters don't understand that you should have some time to yourself for study. Then you are all over the town on committee work between times. Yes, I know you don't neglect what business you now have, but you must prepare for what is coming."

Then another lawyer on the same floor who has often caught me surrounded by women, posters, literature, or invitation cards, lifted up his voice in warning, "What is there to hinder you from being a good lawyer? The men of the bar feel some interest in having the one woman do well but you waste your time working for these women who would probably consult a man rather than you if they had a paying case. The other day when you were trying that E. case, Lawyer T. said, 'What a pity that a girl who has the making of a lawyer and can conduct a case like that should fritter away her time on charities however good.' It is your own business, of course, but you must remember that Law is a jealous mistress and that 'If you keep your office your office will keep you.'"

And last term a new judge supposed to be unfavorable to women in the court room was very gracious and after allowing me a fifty dollar fee, came down from the bench in a little intermission for a pleasant chat. He too had learned of my weakness and among other things said "You let these women go without the ballot if they have not sense enough to see their need of it and you stick to your profession unless these suffragists pay you well. Yes, I thought likely you worked for them for nothing. To be a successful lawyer you must follow the plan of working like a slave and living like a hermit." Of course I thanked them and have been trying hard to follow all this good advice for it is encouraging that they have interest enough to criticize me. But I swallow more advice to the square inch than any young man lawyer in the state. In the last six months since election I have studied more than during the year and a half before and every little case even before a justice has as much careful attention as though thousands were involved. The American and English Encyclopedia of Law has been very helpful to me in this for it has a wider range of subjects than even large law libraries and each subject is about as full as it would be in the ordinary text books.

In regard to woman's health as referred to in the last Annual, we can be sick in comfort easier than in any other profession for the cases can be postponed till next week or next term while the doctor could not so easily shove aside a case of fever or a minister a marriage ceremony. Still if we paid more attention to dress, diet and exercise we might all be strong. My creed includes no corsets, broad, low-heeled shoes, reform under garments, dresses in one piece hanging from the shoulders, no tea, little coffee or pork, few pies and cakes, much sleep, a little hoeing in the flower beds and a day in bed when occasion demands instead of sitting up and suffering. We must not let another woman lawyer die of overwork.

Speaking of the courtesy of attorneys, there is only one here whom I have ever heard of saying anything but kind words and he remarked with the refinement which characterizes all of his utterances, "Let me once meet Miss Waugh in a case and I will wipe the floor with her." We met and he didn't and we met again and still he didn't either literally or figuratively. Then he became kindly and to my disgust referred to me in open court several times as "Kitty" so that an outsider would have thought us great friends. I told him with intense coldness that when he found it necessary to address me, he should call me Miss Waugh, as only my family and *friends* were privileged to call me by my home name. His own sense should have suggested to him that such familiarity was a breach of professional courtesy. He actually blushed, for the first time in his life, much to the edification of listeners. The reason I mention this is because I believe we young women must be extra careful not to let any legal scapegrace be too familiar, especially if he is young. A woman lawyer must be like Caesar's wife in one thing, but she need not follow her example in being wedded to one who was not himself "above suspicion." But there are all varieties of young lawyers, and one quite the reverse to whom I loaned my Annual last year asked if he could not read it the next year too. I wondered whether it might not do to let in a few such to honorary memberships. What do you think?

Before closing I must confess that the Prohibitionists here nominated me for state's attorney last fall. I was truly opposed, fearing I should be charged with all the sins in the category, lying, stealing, murder, being a general in the rebel army or the husband of two wives as is common concerning candidates. The papers however were kind but at once declared me ineligible and so the next evening at our ratification meeting when I had to speak and accept the nomination, I promptly told those young reporters down near the platform that it was the most unkindest cut of all to declare in the presence of all the handsome bachelors of the county that a certain unmarried young woman was not eligible. It might ruin my chances in a way they had not intended if somebody should not understand that they only referred to eligibility for office, but that if there were votes enough to elect me, no one need worry about my eligibility for I should qualify for office or know the reason why even if it had to go up to the supreme court. The good-natured laugh that followed was a sample of my treatment during the rest of the campaign. I told them they need not expect me to set 'em up to the boys in cigars and whiskey or to go around begging or even asking anybody to vote for me; that they should see that a woman could be a candidate for office without any dishonorable wire pulling.

Some lady friend always accompanied me to the political meetings over the county and the men speakers who went along were just as gallant as though we were weak-minded instead of strong-minded. They said the voters of other parties always turned out better when the woman lawyer ("So little she didn't weigh more than fifteen pounds") was to be one of the speakers. I didn't tell smutty stories, nor lie about my opponents, nor did any one lie about me though I was the only one on the Prohibition ticket who was treated so gently. I really believe that my candidacy helped the woman question here more than any convention ever did, for way off in some benighted portions of the county were men who had never heard a woman speak and who supposed a woman lawyer had horns and hoofs or at least wore boots and breeches. My harmless, insignificant appearance amazed them. Was I elected? Oh no, no one expected I would be, but to use a political phrase, I ran ahead of the ticket by about two hundred votes and the Prohibitionists thought it was quite a good scheme to put on a woman. I had quite a little fun out of it and met some very pleasant people but I'll never do it again. It is hard work, no pay, little glory, and a second time, people would call one a chronic office seeker.

Awaiting anxiously the arrival of the next Club Annual,
I remain,

Yours Sincerely,
Catharine G. Waugh

* * *

Chicago, Illinois

June 1, 1889

Dear Equity Club,

Allow me to make a suggestion in a matter not requiring a profound knowledge of the law, viz: "The Bonnet" or "Not the Bonnet" in the courtroom. Let no one lay down the law on that question. Mind I give you all fair warning that I shall wage unending warfare for the freedom of women lawyers.

If one should choose to lay aside her bonnet in the courtroom, whether on account of a heated atmosphere, or the shabbiness of the bonnet, or because she knows, intuitively, that the jury to be addressed would be prejudiced against her argument by either the extremely fashionable style of her hat, or its lack of style; whether one should plead with bonnet on, feeling confident that its beauty and becoming style lends persuasion to her tongue, or conscious that her hair needs the friendly concealment of a hat, in either case, I maintain that it is the inalienable right of each lady to follow her "own sweet will." Her keen intuition will guide her aright.

Your letters, dear friends, have been a source of great pleasure and profit to me. May they never cease.

Yours as ever,
Margaret L. Wilcox

Letters from 1890

Martha Kellum Pearce, December 30, 1892, Chicago, Illinois

Florence Cronise, July 25, 1890, Tiffin, Ohio

Emma Melinda Gillett, July 30, 1890, Washington., D.C.

Mary Anne Greene, May 14, 1890, Boston, Massachusetts

Almeda Eliza Hitchcock [Moore], August 28, 1890, Hilo, Hawaii

Ce Dora Lieuellen, August 12, 1890, White Springs, Florida

Catharine Gouger Waugh McCulloch, May 30, 1890, Rockford, Illinois

Catharine Gouger Waugh McCulloch, November 8, 1890, Chicago, Illinois

Marie Popelin, Lettre de Belgique, n.d.

Lelia Josephine Robinson Sawtelle, September 18, 1890, Boston, Massachusetts

Margaret Lyons Wilcox, September 15, 1890, Chicago, Illinois

Mary Hickey Wilkinson, June 13, 1890, Hutchinson, Kansas

The Equity Club

Annual.

1890

"All the Allies of Each."

* * *

Chicago, Illinois

December 30, 1892

My dear friends,

The letter which I prepared some time ago does not fill the bill now, but this Annual must be sent off right now, and I will write to you individually later. I must say however that I cannot but regret having taken up the work of the Secretaryship again after resigning it in '89. No one seemed ready to undertake it & I deluded myself with the hope I could do it again tho' I was cumbered with unusual cares and anxieties. Quite a number promised to write & I delayed[1] so long hoping to make our list larger that I was ashamed to send off what I had, & so it went on. I hope you will think with kindly forbearances of my failure to do what I had hoped.

We will surely meet during the World's Fair,[2] & we can decide then what is best to be done for the future.

Wishing a Happy New Year to every one of us, I remain,

Yours sincerely,
Martha K. Pearce

* * *

Tiffin, Ohio

July 25, 1890

Dear Equity Club,

It isn't for want of interest in the Club and its members that I'm so late this year in "entering an appearance," but I've been busy both in and out of my professional work; so much so that I've failed to write the usual letter.

This year has gone as the others before it, bringing but little change in its round, except that I've taken a student, Miss Ella Crim

1. Pearce apparently did not distribute the letters of 1890 until December of 1892.
2. Pearce is referring here to the Columbian Exposition in Chicago in 1893.

of Delaware, Ohio, who bids fair to become one of us in time. She has been in my office just a week, and in order that she may see the unpleasant side of the profession as well as the pleasant, I've taken her with me to two long trials in the Justice Court. I had her listen to the statement of a fair client now asking for her second divorce, and adding in her ignorantly innocent way, that if her next husband should turn out so worthless, she wouldn't try it again. I presume she thinks in the third time lies the charm.

I've also taken my student to "my store," for since Dec. 30, 1889 I've had a store on hand—assigned to me for the benefit of creditors. It was what is known as a "Department Store," a general furnishing store, goods mostly second-class and cheap, and of every possible description. To begin with I had not less than one thousand doll babies, shelves of baskets, coffee pots, pans, toys, underwear, hosiery, etc., in value all together averaging not very high. I've done everything under the sun possible for a human being, be he man, or be she woman, to dispose of it and now in sheer desperation I shall get an order of the Court to place it under the hammer for the creditors, if I keep on much longer, will not get so much as a glimpse of a dividend.

In addition to being a lawyer and store helper, I came very near to being a saloon keeper, having been appointed administrator of the estate of a young man saloon-keeper who after involving himself in debt through all classes of dissipation finally wound up by taking poison. For three days I had sole and complete possession of the saloon, though I kept doors tightly closed, had it appraised and sold and off my hands. Though I am frequently called into saloons, and think but little of it, yet this experience was not of the most agreeable kind. I only speak of this that you may know how *real* my daily practice is. While in possession of the saloon, it frequently came into my mind to wonder what course the good sisters of the W.C.T.U. would have advised, whether to proceed under the law to sell out, or to pull out the bungs, break in the heads of the casks and shatter the glasses and bottles. None of them advised me. I obeyed the law and protected my bondsmen, and hope that all women lawyers will do likewise when likewise situated.

Lately I've filed some petitions to quiet title involving considerable money. Also some involving the question of Wife's Right of Dower in mortgaged lands, mortgaged for purchase money, though not held by original grantor. These and other questions such as setting aside wills, Replevin of personal property,[1] foreclosures etc., will take up my spare time for study during the summer.

I am myself sued in my official capacity as executrix for taxes on the estate of decedent not listed, and again am sued in an estate to divert the estate into a different channel on the ground that testator had but a life estate in the property. And so goes on my work, I've scarcely had an opportunity to do anything outside. I longed for Vermont breezes this summer and fully believed I'd get off, but no opportunity has come, and the way seems [blocked] for the month of August. As my avoirdupois[2] hasn't lessened any and my nerves are quiet, I shall be forced to postpone breathing in foreign air until another summer.

And now with hearty congratulations for her who was Miss Robinson, now Mrs. Sawtelle, and for her who was Miss Waugh, now Mrs. McCulloch, and earnest hopes for their happiness both in and out of the profession, and with sincere affection for all of the Club,

Yours,
Florence Cronise

* * *

802 F St. N.W. Washington, D.C.

July 30, 1890

Dear Equity Club,

It is a saying that a busy person always has time for everything, but there certainly are times when the busy woman cannot find time to do what she would like to do as soon as she would like to. I hurried to get my work in hand so that I could attend a reunion of my class at the Seminary at Painesville, Ohio, in June, and since my return I have had an unusual amount of probate work to do, which in addition to other work has kept me very busy indeed.

1. Replevin of personal property refers to a form of action at common law for the recovery of personal property.

2. Here Cronise is referring lightheartedly to her weight.

I think my return to my old associations impressed me with the idea that I am a little insincere or that I am inclined to be satisfied "to seem" no matter what I really am. I wonder if others of us find people expect much of us because we have chosen to step a little to the side of the beaten track where the grass is fresher, and feel an anxiety like the toad in the fable to be an ox, because people seem to think we are an ox. The vastness of the legal field and the little I know makes me feel like a lady who asked me the other day if I knew a lawyer who knew any law.

I have been investigating the status of married women in the District lately, and find the laws most unsatisfactory. A married woman cannot give a note, make a contract, (except in relation to her separate estate) nor is she entitled to her earnings. She cannot carry on business as she cannot contract and her time is her husband's, etc. A bill has been introduced into Congress correcting this but, legislation is slow and, with Silver Bills, Tariff Bills, Force Bills, and other political moves the women can wait.

I received a letter from the *Illustrated American* requesting a short article on Divorce. I did not write it because my ideas are so chaotic on the subject I do not like to put in black and white what I think I believe to-day, I may think just the opposite tomorrow. I am conservative enough to believe in marriage till death parts,—absolutely no divorce. But that is an ideal condition that humanity would certainly groan under and find unbearable. What less than that is practically the best I do not know; if marriage is not a failure, it should be divorce laws making it possible for a victim to escape but still throwing such safeguards around the state as will make trivial reasons for separation insufficient for divorce. Then, if the ideal marriage is not possible, reason sometimes says let divorce laws be very free, take people as they are and apply laws to their conditions, it will lessen crime and unhappiness, and prevent the offspring of ill-mated or criminal parents coming into the world. Then I see reasons on the other side and like a pendulum my mind swings back and forth uncertain if the present law is not good what would be better.

Very truly,
Emma M. Gillett

* * *

Boston, Massachusetts

May 14, 1890

My dear Friends of the Equity Club,

If the writing of a letter were not a condition precedent to the reading of the Annual for 1890, you would hear nothing from me this year, for we are very busy moving ourselves and our Saris[1] and Penates[2] from the harsh Boston climate to the milder air of Providence, Rhode Island.

This step would not have been taken had not three specialists in diseases of the throat warned me away from the Boston east winds.

The woman lawyers of Massachusetts have a great deal to report to the Club. Our ranks have been re-inforced by Miss Alice Parker,[3] a member of the San Francisco bar, who has returned to her native state, and is hereafter to practice in Massachusetts. There are eight ladies studying in the Boston University Law School, three at least of whom we expect to be graduated in 1891.

Socially *the* event of the year has been the marriage of our pioneer—Lelia J. Robinson in April last. She continues in practice under her new name of Lelia Robinson Sawtelle.

The Portia Club[4] is now a flourishing institution with its monthly dinners and discussions. All the Massachusetts women lawyers and most of the students are members. Our last meeting took the form of a reception to our bride, and her husband, and for the first time gentlemen visitors were invited. Eight ladies and seven gentlemen sat down to a bountiful repast. Miss Parker as toast master, presided with dignity and proposed various toasts with comments in rhyme. "Our Guests"—(the gentlemen), "Woman's Sphere," "The New Legal Con-

1. The principle garment of a Hindu woman, the sari is a long piece of cloth wrapped around the body with one end over the head.

2. The penates were Roman gods of the household.

3. In 1890, Alice Parker returned to Boston from San Francisco, where she had studied law and passed the bar in 1887. In Boston, Parker shared an office with Lelia Robinson. She authored amendments to the Massachusetts Constitution broadening women's property rights. She was an active suffragist and later a leader in the League of Women Voters. In 1918, she moved to New York to practice law and became the editor of the *Women Lawyers' Journal.*

4. On the Portia Club, see Robinson letter, 1889, n. 3.

federacy," (i.e. Robinson Sawtelle,) "Law and Letters," "Law and Love," and "The Law School" were all toasted. Of our seven gentlemen, three were lawyers, two were law students and two were business men, but all when called upon to speak, responded with emphatic assertions of their belief in the full equality of woman to man, and her consequent right to all offices and privileges enjoyed by man.

As to my own legal biography I have to report myself as a sort of wandering star, so to speak. Nothing would please me better than to devote myself to practice just as a man does. But I cannot for two reasons. First, the want of physical strength, second, household duties which cannot be delegated to any one else. I have concluded that in future I must sandwich law and housekeeping together as I have done in the past year. I have had a good deal of interesting conveyancing to do, and best of all, have delivered a successful course of six lectures on Business Law for Women at Lasell Seminary, Auburndale, Mass. This educational work I feel to be so necessary, that it has been a delight to me and the result as shown in the interest displayed by the hundred and ten girls as well as in the good written examination they passed has been very gratifying.

Now, in my new home, I hope to continue that kind of work. Rhode Island needs such instruction as a woman lawyer can give to its women citizens.

I hope to open the Rhode Island bar to women, but cannot probably under a year, as the rules of the Supreme Court require an applicant who has been a member of the bar of another state for less time than three years, to spend six months in the office of a Rhode Island lawyer and then to pass an examination. The statutes of the state prescribe no qualifications for admission, they leave the whole matter to the Supreme Court to make its own rules, and fix its own qualifications for admission of attorneys.

There is much I should like to say, but I must ask you to accept this statement of facts and I submit it without argument

Sincerely yours,
Mary A. Greene

Future address,
9 Halsey St.
Providence, R.I.

* * *

Hilo, Hawaii

August 28, 1890

To the Ladies of the Equity Club,
Dear Friends,

Another year in our life's history is to be chronicled, and how it has passed with one of the members of the club in her far away home in the Hawaiian Islands the following will in a measure tell. To say that it has passed profitably and well would express it all but perhaps a more dctailed account would be of interest.

To begin where I left off last year would take us back to May, 1889, but an exact account of each event cannot be given as it would take up too much space and time.

The third Judicial Circuit of the Supreme court sits here in May and last term was of special interest, although I did not take any active part in it. Four men—Americans—were on trial for their lives. Father was employed for the prosecution and I as a reporter for one of the daily papers in Honolulu. There was a good bit of good-natured rivalry between the other reporter and myself to see who could get off the latest news to Honolulu. The telephone, made use of by me and not by the other reporter, helped me to get in the latest accounts.

The business of the past year has been good, and my success in my cases fairly good. As father has attended all of the circuits wherein we had business, my work has been here in Hilo entirely. Father's being away has thrown me on my own resources more and it has been a good thing for me, for I found that I was getting to depend on him more and more and was doing little thinking for myself. Office work is more to my liking, but when father is away the cases that come up have to be tried, and after screwing up my courage to the sticking point I enter the court room ready for work. Two weeks ago I had a Liquor case to defend. My uncle being the Prosecuting Attorney and a keen lawyer, made me feel anything but joyful when I took up the case, but after a two-day fight I came off victorious and went out of the court room feeling much better than when I entered.

The trying of cases is usually hard here, for everything has to be interpreted, and the interpreters never put a question exactly as one asks it. We have the native, Chinese, Japanese and Portuguese languages to contend with here in the courts, and I often wish I were a linguist so as to understand what is being said before it is interpreted.

Perhaps a little diversion from the subject of law, and on that of volcanoes would be of some interest. Our Goddess of the Volcano, Madame "Pele" (pay-lay) has been making herself felt this last few months in a series of Earthquakes. August 6th, 11:20 P.M. this little town was awakened from its peaceful slumbers by two severe shocks; so severe that vases, crockery, easels and anything that was not securely fastened was thrown from position and many broken; so severe that pianos were moved from position. At 12:30 A.M. three shocks followed one another in quick succession, doing very little damage however. Later another shock came, making six in all for one night. The people were pretty thoroughly frightened, and the talk now is "Madame Pele must be getting ready for an outbreak."

Let me assure you, however, that there has never been an earthquake here yet that has done serious damage, and do not let the fact that we do have shakes once in a while deter any of you from visiting these beautiful isles when the opportunity presents itself.

A most cordial welcome will be given to any of my "Sisters-in-Law" who visit these Islands.

Your "Sister-in-Law,"
Almeda E. Hitchcock

* * *

White Springs, Florida

August 12, 1890

Dear Sisters of the Equity Club,

What I have to say will necessarily seem like an advertisement of what is now my most immediate interest, the establishment of a School of Law in connection with the Florida Normal College, with which I have so pleasantly labored for the last six months. Certainly no time in my eighteen years of teaching, fourteen of which have been in this kind of work, have I found more painstaking, wide-awake students in Literature and History than I have found here, and in as much as I have found in one important respect facts to contradict geography, namely, these people of this land of fruit and flowers eat as much as do the Esquimau[s],[1] I think it worth while to say that my observations certainly set aside another commonly received notion, that the Southern people are necessarily slow of movement and lacking in energy. Surely I have not found this true of the large number of students that I have met, in all things faithful to their class-room duties throughout the months of June and July. True, we have had no such sweltering weather as the newspapers report in the Mississippi Valley and on the Atlantic coast, but these were young men and women from different parts of the South, and I have never known finer students, nor a more ideal summer climate.

A law professorship has been the goal towards which I have been striving for ten years, and I gave up College work a year ago to take a course in law school preparatory to three years practice, after which, in about six or seven years, I hoped to secure in some College or University such a position. My physical condition made it imprudent for me to begin the work of a student immediately after my long term of teaching, for in all those years I had taken but one vacation of a summer, which was spent in study and each year I had spent forty-eight weeks in the College halls. The plans that I had made proved unsatisfactory and I turned to teaching again after six months respite, and as soon as I came here I began to feel that here is an opening for just what I want. A thriving school, enterprising young men and women, and a President ambitious to make this the school of the state and a most loyal patronage. There is no law school in the state, and if indications are rightly interpreted a fair demand for one exists. I will have what help I need, and sole charge of the work, and in another year I hope to have something to record of what has been done. Ladies and gentlemen alike are free to enter this as all other courses of the College, and several of our enterprising girls have told me that it is their purpose to do so. I believe too, that our genial summer-land climate will bring those from the North who may wish to test the virtues of White Sulphur Springs stroll along the banks of the beauteous Suwannee and at the same time turn the pages of Blackstone,[2] Greenleaf[3] and Cooley.[4] I shall labor faithfully to make

1. Eskimos.

2. Sir William Blackstone was the author of *Commentaries on the Laws of England,* 4 vols. (1765–69).

3. Simon Greenleaf was the author of *Treatise on the Law of Evidence* (1846).

4. Thomas M. Cooley was the author of a treatise on *Constitutional Limitations* (1868).

this school a means of helpfulness to young men and women and I hope that I have the good wishes of the Equity sisters.

Very truly yours,
Ce Dora Lieuellen

* * *

Rockford, Illinois

May 30, 1890

Dear Sisters of the Equity Club,

I have followed the example set by Jessie E. Wright and Lelia J. Robinson, and "doubled my joys and halved my sorrows" in regular orthodox shape. "He" was a classmate of mine in the Union College of Law and I think quite a brilliant young man doing beautifully in his business. So you see I won't leave the profession but will really step into a wider field of work.

I had promised to go up to South Dakota to speak in the suffrage campaign and so that will be my honeymoon with visiting of friends added at the close. That will be about as practical as Mrs. Sawtelle's. It strikes me as funny even now, but I guess it will be just as sensible as a fashionable watering place.

Yours with bright anticipations,
Catharine G. Waugh

* * *

Chicago, Illinois

November 8, 1890

Dear Friends,

It is over five months now since I wrote my this year's letter for the Club and telling of my contemplated wedding trip. A few days ago

Miss Pearce was in the office and told me the letters were still unfinished and I had better write more or rather something different as to my present existence.

I was married May 30, to Frank H. McCulloch of Chicago, and have gone into law business with him with offices in The Rookery, Room 1167. He was one of my classmates and has practiced here steadily ever since he graduated and has done better than any other of my classmates that I have heard of. We reach the office at 9 A.M. and leave at 6 P.M. We are keeping house with my brother and his wife only married recently, and divide between us the responsibility. We have a good girl in the kitchen and between the successful administration there and our prosperity here at the office, I am more contented and yet more ambitious than ever before. I believe now that instead of crippling my ability to be a lawyer that my prospects are much improved. I believed differently a year ago, but it makes all the difference in the world who one marries, and I should never again oppose a woman lawyer marrying, if she devotedly loved her husband and he was clean and brilliant and honorable and progressive enough to be proud that his wife was a lawyer. Mrs. Sawtelle writes me that she is braver than I in marrying a business man. Well perhaps if I should have fallen in love with a business man, I should have been willing to marry him, but I am thankful he happened to be a lawyer.

As yet I have had very little Chicago business of my own, being generally at work on matters belonging to Mr. McCulloch, but within the last month I had a genuine client and she has sent her friends to me with abstracts to examine and altogether we did $55 worth of work for them. It pleased me that something was coming to me, and she says she has more work to do.

Rents are enormous here. For our not very large rooms we pay $36 a month, but we like the rooms.

I hope you can come and visit our home and office and if not very soon that we can all meet at the World's Fair.

Very sincerely,
Catharine Waugh McCulloch

* * *

Lettre de Belgique
Aux membres de l'Equity Club

I. Comment on devient avocat en Belgique?
II. La Femme peut-elle acquirir le titre d'avocat et exercer la profession?

I

En Belgique, les femmes sont admises aux etudes juridiques depuis la loi de 1876 sur l'Enseignement supérieur et sur la collation des grades académiques qui a supprimé, pour l'admission dans les Facultés, la condition du graduat-grade que les jeunes gens seul pouvaient obtenir dans les colléges et athénées.—

Nos femmes paraissent peu disposées à jouir du bénéfices de la loi; jusque ici une seule a terminé les etudes juridiques et obtenu le diplome de docteur en droit en Juillet 1888.

A elles seules, les etudes juridiques ne pas l'avocat, il reste à remplir deux autres conditions que nous allons examiner—*le serment* et *le stage.*

Le serment. Nos docteurs en droit, pour posseder le titre d'avocat, doivent préalablement être admis à la prestation du serment; pour être autorisés à exercer la profession, ils doivent être inscrits au tableau de l'Ordre ou tout au moins être reçus au stage professionel d'une durée de trois ans.

C'est une Cour d'appel, ou un tribunal de première instance, que reçoit le serment sur les conclusions due ministère public. Le Procureur Général jouit dans l'admission au serment d'un pouvoir discrétionnaire; toutefois, il y a peu d'exemples de refus du serment. Il faudrait évidemment des motifs graves. Le récipiendaire est présenté par un avocat ayant au moins dix ans de barreau; celui ci le prend en quelque sorte sous son patronage, lui sert de parrain et se porte, garant de sa moralité.

Le futur avocat prête le serment suivant; "Je jure fidélité au Roi, obéissance à la Constitution et aux lois du peuple belge; je jure de ne rien dire ou publier de contraire aux lois, aux règlements, aux bonnes moeurs, à la sûreté de l'Etat et à la paix publique; de ne jamais m'écarter dû respect du aux tribuneaux et aux autorités publiques, de ne conseiller ou défendre aucune cause que je ne croirai pas juste en mon âme et conscience."

Cette formalité peut se remplir à tout moment de l'année. Elle a lieu en audience solennelle, une fois l'an, lors de la rentrée des Cours et tribunaux le 1st Octobre. Tous les jeunes gens diplômes en Juillet epoque de la session ordinaire des examens prêtent serment en cette séance solenelle en même temps que les magistrats nouvellement élus. Ce jour la, le Palais est tres anime, les couloirs et les salles sont envahis par les parents, les amis de ceux qui entrent dans la vie active dans le *struggle for life*, et, au silence des longs jours de vacances succèdent, tout à coup, le mouvement et la vie accoutumés en ces lieux.

Le stage. Le Conseil de l'Ordre des avocats, composé de quinze membres élus par l'Assemblée de l'Ordre, reglemente et surveille le stage; il inscrit le docteur en droit assermenté sur la liste des avocats stagiaires.

Les avocats stagiaires travaillent sous la direction d'un avocat qui leur sert de patron. Très souvent, ce patron n'est que nominal. Le stagiaire qui fréquente régulierement le cabinet de son patron, prépare les dossiers, plaide les petites affaires que celui ei vent bien lui confier, differends, qui relevent de la Justice de Paix ou les petites affaires correctionelles. Les plus zélés sont assidus aux audiences, et s'il s'agit d'entendre *l'une gloires du barreau,* l'espace réservé au barreau est envahi par toute la jeunesse désireuse de s'initier à l'art de la profession et heureuse d'admirer un maître.

La défense des indigents est une obligation du stage. Un bureau de consultation gratuite composé de cinq membres, choisis parmi les membres du Conseil de l'Ordre, examine, en sa séance hebdomadaire, les demands des indigents et confie aux stagiaires les causes "qu'il trouve justes." Le stagiaire est tenu d'assister aux séances du bureau de consultation, son nom ne serait point porté au Tableau de l'Ordre s'il ne pouvait justifier d'au moins soixante presences à l'expiration des trois années du stage.

Enfin les stagiaires suivent les séances de la Conférences du jeune barreau,—institution née du bureau de consultation—ils prennent part aux discussions juridiques que la Conférence organise, et plaident devant leurs confrères des procès fictifs, toutefois, sans qu'il y ait la obligation pour eux. Cette institution, d'une utilité incontestable, n'a guère donné de resultats sérieux, jusqu'ici. C'est, du moins, l'opinion des nos jeunes stagiaires, mais, j'imagine qu'il leur plait peu d'être astreint à ces séances régulieres et de se soumettre aux critiques de confrères plus on moins bienveillants.

Le stage terminé, le stagiaire prend rang parmi les avocats du barreau de . . . . , son nom est inscrit au tableau de l'Ordre, et il porte le titre d'avocat près tel Cour d'appel, ou tel tribunal. Il quitte son patron et s'occupe des affaires que lui sont confiées directement.

Voilà donc comme on devient avocat en Belgique.

Les femmes sont admises aux études juridiques, elles peuvent obtenir le grade de docteur en droit à la suite d'un cours d'études de quatre années dans une Université, mais elles ne peuvent devenir avocat parce qu'elles ne sont pas reçues au serment ni au stage.

Avant 1888, la question de l'admission de la femme ne s'était pas posée en Belgique, et un doute subsistait et par conséquent aussi un certain espoir quant à la décision.

Le Procureur Général interrogé officiensement dans le cas Popelin se déclara immédiatement et formellement contre l'admission. En effet, il refusa de viser le diplôme de la postulante et prit des conclusions tendant à la repousser du serment. Il fallut plaider—toute la science de la défense, toute le talent des avocats furent dépensés en pure perte; on se heurtait devant la volonté inebranlable du Procureur Général, bien plus que devant le valeur ou la force de ses arguments. Et voici, à ce propos, un petit bruit de couloir assez significant que je vous rapporte sous toutes reserves.—Le greffier, interrogé sur l'arrêt que l'on attendait, répondit. "Jusqu'ici, la Cour à toujours rendu ses arrêts conformément au réquisitoire du Procureur Général et Mlle. Popelin ne doit pas espérer interrompre la serie"—! En effet, la serie ne fut pas interrompue et l'arrêt fut celui que vous connaissez, ou il est beaucoup question des lois romaines, des coutumes du Moyen Age, du décret de 1810 et du Code Napoleonien, pas du tout des progrès réalisés dans la condition de la femme, de son entrée dans presque toutes les carrières libérales, et en ce qui concerne spécialement la femme avocat, de l'expérience, tentée avec succès aux Etats Unis d'Amérique.

L'arrêt de la Cour d'appel fut soumis à la censure de la Cour de

Cassation. Celle a declaré qu'il ne lui appartenait pas d'examiner si la loi qui permet à la femme d'obtenir le diplôme de docteur en droit est engagée à lui ouvrir le carrière du Barreau; que la solution de cette question est réservée au legislateur 11 *obre* 1889.

Précisément, l'occasion d'interroger le législateur n'allait pas tarder à se présenter. La loi de 1876 sur l'enseignement supérieur n'était que temporaire. Une loi nouvelle sur le même objet devait être discutée au cours de la session 1889–1890. Cette loi vient d'être votée. Elle à paru au Moniteur journal officiel le 25 Avril 1890, et décide 1e que les femmes peuvent obtenir les grades académiques. 2e qu'elles peuvent exercer la médecine et la pharmacie, mais elle garde le silence en ce qui concerne l'exercise de la profession d'avocat par la femme.

Par conséquent, le diplôme de, docteur en droit délivré à une femme reste frappé de sterilité. Sera ce pour long temps?

Marie Popelin
(Dr. en droit.)
Brussels, 14 Vieille Halle aux Blés

* * *

[Letter from Belgium
To the members of the Equity Club

I. How one becomes a lawyer in Belgium?
II. Is it possible for the women to acquire the lawyer's title and to work within the profession?

I

In Belgium, women are admitted to study law since the law of 1876 on the graduate educational system and on the awarding of the academic grades abolishing, for the admission in Faculties, the status of the "graduate-grade," only obtained by the young men in colleges.

The women here seem little disposed to enjoy the benefits of the law; until now, only one has finished the judicial studies and has obtained a Ph.D. in law in July of 1888.

The judicial studies, alone, do not permit one to become a lawyer;

two other conditions have to be fulfilled, which we are going to study: *the oath* and the *probationary period.*

The oath: our Doctors in Law, in order to obtain the lawyer's title, have first to be admitted to the "taking of the oath;" in order to be authorized to enter the profession, they must be registered on the Board of the Order, or at least they must be admitted to the probationary period which lasts three years.

It is an appellate Court, or a "first instance" Tribunal which receives the oath according to the conclusions of the public ministry. The Attorney General enjoys a discretionary power for the admission of the oath; nevertheless, there have been few examples of refusals of the oath. It should be evident that those that are not admitted, are not admitted because of grave motives. The inductee is introduced by a lawyer having at least ten years of experience at the bar; in other terms, this lawyer takes the inductee under his patronage, acting as a sponsor and guaranteeing his morality.

The future lawyer swears to the following oath: "I swear fidelity to the King, obediance to the Constitution and to the laws of the Belgium people, to the rules, to the upstanding morals, to the safety of the State and to the public peace; I swear to never waiver from the respect due to the Courts and to the public authorities, to never advise or defend any cause I won't believe in my soul and conscience."

This formality can be fulfilled any time in the year. It takes place before a solemn audience, once a year, at the beginning of the courses and courts, the first of October. All the new students who graduated in July, the time of the ordinary exams' session, swear to the oath during this solemn session, at the same time as the magistrates newly elected. During this day, the Court is very animated, the corridors and rooms are invaded by the parents, the friends of those who are going to enter active life in the "struggle for life," and, after the silence of the long holidays, come, suddenly, the movement and the life which are usual in this place.

The probationary period: the Council of the Order of the lawyers, composed of fifteen members elected by the Assembly of the Order, regulates and controls the probationary period; it registers the Doctors in Law who are under oath on the list of the apprentice lawyers.

The apprentice lawyers work under the direction of a lawyer who acts as a sponsor. Very often, this sponsor is only nominal. The apprentice who regularly frequents the office of his sponsor prepares the dossiers, pleads the little cases the latter accepts to give him and which depend on the Justice of the Peace, or the little correctional cases. The most zealous are attentive to go to the audiences, and if a "star of the bar" is expected to speak, the space reserved to the bar is invaded by all the youth desirous to initiate herself to the art of the profession and glad to admire a master.

The defense of the poor is an obligation for the apprentice. An office of free consultation and composed of five members, chosen among the Council of the Order, examines, during its weekly session, the requests and entrusts the apprentices with the causes "it considers fair." The apprentice must attend the sessions of the office of consultation; his name would not be written on the Board of the Order if he couldn't at least justify sixty attendances at the end of the three years of probationary period.

Finally, the apprentices attend the sessions of the Conference of the young bar, an institution born from the office of consultation. They participate in the legal discussions organized by the Conference, and plead in fictive trials in front of their colleagues; but there is nevertheless no obligation for them to do so. This institution, of an unquestionable utility, did not yet give serious results. It is, at least, the opinion of our young apprentices, but I can imagine they do not really like to be forced to attend those regular sessions and they do not like to be submitted to the critics of colleagues more or less benevolent.

When the probationary period is finished, the apprentice takes rank among the lawyers of the bar of . . . . , his name is written on the Board of the Order, and he carries the title of lawyer appointed to such and such appellate Court or Tribunal. He leaves his sponsor and takes care of the cases which are directly given to him.

This is how one becomes a lawyer in Belgium.

Women are admitted to the legal studies, they can obtain the title of Doctor in Law at the end of a four-year cycle in a University, but they cannot become lawyers because they are not accepted to the oath or to the probationary period.

Before 1888, the problem of the admission of women had not been posed in Belgium; a doubt subsisted and, thus, also a certain hope concerning the decision.

The Attorney General, unofficially questioned in the case "Popelin," immediately declared he was against the admission. As a matter of fact, he refused to sign the diploma of the candidate and took dispositions as she could not make the oath. She had to plead—all the science of the defense, all the talent of the lawyers did not help her in any way; nothing could be done against the unshakable will of the Attorney General, much more than against the value of the force of his arguments. Here is, in this connection, a little "gossiping" quite significant and which I report to you under all reserve. The clerk of court, questioned on the issue of the case, answered: "Until now, the Court has always decreed according to the indictment of the Attorney General and Miss Popelin should not hope to end this tradition!" Actually, the tradition was not ended and the issue was the one you already know, where the roman laws, the customs of the Middle Age, the decree of 1810 and the Napoleonic Code were much talked of, but no one discussed the progress made in the woman's condition, of her entry in most of the liberal careers, and especially of the woman lawyer, and the experience, tried with success in the United States.

The decree of the appellate Court was submitted to the censure of the Supreme Court of Appeals. The latter declared that it was not allowed to examine if the law allowing the woman to obtain the diploma of Doctor in Law is ready to accept her to the bar; it also declared that the solution to this question was reserved to the legislator's conclusion, October 11, 1889.

Precisely, the occasion to question the legislator was not very far to go. The law of 1876 on the graduate educational system was only temporary. A new law on the same subject was to be argued during the 1889–1890 session. This law has just been passed. It came out in the official newspaper "Moniteur" on the 25th of April of 1890 and has decided: First, that women can obtain the academic degree; second, that they can practice medicine and pharmacy; but it remains silent concerning the practice of the legal profession by the woman.

Consequently, the degree of Doctor in Law delivered to a woman remains sterile. Will it be for a long time?

Marie Popelin
(Doctor in Law)
Brussels, 14 Vieille aux Bles][1]

1. Translated for the author by Barbara Pajot.

* * *

5 Pemberton Square,
Boston, Massachusetts

September 18, 1890

Dear Equity Club,

I fear this letter is too late for the Annual, but I hope not, for as I am owing a personal letter to nearly every member of the Club, I want my sisters in the law to know that I am still alive and in my office.

It is a little odd, to say the least of it, that my last Club letter concluded with the question—"Is it practicable for a woman to successfully fulfill the duties of wife, mother and lawyer at one and the same time?" and the request that some of our members would discuss the question in its pros and cons. I was not seriously contemplating marriage for myself at that time, and yet it has come to pass that I am now a wife of nearly six months standing. Nor have I married *into* the profession, for my husband is a business man who spends all his odd hours in reading philosophy, and who has little fancy for any but the ethical side of law. Miss Alice Parker,[1] a bright young lawyer who is now my office mate, in turning over my scrap-book the other day, came across another owl-like saying of mine in a letter to one of our earlier Annuals, to the effect that if a woman lawyer marries at all, it should be into the profession and not out of it. Thus do we preach and not practice. But really, my legal business has taken on such comfortable proportions during the last year or two that when I could get away from the office, I have not wanted to see anybody who had ever seen a volume of reports or looked into a statute-book. I have been too tired to go from law at the office to law at home, hence a lawyer was not the best husband for me. However, if I had happened to fall in love with a representative of bench or bar (and he had reciprocated) I should probably now be arguing just the other way. It is one of those cases where one may take up either side that first brings in a retainer.

This sounds frivolous, but I do not mean it to be so. My husband is proud of my professional ambition and does everything that a husband can do to encourage and sustain me in it. His wedding

1. See letter from Mary Greene, 1890, n. 3.

present was a fine new roll-top desk for my office, and he does not fret very much when it is discovered that every pair of his socks is in need of mending. To be sure, I sit down the same instant, usually and have a pair ready in about three minutes.

The past summer, my vacation has been rather longer than usual—two delightful months at my husband's summer home in New Hampshire; but I came to the city occasionally, did some business by letter, and the rest of it Miss Parker good-naturedly looked after for me. And the two weeks that I have been back in Boston have been largely spent in vain efforts to find a servant who both would and could keep the domestic machinery running. But I have her at last—a jewel, I think—and am getting back to business in earnest.

Probably Miss Greene has written you of the increase of women students in Boston Law School. Ten women were attending the spring term. Next June, Mrs. Fall will graduate,—a lawyer's wife with two little children, and one of the brightest women and best students I ever knew.

Have you seen the article in the New York *Illustrated American*[2] of July 26th on the Women of the United States Supreme Court? It says the day of women lawyers has at last come—and I believe it.

Hastily but always truly yours,
Lelia Robinson Sawtelle

* * *

Chicago, Illinois

September 15, 1890

Dear Friends of the Equity Club,

Dare I write when my past year has not been spent in legal work? Perhaps you may pardon one who hesitates. Why such hesitation? Well, I acknowledged that the sordid matter of sufficient pecuniary reward is the cause. I am enjoying a comfortable salary for my work

2. The article Robinson refers to is "Women of the American Bar," by former Equity Club member, Belva Lockwood, in the *Illustrated American* 45–47 (July 26, 1890). Lockwood refers to a number of pioneer women lawyers including Equity Club members Laura de Force Gordon, Ada Bittenbender, Emma Gillett, and Lelia Robinson Sawtelle.

as a teacher which I should miss probably during the earlier years of my law practice.

Are women lawyers, even after several years of experience, successful in the matter of large fees? If one could see the prospect of future remuneration, it would be easier to take up the new profession. My case is somewhat different from that of a young woman who at the outset of her career is fitting herself for a profession. For her, the amount of salary or income will be of slow growth in any chosen work. It seems a greater risk financially for one to begin a law practice after years of success in teaching. I still enjoy it, although I think work in the law would be deeply interesting to me.

Many a woman has the same problem to solve. Will it pay to relinquish a certainty for an uncertainty? Women lawyers in active practice may help us to answer this question. What some have done more can do. True it is that only the brave deserve reward. While we timidly hesitate others may be reaping rich fruit.

Yet I do not hesitate to advise young women to study law, if so inclined. No closer discipline of mind can be attained than that given by tracing out legal principles, and there is no better preparation for business of any sort. My legal studies have been of great value to me as a teacher. They have given me a clearer insight into the past, a closer analysis of human thought and progress, a more comprehensive mental grasp, more flexible habits of mind, in a word, a broader culture. I can, then, see no loss in studying law.

Now do not imagine that I shall always hesitate. Your letters are giving me courage. The final step shall be taken ere long, I hope. I shall burn all the bridges I have crossed, and be with you in active work, as I am in spirit.

Yours fraternally,
Margaret L. Wilcox

* * *

Hutchinson, Kansas

June 13, 1890

Ladies of the Equity Club,
Dear Friends,

I am much pleased to have an opportunity to come into communication with women who have chosen the Law. I come empty-handed so far as anything interesting or instructive is concerned. It is now seventeen years since I graduated from Iowa's Law School, and to all appearance abandoned the profession from that day to this. I married and my family engrossed my time principally. But all this time I have still loved to read law and have done so to some extent. I have now reached a time of more leisure and a desire to do something in the line of the Law comes back very strong to me. I have lived a retired life so long that how to make the start is the question with me. I have no need that urges me to cast about for an opportunity to start.

I look forward to the coming of the Annual.

Yours truly,
Mary B. Wilkinson
312 Avenue B. East

Profiles of the Members of the Equity Club

Cora Agnes Benneson
Addie Melvina Stephenson Billings
Ada Matilda Cole Bittenbender
Letitia Lavilla A. Burlingame
Eliza Anne Chambers
Florence Cronise
Corinne Williams Douglas
Emma Millinda Gillett
Laura de Force Gordon
Mary Anne Greene
Mary Emily Humphrey Haddock
Almeda Eliza Hitchcock [Moore]
Ada Harriet Miser Kepley
Laura A. Woodin LeValley
Ce Dora Lieuellen
Belva Ann Bennett McNall Lockwood
Leona Taylor Lounsbury
Ellen Annette Martin
Rebecca May
Catharine Gouger Waugh McCulloch
Martha Kellum Pearce
Lelia Josephine Robinson [Sawtelle]
Jane Mariah Slocum
Marion Marsh Todd
Catharine Van Valkenburg Waite
Sarah Killgore Wertman
Jessie Elvira Wright Whitcomb
Margaret Lyons Wilcox
Mary Hickey Wilkinson

European Members:
Emilie Kempin
Eliza Orme
Marie Popelin

Cora Agnes Benneson

Cora Agnes Benneson was born June 10, 1851, in Quincy, Illinois, to Robert S. Benneson of Delaware and Electa Ann Park of Vermont. Benneson was the youngest of four daughters. Unlike her sisters, all of whom married, Benneson remained single and followed a less traditional path for women of her day. She attended college and law school, practiced law, and traveled by herself around the world.

Benneson's father was an avid advocate of educational reform. Having made his fortune in the lumber business, he became a leader in Quincy, Illinois, where he was elected mayor in 1861. He used his influence to introduce a system of public school education to Quincy. Cora Benneson shared her father's passion for education and devoted much of her adult life to her quest for knowledge. Benneson's early education was typical of young girls of her social class. She attended the local girls' school, Quincy Female Seminary. After graduating she stayed at the school as a teacher of English, reading, history, and physiology. While many young women in Benneson's generation taught temporarily before settling down to marriage and motherhood, for Benneson teaching was merely a preliminary step before she embarked on her pursuit of higher education. In 1875 she entered the University of Michigan. When she graduated in 1878 with a B.A., she became part of the first generation of college-educated women in America. Immediately upon graduation, Benneson entered the law department of the University of Michigan and received her LL.B. in 1880. Her study of law seemed to be motivated less by professional aspirations than intellectual curiosity. While she was admitted to both the Michigan and Illinois bars immediately upon receiving her LL.B., Benneson did not embark upon law practice. Instead she continued her pursuit of higher education at the University of Michigan, studying for a master's degree in jurisprudence and German, which she earned in 1881.

After almost a decade of study at the University of Michigan, and three degrees in hand, Benneson left her alma mater a loyal and appreciative alumnae. In 1889, in an essay entitled "Life of Women at Michigan University," published in the *Women's Journal,* she fondly praised the coeducational experience and life for women at her alma mater and revealed her deep appreciation for the precious educational opportunities the University of Michigan offered to women.

After leaving the University of Michigan in 1883, Benneson set out to travel around the world to study legal procedures in other countries. She was particularly interested in the status of women in the legal profession in other countries and shared some of her observations in her Equity Club letter. Her travels kept her abroad for over two years. When she returned, she supported herself by writing and lecturing on her travels. In addition, she worked briefly as an editor of the *Atlantic Reporter,* issued by the West Publishing Company of St. Paul, Minnesota.

But in 1887, Benneson returned to the familiar environs of academe, this time as the recipient of a fellowship in history from Bryn Mawr College in Pennsylvania. While a fellow at Bryn Mawr, Benneson studied administration with Woodrow Wilson, who was then a young professor at the college, and continued her studies in jurisprudence and political history.

Benneson then moved to Cambridge, Massachusetts. In 1894, she was admitted to the Massachusetts bar and began her legal practice. Thus, it was fourteen years after she received her LL.B. that Benneson first settled down to practice law. But still she did not give up her passion for education, and that same year she applied to become a candidate for a doctorate of philosophy at Harvard University. Harvard, with its strong stand against coeducation, rejected her, but Benneson received graduate status at Radcliffe.

Benneson spent the rest of her life in Cambridge where she practiced law and was a justice of the peace. In 1899, she was elected a fellow at the American Association for the Advancement of Science. She died June 8, 1919, just two days before her sixty-eighth birthday.

Selected Sources

Biographical information on Benneson is in *Portrait and Biographical Record of Adams County, Illinois* (Chicago, 1892); Carl Landrum, "Girls School opened doors in 1867" (*Quincy Herald Whig,* July 13, 1969, in Quincy Public Library, Quincy, Ill); Theodore R. Chase, ed., *The Michigan University Book, 1844–1880* (1880); *Calendar of the University of Michigan* (1876 and 1880); and *Bryn Mawr College Calendar Register of Alumnae and Former Students* (1915). Benneson is included in Ellen Martin, "Admission of Women to the Bar" (1 *Chicago Law Times* [1886]) and in Lelia J. Robinson, "Women Lawyers in the United States" (2 *Green Bag* [1890]). Her application to Harvard University for admission as a Ph.D. candidate is in the Radcliffe College Archives, Schlesinger Library, Radcliffe College, Cambridge, Massachusetts. Benneson's writings include "Life of Women of Michigan University" (20 *Woman's Journal* [1889]) and "Palestine To-day," a twelve-part essay in 5 *Unitarian* (1890).

Addie Melvina Stephenson Billings

The economic growth and westward movement of people in the latter half of the nineteenth century opened a wide array of opportunities for industrious and ambitious individuals. Addie Stephenson Billings's life followed a western trail. With each stop along the way she tried something new—first teaching then marriage and motherhood combined with a legal career finally investing in the fertile California farmlands to profit from the emerging grape and wine industry. Her participation in public life fed her political view, helping to fashion a woman who held firm beliefs about equal rights, woman suffrage, and economic opportunity freed from government constraints.

Addie Melvina Stephenson Billings was born on January 4, 1858, in Pecatonica, Illinois. The daughter of a schoolteacher, James Stephenson, she developed reading skills at an early age. The family moved frequently, first to Wheaton, Illinois, and later to Waverly, Iowa. By the time she was sixteen years old, Billings was also teaching in a small school in Iowa to teenage boys not much younger than herself. She attended the Iowa State Normal School in Cedar Falls, graduating in 1877 with high academic standing. After receiving her teaching certificate she began a brief career teaching school in various towns in Bremer County, Iowa.

Billings's adolescent writings do not reveal the piety of young girls of the Victorian era, but rather the psychological battles faced by youth struggling to adjust to life in a modern industrialized society. The poems from her teenage years reflect both a level of insecurity about her appearance and a fierce independence to follow her own dreams. She lamented that she was homely and would need to develop her mind if she were to find a place in the world. She was also keenly aware that a number of opportunities existed that would help her lead a full and happy life: "There are many ways in this life / For you to have plenty of fun / All nature is full of delight, / And pleasure like rivulets run." In a poem entitled "Don't be Spongy on the Boys," she expressed her belief that women must fight for their independence and defend woman's rights ("you must ever defend / With a vigor both firm and true"). Billings held on to her adolescent views as she matured into a strong, independent woman unafraid to take risks or express controversial views.

In 1880, Addie Melvina Stephenson married a young attorney, Elmore M. Billings, and moved with him to Geneva, Nebraska. Assisting her husband to establish his practice, Addie Billings developed an interest in the law and began to read law with him in preparation for admission to the bar. In the early years of their marriage, she worked as a secretary in his law office and submitted news articles to the Omaha papers. Billings's position as a newspaper correspondent allowed her to generate publicity and business for her husband's practice by reporting cases he had won while judiciously avoiding news of lost ones. On November 19, 1887, she was admitted to the bar in Nebraska and immediately joined her husband in his practice. The firm of Billings and Billings tried both criminal and civil cases and Addie Billings made frequent appearances in court to present cases. In one noteworthy case, Mrs. Billings won an acquittal for a client accused of murder by proving that the death was a suicide. She became one of the first women in Nebraska to be admitted to all courts for the practice of law. She was also admitted to the bar in Iowa in the 1880s and in California in 1891.

Billings was a woman of indefatigable energy. Early in their marriage the couple adopted three children, two girls and one boy. When the Billings decided to move to California in 1891, the boy ran away and never appeared to have made contact with the family again. Addie Billings developed close relationships with her two adopted daughters, eventually living with them in her retirement. Apart from assuming domestic responsibilities, Billings also became involved in political and social activities. She was an avid suffragist and an eloquent speaker on the issue. Her public speeches urged women to stay loyal to the Republican party while vehemently criticizing the various third parties that arose in the 1890s and attempted to sway women with promises of immediate suffrage and improved economic and social standing. Billings was an active member of the Order of the Eastern Star, an all-women's Protestant society modeled after the Masons, and served as Grand Matron in the early 1890s.

The Billings family moved to California in 1891 in hopes of improving Elmore Billings's failing health. Shortly after arriving in Benicia, California, Addie Billings entered into a legal partnership with Wallace Rutherford in nearby Napa. The fertile fields of the Napa Valley produced more grapes than legal business and in 1908 the

Billings invested in a wine vineyard near Calistoga, California. The wine business proved financially lucrative, and Addie Billings devoted more and more of her time to it, serving as executive secretary of the California Grape Protective Association for several years.

Having achieved success as a grape grower while still a member of the Women's Christian Temperance Union, Addie Billings faced an interesting dilemma: how to promote her business while not jeopardizing the ideals of the WCTU. She attempted to resolve the problem by explaining that wine was more of a food than it was an alcoholic beverage. In her speeches and writings for the California Grape Protective Association she reported that the beverage was a staple on the dinner table in many European countries—as the soldiers who fought in the first World War could attest—and should not be banned by the Prohibition Amendment. When this patriotic appeal failed to win supporters to her cause, she drew on a more personal approach and began to deliver a speech titled "How the Bone Dry Amendment Would Affect Me and My Family," hoping that a plea for the welfare of her family might be more persuasive. Temperance workers accepted none of Billings's arguments and the conflict eventually resulted in the termination of her long-standing membership with the WCTU.

After her husband's death in 1920, Addie Billings moved to Berkeley, California, so that her daughters could attend the University of California. They both graduated, one becoming a teacher and the other a social worker, and continued to live with their mother for the rest of their lives. Addie Billings kept house for her daughters, took up rug-hooking as a hobby, and remained involved in the Republican party throughout her adult life, keeping a close eye on international and domestic affairs. She died in Berkeley, California, on February 7, 1948, one month after her ninetieth birthday.

Selected Sources

There are papers on Addie Billings in the Mary Earhart Dillon Collection, Schlesinger Library, Radcliffe College, Cambridge, Massachusetts. Hal Johnson, "So We're Told" (9 *Berkeley Gazette* [1948]) is a biographical sketch of Billings. Billings is mentioned in Lelia J. Robinson, "Women Lawyers in the United States" (2 *Green Bag* [1890]).

Ada Matilda Cole Bittenbender

Social reform efforts undertaken in the last two decades of the nineteenth century attempted to keep white, Protestant, middle-class values at the heart of American culture. Women like Ada Bittenbender played a leading role in the dramatic clash of lifestyles and social values that occured between traditional Yankee stock and the immigrants from Southern and Eastern Europe who began to arrive in huge numbers during the Industrial Revolution. Bittenbender brought her legal knowledge to several of the social reform efforts of the day including temperance, social purity crusades, and the suffrage movement.

Ada Bittenbender was born on August 3, 1848, to Emily Madison and Daniel Cole of Macedonia, Bradford County, Pennsylvania. Her early schooling took place near home until she left Pennsylvania to enroll in Lowell's Commercial College in Binghamton, New York, graduating in 1869. Unsatisfied with this preparation for life, she trained for a teaching career at the Pennsylvania State Normal School at Bloomsburg from 1874–75 and the Froebel Normal Institute in Washington, D.C., in 1876–77. After serving as principal for a year at her alma mater in Bloomsburg, she resigned because of declining health attributed to overwork.

On August, 9, 1878, Ada M. Cole married Henry Clay Bittenbender and three months later moved with him to Osceola, Nebraska. After a year of teaching school, she became editor of the *Osceola Record,* a Republican, reform-minded newspaper, holding the position until 1881. Her editorial career included a brief stint working for a local journal of the Farmer's Alliance in 1881, an experience that increased her involvement in agricultural affairs, and that ultimately led to her appointment as the first woman delegate to the Nebraska State Board of Agriculture in the same year.

Bittenbender became a leader in organizing local suffrage societies on behalf of the Nebraska Woman Suffrage Association. As president of that group in 1882 she delivered many speeches in favor of a state suffrage amendment. Her efforts were thwarted by male voters who feared, in part, that women would sway the vote in favor of prohibition.

Two years of reading law under her husband's supervision prepared her to become the first woman lawyer in Nebraska. She was admitted to a Nebraska District Court in 1882 and the Nebraska Supreme Court in 1883. The Bittenbenders opened a legal partnership in 1882, primarily involving court practice. Though most married women lawyers who practiced with their husbands took over the responsibilities of the office while their husbands went to court, Ada Bittenbender had an active court practice. She made many appearances in state and federal courts including a groundbreaking case that gave women equal guardianship rights over their children.

Bittenbender became a leader in the Women's Christian Temperance Union. Between 1883 and 1889 she worked as superintendent of temperance legislation in Nebraska. In 1887, her role took on a broader scope when she went to work as superintendent of temperance legislation for the national WCTU in Washington, D.C. A year later, she was named attorney for the national WCTU. Her work involved analyzing legal questions arising from the war on liquor traffic and serving as an expert before Congressional committees addressing issues of prohibition. On October 15, 1888, during her tenure in Washington, she became the third woman admitted to the bar of the Supreme Court of the United States.

Bittenbender used her legal knowledge to work for social reforms that attempted to improve the quality of women's lives. In 1887, she wrote a bill for the Nebraska legislature which established an industrial school and home for women and girls with the explicit aim of reducing prostitution. Two years later she drafted a bill to raise the statutory age of consent for women in the District of Columbia to sixteen years, another measure designed to enhance the social purity of the nation. Working with Senator Blair, another temperance advocate, she was influential in the passage of Congressional legislation ensuring the protection of women.

After two years as the attorney for the national WCTU, Bittenbender returned to Nebraska in 1890 to resume her private practice. The next year she was nominated to run on the Prohibition ticket for Supreme Court Judge in Nebraska. She received five percent of the all-male vote, a credible appearance for a third-party candidate and the greatest percentage of the vote ever achieved by a candidate on the head of the Prohibition ticket.

Bittenbender's work in temperance and suffrage and her close

Laura A. Woodin LeValley *with her male classmates in the Law Department, University of Michigan, 1882. (Michigan Historical Collections, Bentley Historical Library, University of Michigan.)*

James Valentine Campbell,
first dean of the Law Department of the University of Michigan. (Michigan Historical Collections, Bentley Historical Library, University of Michigan.)

Thomas McIntyre Cooley,
one of the first professors of the Law Department of the University of Michigan and dean of the Law Department, 1871–1883. (Michigan Historical Collections, Bentley Historical Library, University of Michigan.)

Harry B. Hutchins,
professor and dean of the Law Department and later president of the University of Michigan. (Michigan Historical Collections, Bentley Historical Library, University of Michigan.)

Cora Agnes Benneson,
graduate of the Law Department of the University of Michigan, 1880, fellow in History at Bryn Mawr College, and practicing lawyer in Cambridge, Massachusetts. (Michigan Historical Collections, Bentley Historical Library, University of Michigan.)

Addie Melvina Stephenson Billings, *lawyer, suffragist, and temperance advocate pictured with her husband and law partner, Elmore M. Billings and their "runaway" son. (The Schlesinger Library, Radcliffe College.)*

Ada Matilde Cole Bittenbender, *first woman lawyer in Nebraska, suffragist, temperance leader, and attorney for the National Woman's Christian Temperance Union. (Frances E. Willard and Mary A. Livermore, eds.,* A Woman of the Century.*)*

Letitia Lavilla A. Burlingame, *graduate of the Law Department of the University of Michigan, 1886, and one of the founding members of the Equity Club, practiced law until her untimely death in 1890 at the age of thirty-one. (O. C. Burlingame, ed.* Lettie Lavilla Burlingame: Her Life Pages. Stories, Poems, and Essays.*)*

Mary Anne Greene,
second woman admitted to the Massachusetts bar, first woman to argue a case before the Supreme Court of Rhode Island and author of articles on women's legal condition. (Frances E. Willard and Mary A. Livermore, eds., A Woman of the Century.*)*

Almeda Eliza Hitchcock [Moore],
graduate of the Law Department of the University of Michigan, 1888, and lawyer in practice with her father in Hawaii until her untimely death in 1895 at the age of thirty-two. (Michigan Historical Collections, Bentley Historical Library, University of Michigan.)

Ada Harriet Miser Kepley,
first woman in the United States to graduate from a law school (Union College of Law), originator with her lawyer-husband of the bill to admit women to the Illinois bar, and active suffragist and temperance advocate. (Frances W. Willard and Mary A. Livermore, eds., A Woman of the Century.*)*

Belva Ann Bennett McNall Lockwood,
best known as the first woman admitted to the bar of the Supreme Court of the United States, advocate of women's rights, temperance, and peace, and presidential candidate for the Equal Rights Party. (Syracuse University Archives, Syracuse University.)

Catharine Gouger Waugh McCulloch,
lawyer in practice with her husband in Chicago, advocate of suffrage, temperance, and women's legal rights and leader in the women's rights movement in Illinois. (The Schlesinger Library, Radcliffe College.)

Sarah Killgore Wertman,
first woman to graduate from the Law School of the University of Michigan and the first woman admitted to the Michigan bar. (Michigan Historical Collections, Bentley Historical Library, University of Michigan.)

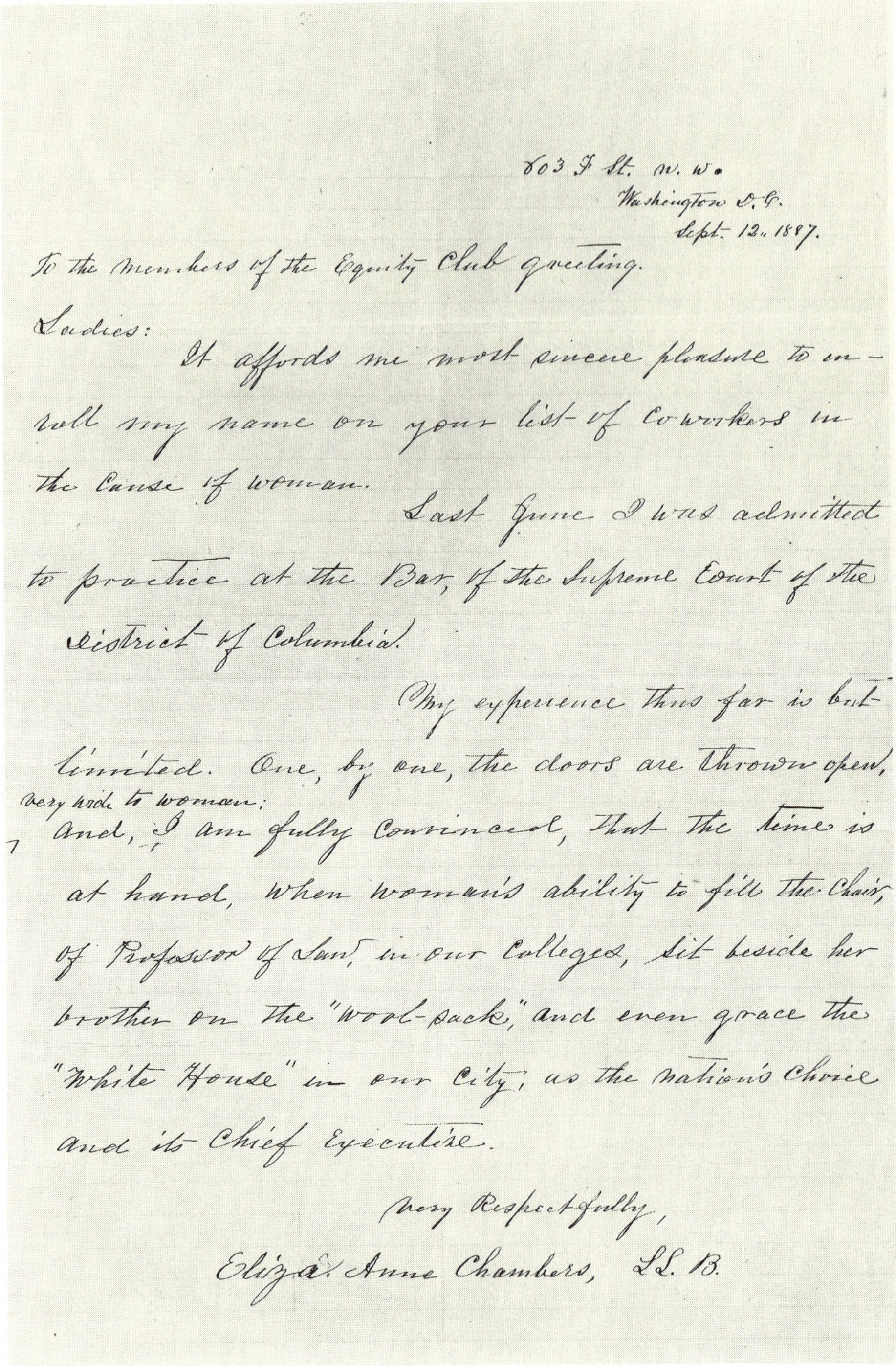

603 F St. N. W.
Washington D. C.
Sept. 12. 1887.

To the Members of the Equity Club greeting.

Ladies:

It affords me most sincere pleasure to enroll my name on your list of coworkers in the Cause of woman.

Last June I was admitted to practice at the Bar, of the Supreme Court of the District of Columbia.

My experience thus far is but limited. One, by one, the doors are thrown open, very wide to woman; And, I am fully convinced, that the time is at hand, when woman's ability to fill the Chair, of Professor of Law, in our Colleges, sit beside her brother on the "wool-sack," and even grace the "White House" in our City; as the nation's Choice and its Chief Executive.

Very Respectfully,

Eliza Anne Chambers, LL. B.

Letter from Eliza Anne Chambers to the Equity Club, September 12, 1887. (The Schlesinger Library, Radcliffe College.)

ANNOUNCEMENT.

MEETING OF WOMEN LAWYERS.

There will be a meeting of women lawyers in Chicago, Illinois, August 3d, 4th and 5th, next, under the auspices of the Law Department of the Queen Isabella Association.

There will be papers, discussions and conference meetings, the leading object being to promote acquaintance among those interested in the practical work of the profession. The arrangements are in charge of practicing lawyers.

All women in the United States and elsewhere who have been admitted to the bar of a court of record or graduated from a law school, are especially invited to be present.

The committee in charge consists of Ellen A. Martin, Chairman, Florence Cronise, Elizabeth Eaglesfield and Catharine Waugh McCulloch.

The meeting will be held at the Isabella Club House, corner 61st Street and Oglesby Avenue, (four blocks from the 60th Street entrance to the World's Fair Grounds) and the first session will begin at 10 a. m., August 3d.

ELLEN A. MARTIN,
Chairman Law Dep't,
Room 516, 84 La Salle St., Chicago, Ill., U. S. A.

Announcement of a meeting of women lawyers of the Queen Isabella Association in Chicago organized by Equity Club members Ellen Martin, Florence Cronise, and Catharine Waugh McCulloch. (Michigan Historical Collections, Bentley Historical Library, University of Michigan.)

M. FREDRIKA PERRY. ELLEN A. MARTIN.

PERRY & MARTIN,

ATTORNEYS AND COUNSELORS AT LAW,

AND LOAN BROKERS,

ROOM 516, 84 LA SALLE STREET, CHICAGO, ILLINOIS.

Business card for the law partnership of Ellen Annette Martin and Mary Fredrika Perry. (Michigan Historical Collections, Bentley Historical Library, University of Michigan.)

LELIA J. ROBINSON,
Attorney and Counsellor at Law,
5 Pemberton Square, Room 25, Boston.
Consultation free to Women Saturdays (2 to 4 P. M.)

Lelia Josephine Robinson [Sawtelle's] notice of legal services advertised in the Woman's Journal, *December 28, 1889. (The Schlesinger Library, Radcliffe College.)*

Thirtieth anniversary reunion in 1911 of the University of Michigan Law Department, Class of 1881, with Equity Club members Leona Taylor Lounsbury (no. 4) and Laura A. Woodin LeValley (no. 20). (Michigan Historical Collections, Bentley Historical Library, University of Michigan.)

association with leaders of the Woman Movement made her keenly aware of the historical significance of women's entry into the legal profession. In the 1890s, she wrote essays on women lawyers in which she proudly outlined their accomplishments and progress. Bittenbender's final years were spent in Lincoln, Nebraska. By 1910 she had abandoned legal work to pursue an interest in philosophical studies. The next year she published *Tedos and Tisod: A Temperance Story,* a book that mixed fact and fiction with a heavy dose of spiritualism. The book symbolized her departure from the professional world of the law and distanced her from an emerging group of reformers who held a more scientific outlook of social reform. Bittenbender spent the last seven years of her life as a widow and died of pneumonia on December 15, 1925, in Lincoln, Nebraska.

SELECTED SOURCES

There is a biographical essay on Bittenbender in Edward T. James et al., *Notable American Women* (1971). Several general sketches of Bittenbender which were written in the late nineteenth century include Frances E. Willard and Mary A. Livermore, eds., *A Woman of the Century* (1893); 22 *Chicago Legal News* (1890); 1 *Law Student's Helper* (1893); and 14 *Woman's Journal* (1883). Bittenbender is also included in Lelia J. Robinson, "Women Lawyers in the United States" (2 *Green Bag* [1890]); Dr. Louis Frank, "The Woman Lawyer" (3 *Chicago Law Times* [1889]); and Elizabeth C. Stanton et al., *History of Woman Suffrage* (vol. 3, 1886 and vol. 4, 1902). Her essays on women lawyers include "Women in Law," in Lydia Hoyt Farmer, ed., *National Exposition Souvenir: What America Owes to Women* (1893) and "Woman in Law," in Annie Nathan Meyer, ed., *Woman's Work in America* (1891). There are papers of Bittenbender in the Nebraska State Historical Society, Lincoln, Nebraska.

Letitia Lavilla A. Burlingame

A strong network of female friendships provided a web of support to the women who began to enter the world of male-dominated professions at the end of the nineteenth century. Letitia Burlingame received care and nurturance from her female friendships that allowed her to establish a thriving professional law career and sustained her through periods of poor health. The traditional boundaries of the female sphere offered safety from the adversities attendant upon those who sought to break the constricting confinements of female roles. Letitia L. Burlingame's life story serves as an example of a woman who relied on the private world of female associations to face the promises and perils that faced women entering the public sphere.

Born to Harmon R. and Olive C. Burlingame on August 6, 1859, Letitia Burlingame was raised in a pious, Christian home in Lockport and Joliet, Illinois. Poor health afflicted Burlingame as a child, and during her continual confinements her parents encouraged her to develop her intellect. She read broadly, studied music and foreign languages, kept a diary, and wrote poetry. When not ill, she attended public schools and enjoyed the company of an older sister and numerous girl friends. Following her graduation from the Joliet East Side Academy in 1879, she remained to teach at the high school and in the grammar department of the Joliet school system.

Teachers' salaries were too low to satisfy the aspirations of the bright young scholar. A career as a lawyer appealed to Burlingame as a way to use her knowledge and intelligence to improve the world around her. In 1883, Burlingame began to read law in the Joliet-based firm of Fithian and Avery. Two years later, the family agreed that she should complete her legal education at the law school of the University of Michigan. The years at Ann Arbor were some of the most exciting of Burlingame's life. There, she enjoyed the company of a community of women studying for professional careers in law, medicine and the sciences. The strength and aid she received from these friendships encouraged her to find a way to establish and maintain ties with other female members of her chosen profession around the country. With some of her fellow law students, she was instrumental in the founding of the Equity Club.

Burlingame's female world of support at law school included her family. Mrs. Burlingame went to Ann Arbor with her daughter where she ran a boarding house near the law school and watched over Letitia, who, because of her sickly constitution, had always received special attention. The gesture provided another level of female companionship for Letitia, but was a deep sacrifice for her mother who had to leave her husband for two years. Still, the family agreed to the temporary separation so that Mrs. Burlingame could care for her daughter.

Burlingame was admitted to the Michigan bar immediately upon graduating from the University of Michigan in 1886. She spent the next year in Ann Arbor attending lectures, arranging meetings with the new group of women law students entering the university, and visiting among her friends. She returned to Joliet in 1887, was admitted to the Illinois bar, and opened her own law office. Burlingame reveled in the excitement of being a practicing attorney and her health seemed to thrive on the activity. Her legal practice involved courtroom appearances as well as office work and she also held a commission as a notary public. The practice was busy and kept her occupied on a full-time basis, but it was not enough to satisfy the strong moral training of her Christian upbringing. Burlingame began an active avocation as a temperance and suffrage lecturer, speaking and writing on behalf of the Women's Christian Temperance Union and the Joliet Equal Suffrage Association.

Her brisk and successful practice combined with her voluntary commitments became too much for Burlingame to handle on her own. In May of 1890, she invited fellow Equity Club member Rebecca May, a friend from Ann Arbor days and at the time an attorney in Topeka, Kansas, to join her practice in Joliet, but the partnership was never to occur. Overwork taxed Burlingame's poor physical stamina. At the end of May, 1890, she contracted influenza. The illness weakened her already frail constitution, and over the next year and a half developed into a severe case of nervous prostration. A trip to the world-renowned sanitarium in Battle Creek, Michigan, failed to improve her health. As she had foretold in the diary kept during her sickly adolescence, Letitia L. Burlingame died at the tender age of thirty-one, succumbing to "brain disease" on December 12, 1890, at her parents' home in Joliet.

Burlingame's death brought a new level of influence to her name. In 1895, her grief-stricken mother, Olive Burlingame, published a memorial to her ambitious and pious daughter entitled *Lettie Lavilla Burlingame: Her Life Pages. Stories, Poems, and Essays.* The book contained selections from Lettie Burlingame's diaries, poems, letters, and speeches as well as obituary notices. Cast in the light of dutiful daughter and God-fearing professional woman, the book promoted Burlingame's reputation as an upstanding member of the female sphere and attempted to set an example for all young women who sought to combine the traditions of Victorian womanhood with the pathbreaking possibilities available to women pursuing professional careers. Burlingame's brief career as an attorney drew her deeper into a female world of support and sustenance even as it forced her to move within the male-defined public sphere. The story of her life, death, and memorial speaks to the tenacity and importance of a traditional community of female friendship for women entering the professions at this turbulent period of change in American social history.

Selected Sources

The best source on Letitia Burlingame is the collection of her writings published by her mother (Olive C. Burlingame, ed., *Lettie Lavilla Burlingame: Her Life Pages. Stories, Poems, and Essays* [1895]). Burlingame is also included in Ellen Martin, "Admission of Women to the Bar" (1 *Chicago Law Times* [1886]), and in Lelia J. Robinson, "Women Lawyers in the United States" (2 *Green Bag* [1890]). Additional information is available at the Bentley Historical Library, University of Michigan, Ann Arbor, Michigan.

Eliza Anne Chambers

The hectic pace of life in Washington, D.C., provided many opportunities for women seeking a foothold into professional fields. During the Civil War women from around the country flocked to the Union Capitol to secure jobs as clerks and nurses when men were needed on the battle front. While these were initial steps on the long road to women's acceptance into the professions, Washington attracted a large number of the first generation of professional women. The fact that federal offices for pension and land claims were located in Washington, D.C., made it possible for several women attorneys including Eliza Chambers and fellow Equity Club members Belva Lockwood and Emma Gillett to enjoy lucrative office practices that reduced the need to make frequent courtroom appearances.

Eliza Chambers enrolled at the Howard University School of Law and received the LL.B. and LL.M. degrees in 1886. Normally, all graduates receiving these degrees were automatically admitted to the bar of the District of Columbia. Chambers, however, reported that she encountered overt sex discrimination when the male faculty of the university refused to submit her name to the board of examiners because she was a woman. Her claim is especially interesting since Howard University admitted students regardless of race or sex and proved to be one of the only law schools then open to women in the nation's capitol. It is possible that university officials were beginning to feel pressure from other institutions for helping to promote women's advancement into the professions. Perhaps the faculty hoped that their actions would go unchallenged and would help to arrest any further encroachments by women into the public sphere. But Howard had trained their student well and Chambers would not be thwarted by the faculty's inaction. She forced them to resubmit the list and was rightfully admitted to the bar of the District of Columbia in June, 1887. Within a year of her admittance, she followed the example of many of her Washington-based sisters in the law and opened a legal practice specializing in equity, patents, pensions, and land claims. The office practice kept her out of the immediate public eye while securing a steady income. As a victim of discrimination, Chambers knew firsthand the difficulties women faced in American society. Her own experience revealed that women's opportunities in the public sphere were increasing, if incrementally. Still, in her letter to the Equity Club shortly after her conflict with the Howard University faculty, she expressed the hope that one day women would soon become law school professors, judges, and perhaps, president of the United States.

Selected Sources

Little remains about Eliza Chambers beyond her letter to the Equity Club. Lelia J. Robinson includes her in "Women Lawyers in the United States" (2 *Green Bag* [1890]), and mentions the discrimination Chambers experienced at Howard University Law School. She is listed as a graduate of the law school in Walter Dyson, *Howard University: The Capstone of Negro Education* (1941). Chambers is also listed in the city directories of Washington, D.C., 1886–1923.

Florence Cronise

Florence Cronise was born on October 28, 1845, in Republic, Ohio, to Jacob Staub and Katharine Barbara Cronise. Her father, one of the early doctors of Tiffin, was a drinker. When Cronise was young, her mother divorced Staub and returned to the home of her father, a judge and prominent citizen of the community. In addition, her mother legally returned to her maiden name of Cronise and changed her children's names to Cronise as well.

Florence Cronise grew up in her grandfather's home with her mother and sister, Nettie. She graduated from the public high school in Princeton, Illinois, and then enrolled in the classics course at Heidelberg College. She was an excellent student and graduated in 1865 at the head of her class. But she did not receive the honor of speaking as valedictorian, for Heidelberg College frowned on a woman speaking at the graduation ceremony. Instead, a man who was second in the class gave the "Heidelberg Oration" rather than Cronise.

After she received her B.A., Cronise began her pursuit of a masters degree at Heidelberg. At the same time, she began to teach, first in Peru, Illinois, and then for several years in Princeton, Illinois. While teaching in Princeton, Cronise lived at the home of Charles Baldwin, a prominent Illinois attorney, and his wife, Louise McArdel Baldwin, a longtime family friend of the Cronises's in Tiffin.

Cronise's years in the Baldwin household marked a turning point in her life. She frequently spent evenings in Charles Baldwin's study conversing about law. Her sister, Nettie, often visited and participated in the legal discussions. This experience encouraged both sisters to pursue legal education. In addition, their interest in law was reinforced by the marriage of their mother to Eban Harrington, an attorney from Cincinnati.

In 1869, Cronise received her masters of arts from Heidelberg College and returned home to Tiffin where she began to teach at Tiffin High School. But Cronise did not want to teach for the rest of her life. Her interest in law had been sparked during her stay with the Baldwins. In addition, she found that the pay for teaching was too low, as she explained to the Equity Club. With the goal of earning more money than she could as a teacher, she began to read law with a local attorney, John McCauley. In September, 1873, she became the second woman, the first being her sister, Nettie, to gain admission to the bar in Ohio.

Florence Cronise opened a law office with her sister, and they practiced together until 1880 when Nettie left to work with her husband, Nelson Burgess Lutes. Florence Cronise continued to practice law on her own for almost fifty years. While she wrote to the Equity Club that she did not permit sentiment and emotion to interfere with her law practice, she nevertheless earned a reputation for being a sympathetic friend to widows in need of legal counsel and emotional support. In addition Cronise helped other young women to become lawyers, training at least two women who successfully passed the Ohio bar. One of her students joined Cronise in practice for a few years before she married and went into practice with her husband.

In addition to her law practice, Cronise was active in voluntary activities. She was a founder and early president of the Tiffin Public Library and a member of the Seneca County Board of School Examiners. She was also vice-president for the state of Ohio of the Queen Isabella Association which oversaw women's activities during the World's Columbian Exposition in Chicago.

Cronise continued to practice law until 1926 when her health and eyesight deteriorated, and she moved to Philadelphia to be with her family. She died there on January 28, 1930, and was buried in Greenlawn Cemetery in Tiffin, Ohio.

Selected Sources

Biographical information on Cronise is in *History of Seneca County from the Close of the Revolutionary War to July, 1880* (1880); "Biographical Sketch of Nettie and Florence Cronise" (unpublished essay in Cronise File, Heidelberg College Archives, Tiffin, Ohio); Ellen Martin, "Admission of Women to the Bar" (1 *Chicago Law Times* [1886]); and Lelia J. Robinson, "Women Lawyers in the United States" (2 *Green Bag* [1890]). The information in *History of Seneca County, Ohio* (1886) confuses Florence and Nettie Cronise. An obituary of Cronise is in the Tiffin *Tribune* (January 29, 1930).

Corinne Williams Douglas

Changes in the prescriptions assigned to women's roles and responsibilities occurred slowly but steadily during the late nineteenth century. Even in the social structure of the tradition-bound culture of the deep South, the social barometer of the period measured changes in the expectations of women's appropriate behavior and activities. Corinne Williams Douglas was an ideal candidate to help initiate social change in her adopted city of Atlanta, Georgia. She had been raised in the knowledge of the rituals and customs appropriate to a young lady of her social standing, while her educational background provided her with the tools necessary to analyze and address social problems. This combination of social gentility with social consciousness helped to ease the disruptions that might have occurred when a Southern lady left the confines of the private home to address social problems in her neighborhood. Douglas adopted a socially and intellectually progressive approach to the problems she identified, while addressing them with traditional and conservative methods.

Corinne Williams Douglas was born on November 15, 1860, the only daughter in a family of three children. Related to President Grover Cleveland and Lincoln's secretary of war, Edwin Stanton, the Williams family enjoyed a level of social prominence within their hometown community of Wyoming, Iowa. The family's economic position was strong enough to allow the young woman a college education. She enrolled at Rockford Seminary in Rockford, Illinois, and graduated in 1880. For a few years after graduating from Rockford, Douglas enjoyed a brief but rewarding teaching career. In 1886 she met and married Hamilton Douglas. Together, the couple moved to Ann Arbor, Michigan, where they both enrolled in the University of Michigan Law School, received their LL.B. degrees in 1887, and were immediately admitted to the Michigan bar.

Rockford Seminary was Douglas's first introduction to the power and support available from a community of women friends. Her tenure at the University of Michigan coincided with the existence of a strong network of women lawyers and law students who encouraged her in her studies and influenced her views on the social issues of the day. Corinne Douglas joined with five of these women to help found the Equity Club in 1887, serving on the group's executive committee in its founding year with fellow members Almeda Hitchcock, Lettie Burlingame, Margaret Wilcox, Rebecca May, and Martha Pearce.

A few weeks after graduating from the University of Michigan, Corinne and Hamilton Douglas moved to Atlanta, Georgia. In November, 1887, Mrs. Douglas marked the occasion of the birth of her first child with an announcement introducing the infant as "Donald Douglas, Lawyer." The joys of motherhood, and the fact that Georgia did not admit women to legal practice, encouraged Douglas to turn her attention to the more traditional women's work of childrearing, housekeeping, and socializing.

Though Corinne Douglas gave birth to and raised five children, she still found time to cultivate her interests in advancing women's educational opportunities in her adopted city of Atlanta. Douglas had always believed that education helped women to be better mothers to their children. In 1890, she organized and became the first principal of the Commercial High School for Girls. The course of study included traditional training in domestic arts and offered women from less affluent families some job skills, but Douglas also introduced courses in history and science, a radical innovation for Atlanta's young society women. She also helped to found the Business Woman's Club, an association that brought together middle-class matrons with women workers for social and professional improvement. The group was absorbed into the Atlanta Women's Club where Douglas served two terms as president.

In addition to improving women's educational opportunities, Douglas devoted time and energy to other needed social programs. At different points in her life she belonged to the Hospital for Incurables, Associated Charities, and the Anti-Tuberculosis Association. She held a two-year appointment as chair of the Red Cross committee for the blind working extensively to assess the condition of the blind in Atlanta. Her devotion to social improvements was honored in 1930 when she received an honorary master of arts degree from Rockford College and was accepted as an honorary member in the United Daughters of the Confederacy, perhaps the ultimate recognition that this northern lady had been fully accepted into the region's culture.

By 1920 the Douglas children had reached maturity. Her daughter, Mrs. Helen Mankin, had completed law school that year and was ready to apply for admission to the Georgia bar, opened to women just four years earlier. Mrs. Mankin persuaded her mother to join her in applying for admission to the bar. Sponsored by Hamilton Douglas, Sr., and Hamilton Douglas, Jr., the two women were admitted to the bar in 1920. For Mrs. Douglas the professional recognition came more than three decades after her graduation from the University of Michigan Law School. After her husband died in 1922,

Corinne Douglas took his place in the family firm of Douglas, Douglas, and Andrews.

While Douglas devoted most of her adult life to the roles and responsibilities of traditional female domestic chores, she also found ways to influence changes in the world around her. Similar to the reform agenda of the settlement-house workers in northern cities, Douglas extended the women's sphere into the neighborhood by working to introduce programs and activities that improved the social and physical conditions of many of the city's poor and ill. She had employed her own education to help her own children, clearly influencing the choice that two of them made to become lawyers, but also put her education to use for children throughout the city through her voluntarism and charity work. She died of pneumonia on January 20, 1934.

Selected Sources

Information on Corinne Douglas is in John William Leonard, *Woman's Who's Who of America* (1914–15). She is also included in Lelia J. Robinson, "Women Lawyers in the United States" (2 *Green Bag* [1890]). Additional information is in her obituary, "Mrs. Douglas Sr. Dies at Hospital," in *The Constitution,* Atlanta, Georgia (January 21, 1934). There is material on Douglas in the Rockford College Archives, Rockford, Illinois, and in the Bentley Historical Library, Michigan University, Ann Arbor, Michigan.

Emma Millinda Gillett

Many a roadblock had been created to thwart the initial entry of women into the professions of law, medicine, and science. Often it took emotional toughness, a maverick attitude, and straightforward perseverance for members of the first generation of women lawyers to establish themselves and simply make a living. Emma Gillett's experience represents the difficulty a woman faced in breaking new ground to become a practicing lawyer, and how one woman used her accumulated wisdom to improve the conditions for those who would follow her into the profession.

Born on a homestead in Princeton, Wisconsin, on July 30, 1852, Emma Gillett was the second daughter sent back to Girard, Pennsylvania, to be closer to members of her own family. Gillett attended public schools and graduated from Lake Erie Seminary in 1870. For ten years she taught school until two developments challenged her to think about another way to make a living. First, the process of settling her mother's estate in 1875 revealed the complexities of financial and legal matters; and second, the pittance of a salary paid to teachers frustrated the single woman struggling to make ends meet.

Gillett drew hope from the story of Washington, D.C., attorney Belva Lockwood. In 1880, against the advice of her friends, Gillett took her life savings and went to Washington, D.C., to study law. By the time Gillett arrived at the National University, where Lockwood had been educated, the law school had closed its doors to women. Lockwood invited Gillett to apprentice with her while searching for a law school that would admit women. Gillett enrolled in the law department of Howard University, a predominantly black institution that admitted students without regard for race or sex, and received the LL.B. and LL.M. in 1883. Gillett and other white women who took their degrees at Howard were always quick to note that most of the law school's faculty were white.

After being admitted to the bar in the District of Columbia in 1883, she began to work in the law office of Watson J. Newton, an advocate of women lawyers. Around the same time, Newton arranged to have her appointed as a notary public, making her the first woman to receive the appointment from the president of the United States. Gillett established a successful career in real estate and pension law,—increasing her salary to four times what she had earned as a school teacher—eventually serving as vice president and treasurer of the Realty Appraisal and Title Company from 1908 to 1913. She was admitted to practice before the Supreme Court of the United States in 1890. In 1900, Newton and Gillett formed a partnership that operated until his death in 1913.

Gillett made few courtroom appearances and attempted to keep a fairly low profile within the world of practicing attorneys. Gillett spoke firmly against the practice of taking charity cases, especially when it was done to show the philanthropic qualities and large-heartedness of female lawyers. On the contrary, she was a strong believer that the best way to promote women in the legal profession was by proving one's competence. She held to the idea that women should follow the routine of male lawyers—using after-work hours for relaxation and physical exercise out-of-doors, not housework. Her independence and conservatism notwithstanding, Gillett was in sympathy with the women's issues of the day. She campaigned with Alice Paul for the passage of the Nineteenth Amendment serving in various capacities for the National Woman Suffrage Association and the Congressional Committee. After equal suffrage was won, Gillett continued her involvement in political action for women by serving as chairman of the Legal Branch of the national Woman's Party to work for equal rights for women.

Gillett's greatest contribution to women's lives came in her efforts to open the doors to legal education for women. In 1896, she and Ellen Spencer Mussey, another Washington, D.C., attorney, started a law class for women. Two years later they formalized the instruction by opening the Washington College of Law. Concerns about both race and gender motivated them to take this step. Their primary objective was to provide women with legal education, even though they opened their school to men and women alike. But racial prejudice coexisted with Gillett's and Mussey's commitment to women, for they proudly claimed that Washington College of Law was the only all-white law school open to women in the District of Columbia.

Mussey held the public role of dean while Gillett took responsibility for the administrative work behind the scenes. In addition to her administrative tasks, Gillett found time to help many women students over rough spots, softening the forcefulness of her personality and firm beliefs with a dose of sympathy based on her own hard-won personal knowledge. In 1913, Mussey's failing health forced her to resign and Gillett, following the death of her partner, Watson J. Newton, found that she had the time and the interest to assume the more public role. She served as dean of the school until her retirement in 1923.

The position of dean gave Gillett a forum in which to expound her views about the status of women in law. She took advantage of her appointments as president of the Women's Bar Association (1921) and vice-president of the Washington, D.C., chapter of the American Bar Association (1922) to speak out on behalf of women lawyers' collective struggle in public settings as well as through private letters to individuals.

During Gillett's deanship, the law school found a permanent home in Washington, D.C. Graduates of the school went to work in all parts of the United States, often achieving distinction in their fields. Gillett was always especially quick to point out the women graduates of Washington College of Law who achieved positions as judges or attorney generals.

In October, 1926, Gillett fell and broke a hip. She contracted pneumonia while confined to her bed and died from the illness at her home on January 23, 1927. Members of the National Women's Party organized a memorial service for her on May 15, 1927. Representatives from nearly every national women's organization attended, an attendance record that speaks to the influence Gillett enjoyed when she applied the wisdom gained from her personal experience to create opportunities for other women.

Selected Sources

Emma Gillett is included in Edward T. James, ed., *Notable American Women* (1971) and in *The National Cyclopedia of American Biography* (1967). Her work with Ellen Spencer Mussey at the Washington College of Law is described in Grace Hathaway, *Fate Rides a Tortoise: A Biography of Ellen Spencer Mussey* (1937). She is included in Lelia J. Robinson, "Women Lawyers in the United States" (2 *Green Bag* [1890]). Obituaries of Gillett are in the *New York Times* (May 16, 1927) and 15 *Women Lawyers Journal* (1927). Some of Gillett's papers are in the Mary Earhart Dillon Collection, Schlesinger Library, Radcliffe College, Cambridge, Massachusetts.

Laura de Force Gordon

Laura de Force Gordon's life reflected many of the forces of social change that shaped the development of American society and led to greater independence for women in the late nineteenth century. She joined the migration across the Great Plains, became the first woman newspaper editor and publisher in the country, maintained a highly visible campaign for women's suffrage throughout her adult life, lived as a divorcee raising an adopted son, and became a developer of California's fertile farm lands.

One of nine children of Abram and Katy Allen de Force of Erie County, Pennsylvania, Laura de Force Gordon was born on August

17, 1838. Receiving an academic education, she developed outstanding speaking and writing skills early in life. In 1862, she married Charles Gordon, a Union Army captain and surgeon. After the Civil War, they traveled by covered wagon to White Pine, Nevada, where Gordon was the first white woman to arrive. By 1870, the couple had moved to California, finally settling in Lodi, a town in the San Joaquin Valley.

Almost immediately upon her arrival, Gordon began to work for woman's suffrage. Often traveling alone by stage coach, her public speaking and organizational work to establish suffrage societies in California, Oregon, and the Washington Territory put her in the public eye. In 1871, she took advantage of a nomination to run for state senate to publicize the need for suffrage. Gordon responded to criticism of her campaign in the statewide press by buying out two newspapers in 1873 and 1874, combining them, and publishing her own daily paper, the *Stockton Daily Leader*. She used this public forum to advocate the cause of women's suffrage.

In 1878, while covering a state legislative debate on women's right to practice law, Gordon met Clara Shortridge Foltz and together they studied law and worked for the passage of the "woman lawyer's bill" in 1878. The two women petitioned for admission to the Hastings College of Law, a department of the University of California located in San Francisco. Both women were denied admission and both appealed the denial; Gordon in the state supreme court and Foltz in the federal district court. The two suits were consolidated and arguments in the case of *Foltz v. Hoge* (54 Cal. 28 [1879]) were heard by Judge R. F. Morrison. On March 5, 1879, Judge Morrison ruled in favor of Foltz and Gordon, resulting in an immediate appeal by the Hastings board of directors. Judge Morrison's decision was upheld and Gordon and Foltz enrolled in Hastings College of Law shortly after the California Supreme Court's decision in November of 1879. The decision established the practice of coeducation in California's colleges and universities. Gordon and Foltz had spent the months during the appeal studying for the bar examination. Both women passed the examination and were admitted to the California bar in December of 1879. The following year, Gordon divorced her husband of eighteen years on the grounds of adultery. A few years later she adopted her nephew and raised him alone.

Once admitted to the California bar, and out of her marriage,

Gordon began a highly successful practice as a criminal lawyer. Already known throughout the state for her eloquence on behalf of women's suffrage, she heightened her visibility through the successful defense of a Mexican charged with murdering a fellow countryman in San Francisco. Later, she defended an Italian immigrant against the death penalty for murder. The defense won her an honorary membership from the Royal Italian Literary Society of Rome.

A noted success and courageous entrepreneur in the fields of law and journalism, Gordon's life work centered on achieving suffrage for women, often sacrificing her legal practice to work on behalf of the vote. Yet her skill as a criminal lawyer also earned her the right to practice before the United States Supreme Court, an honor bestowed upon her in 1885, just a few weeks after Foltz had been admitted. In 1887, Gordon declined the nomination for California attorney general in order to continue her suffrage work as well as to devote time to her legal practice. Throughout the 1890s, she corresponded regularly with suffragists around the country, detailing her efforts in California and requesting assistance from other women's suffrage associations.

By 1901, Gordon retired from her legal practice to devote her professional training toward the acquisition and management of farm lands in the San Joaquin Valley. For legal work done for the Southern Pacific Rail Road—the prime developer of California agriculture—she received a "life pass" to travel on its lines. She died of pneumonia on April 5, 1907.

Selected Sources

A biographical essay on Laura de Force Gordon is in Edward T. James, ed., *Notable American Women* (1971). Additional information on Gordon is in *An Illustrated History of San Joaquin County, California* (1890); *National Cyclopaedia of American Biography* (1899); and George Tinkham, *History of San Joaquin County, California with Biographical Sketches of the Leading Men and Women of the County* (1923). There are several articles on Gordon in *The Lodi News-Sentinel,* from August 5 to 7, 1947. Gordon is included in Lelia J. Robinson, "Women Lawyers in the United States" (2 *Green Bag* [1890]); Dr. Louis Frank, "The Woman Lawyers" (3 *Chicago Law Times* [1889]); and in Frances E. Willard and Mary E. Livermore, eds., *A Woman of the Century* (1893).

Obituaries of Laura de Force Gordon may be found in *Stockton Independent* (April 6, 1907); *The Lodi Sentinel* (April 9, 1907); and *Progress* (May 10, 1907). On her case with Foltz against Hastings College of Law, see Mortimer D. Schwartz, Susan L. Brandt, and Patience Milrod, "Clara Shortridge Foltz: Pioneer in the Law" (17 *The Hastings Law Journal* [1976]) and Barbara Allen Babcock, "Clara Shortridge Foltz: Constitution-Maker" (66 *Indiana Law Journal* [1991]). Materials on Gordon are at the California State Library, Sacramento, California; Schlesinger Library, Radcliffe College, Cambridge, Massachusetts; and State Historical Society of Wisconsin, Madison, Wisconsin.

Mary Anne Greene

An unmarried, professional woman, Mary A. Greene devoted her keen intelligence and fine speaking skills to explaining to the pillars of Victorian domesticity—wives, mothers, and widows—the legal rights they possessed as women in American society. Greene wrote and spoke for professional audiences, students, mothers, and shop girls on topics ranging from real estate and wills to check writing and laws for travellers.

Born to John and Mary Frances (Low) Greene on June 14, 1857, Mary A. Greene grew up in Warwick, Rhode Island, graduating from the Rhode Island State Normal School in 1877. Caught unawares over the complexities of a legal matter concerning the family business, Greene entered the Boston University Law School in 1885. She took up the study of law to prepare herself to improve the management of her own affairs and to assist other women to do the same. She completed the three-year program on schedule, in spite of a lengthy illness in her middle year, and received the LL.B. magna cum laude in 1888. That same year Greene became the second woman admitted to the Massachusetts bar, preceded only by her friend and fellow Equity Club member Lelia J. Robinson, in 1881. Robinson served as a mentor for Greene during Greene's student days at Boston University and in the early days of her legal career in Boston. The two shared a commitment to educating women about their legal rights and frequently met to discuss cases.

Poor health and family responsibilities called Greene home to

Providence in 1890, only eighteen months after graduating from law school. The Greenes were a leading Rhode Island family, tracing their genealogy to Nathanael and Christopher Greene, heroes of the American Revolution. Pride in her lineage promoted her interest in the Daughters of the American Revolution [DAR]. She served as a DAR state regent from 1895 to 1897 and wrote articles on both Nathanael and Christopher Greene. While Rhode Island was clearly home to Greene, her connection to Boston remained strong. She was an active member of the Portia Club, a monthly dinner and discussion group for Massachusetts women lawyers and law students throughout the 1890s. From 1894 to 1914, Greene served as vice president and legal counsel for the Woman's Baptist Foreign Missionary Society, making frequent trips to the society's offices on Tremont Street in Boston.

Greene's Providence practice was restricted to conveyancing law and handling of estates, work that typically did not involve courtroom appearances. In spite of her belief that she lacked the stamina to appear in court, she became the first woman to argue a case before the Supreme Court of Rhode Island. With her legal practice based in her home, Greene found the time and energy to begin a prestigious career as a prolific author and effective public speaker. From 1889 to 1906, she offered an eight-session lecture series on practical business law for young women at Lasell Seminary in Auburndale, Massachusetts. The first woman contributor to the *American Law Review,* Greene used the national forum to advocate wives' legal rights in her 1890 article, "Privileged Communications in Suits between Husband and Wife." The fortieth anniversary of the National Women's Rights Convention in 1891 included a lecture by Greene on "Women in the Law." In 1893, Greene's prominence in domestic relations law brought her an invitation to address the Columbian Exposition, an honor extended to only two American and two foreign women lawyers. She travelled to Chicago to speak on "Married Woman's Property Acts In the United States and Needed Reforms" at the World's Congress of Jurisprudence and Law Reform.

Greene's insights into women's legal condition added to the existing scholarship on domestic relations. She analyzed the American cases for the fifth edition (1894) of James Schouler's *Law of Domestic*

Relations, the standard authority in the courts. Her experience and knowledge attracted a popular audience as well. In 1902 she published *The Woman's Manual of Law.* This small, easily readable reference book introduced women to laws that affected them throughout their lives, including domestic relations, real estate, wills, and inheritance. Her popular writings in newspapers and pamphlets included a translation from French of Dr. Louis Frank's essay, "The Woman Lawyer," in serial form in the *Chicago Legal News* in 1889, "Legal Status of Women under the Laws of Rhode Island, 1892" (revised in 1900), "Women and Children under the Laws of Rhode Island" (1915), and a series of articles on law for women in the *Chautauquan* (1891–92). Greene's intellectual independence was mixed with a dose of conservatism. She advocated reform over radical change in the existing legal relations between the sexes. Her articles explained the restrictions imposed by law on women's position and pointed out reform measures, offering her readers a map to the legal world in which they lived.

In 1920, Greene moved to Pasadena, California, where she continued her practice in domestic relations and probate and participated actively in private philanthropies and education related to her lifetime involvement with the Women's Baptist Foreign Missionary Society and the DAR. She was admitted to the California bar in 1923 and the United States District Court in 1928. At the age of 79, Mary A. Greene died of a heart attack at her home in Pasadena on August 9, 1936.

Selected Sources

Biographical sketches of Mary Greene appear in Frances E. Willard and Mary E. Livermore, eds., *A Woman of the Century* (1893) and Julia Ward Howe, ed., *Representative Women of New England* (1904). Additional biographical sources include John William Leonard, *Who's Who in Jurisprudence* (1925) and Justice B. Detwiler, *Who's Who in California* (1929). An article on Greene appears in the Pasadena *Star News* (December 3, 1931). She is included in Lelia J. Robinson, "Women Lawyers in the United States" (2 *Green Bag* [1890]). A scrapbook of Greene's is in the Pasadena Historical Society. Additional information is available at Boston University, Lasell College in Auburndale, Massachusetts, and Pasadena Public Library.

Mary Emily Humphrey Haddock

In the shifting social climate of the late nineteenth century, the choice to pursue a professional career forced women to reinterpret the boundaries of women's sphere. A companionate marriage to a fellow attorney, the privacy of an office practice, and a commitment to studying legal issues affecting women allowed Emma Haddock, a pioneer woman lawyer in Iowa, to become an active member of the legal profession without sacrificing her womanhood. Throughout her life, Haddock expanded the notion of "woman's place" beyond the privacy of her home, striking a delicate balance between her career, her politics, and her private life.

Mary Emily Humphrey Haddock was born in Tipton, Iowa, in 1845. She grew up and attended schools in Iowa, eventually graduating from the State University of Iowa in 1865 with a bachelor of didactics degree. On August 2, 1865, she married William J. Haddock, an Irish immigrant who had moved to Iowa to enter the legal profession. He was admitted to the bar in 1861 and joined the firm of G. W. and Rush Clark, where he had read law in preparation for the bar examination. The firm changed its name to Clark and Haddock and existed until the death of the senior partner in 1879.

As a young bride, Emma Haddock devoted herself to the traditional role of homemaker. The couple never had any children and Haddock found teaching school to be unfulfilling. After ten years of living in a traditional Victorian marriage where her life revolved around housekeeping and advancing her husband's career, Haddock yearned for other activity. Feeling trapped, she discussed the problem with her husband who encouraged her to enroll in the law school at the State University of Iowa to prepare herself for office work in a legal practice.

Emma Haddock studied law while continuing to perform all of her usual household and wifely duties. The demands of full-time study and housework tasks threatened her health, but she completed the program and graduated in 1875, just two years after fellow Equity Club member Mary B. Hickey Wilkinson, the first woman graduate of the State University of Iowa Law School. Haddock was admitted to the bar in Iowa shortly after graduation and became the first woman to practice law in the state. Another year of study at the law school earned her a certificate for special proficiency in law. With academic credentials in hand, Haddock joined her husband's firm, pursuing a career in office practice. Most of her work consisted of assisting with her husband's cases. She conducted legal research, wrote briefs, and helped to prepare cases.

Haddock's interest in legal research was increasingly directed toward laws that directly affected women. Aware of women's ignorance of the law, she began to teach women about their legal rights. She sought invitations to speak to women's organizations about the financial and legal matters incumbent upon married women. She was founder and first president of the Nineteenth Century Club, the first women's literary club in Iowa City. Using the club as a platform, she delivered a series of lectures on the property rights of women in Iowa. She also traveled to the Women's Congress of Louisville, Kentucky, in 1886 to speak on "Women as Landholders in the West." In this way, she used her professional expertise to help other women better understand the American legal system and its effects on their personal lives.

In 1887, Judge Haddock left his practice to work full time as an administrator at the State University of Iowa. Emma Haddock went with him to work as his assistant. They remained at the university until retiring in 1902. Haddock's position in the university combined with her years of experience as a practicing attorney won her a three-year appointment from the state supreme court to examine students of the university for graduation and admission to the bar.

Haddock had a reputation among Iowa's young female attorneys as a woman lawyer they could turn to for advice and counsel. Her status as a pioneer set an example for other female attorneys to follow. Her lectures on women's legal rights increased her popularity among the region's middle-class women's groups. When she died of a spinal disorder in a Los Angeles sanitarium on March 31, 1907, she left behind many devoted women friends who were grateful for the friendship she shared with them.

Selected Sources

Information on Mary Emily Haddock is in Phebe A. Hanaford, *Daughters of America* (1882). She is included in Lelia J. Robinson, "Women Lawyers in the United States" (2 *Green Bag* [1890]). There are several obituaries on Haddock, including "Death of Mrs. Haddock" (Iowa City *Citizen* [April 1, 1907]); "Mrs. Haddock Died in West" (Iowa City *Republican* [April 1, 1907]); "Mrs. Haddock is No More" (Iowa City *Press* [April 1, 1907]); and "Mrs. Haddock Buried Yesterday" (Iowa City *Citizen* [April 8, 1907]). Haddock is mentioned in 16 *Annals of Iowa* (1928) and in the *History of Johnson County, Iowa* (1883). She is also included in Teresa Opheim, "Portias of the Prairie: Early Woman Graduates of the University Law Department" (67 *The Palimpsest* [1986]).

Almeda Eliza Hitchcock [Moore]

Almeda Hitchcock, the first woman lawyer in Hawaii, was born in Hilo, Hawaii, in 1863. She attended the local missionary school where her quick intelligence often allowed her to finish her schoolwork early and just as often found her engaged in mischief with her brothers. A tomboy in character, Hitchcock preferred exploring the countryside around her to playing with dolls. At age fifteen, she and her older sister, Clara, enrolled at Oahu College, a coeducational institution offering four years of high school and two years of collegiate education. A back injury kept her from completing the full course. After recovering she taught for one year in a country school on Oahu.

Frustrated with teaching young children, Hitchcock left the position, taking advantage of her father's professional reputation to find more satisfying work. She went to work with her father, a prominent attorney and circuit judge based in Hilo, learning enough law to be able to run the office efficiently. Hitchcock had not given much thought to attending law school, finding sufficient satisfaction in assisting her father with the operation of his firm. Her attention was turned when future Equity Club member Cora Benneson, an 1880 graduate of the University of Michigan Law School, visited the Hawaiian Islands in 1886 while on a world tour. David H. Hitchcock approved of his daughter's desire to attend law school, especially since his oldest son had failed to follow in his father's footsteps. Together they reviewed catalogues and information from law schools in the United States, finally choosing between two and selecting the University of Michigan over California.

The community of women law students at the University of Michigan offered Hitchcock a network of female support she had only begun to experience when Cora Benneson offered her the advice and counsel derived from her own law school years. Hitchcock was admitted to the Michigan bar on December 27, 1887, and graduated from the University of Michigan in 1888. The women's network at the University of Michigan offered her the support to undertake several activities at the law school that would have been considered outside the realm of women's sphere, even for those pioneers in professional schools. She pursued intellectual excellence, winning her degree with honors for her thesis on jurisprudence of the Sandwich Islands, was elected class president one year, and delivered one of the speeches at her graduation exercises.

After a tour of the eastern United States with her mother in the summer of 1888, she returned to Hawaii, was admitted to the bar, appointed a notary public, and joined her father's legal practice under the name Hitchcock and Hitchcock. Life as a country lawyer combined Hitchcock's legal training with her love for the out-of-doors. The firm's practice served a number of rural clients and in order to try cases she had to ride horseback more than two hundred miles around the island to meet with them. The hard life of a circuit-riding attorney caught up with her, and in 1890 she explained to the Equity Club members that she preferred to work in the office, leaving the courtroom appearances and the traveling to her father.

Hitchcock's legal expertise opened the door to other professional experiences. She enjoyed a brief appointment as "Sheriff" of Oahu, equivalent to the position of governor in the continental United States. For a brief period she worked as a newspaper reporter covering a case being prosecuted by her father. She outwitted a reporter from a competing newspaper by using the new invention of the telephone to submit her reports and repeatedly "scooping" the news stories away from him.

In 1893, Hitchcock ended a five-year, long-distance correspondence with William Levi Moore, a physician she had met while studying at the University of Michigan, when she accepted Moore's proposal of marriage. The two were wed at her parents' home on May 29, 1893, one week after his arrival in Hawaii. The couple stayed in Hawaii where Moore's medical training was immediately put to use. Hitchcock left her legal practice, apparently as a temporary gesture, and joined her husband on his frequent travels around the island, where he provided medical assistance to rural inhabitants. The lengthy visits in primitive conditions taxed Hitchcock's physical constitution. After two years of constant travel and declining health, she died of "bilious fever" in Hilo, Hawaii, on May 4, 1895, at the age of thirty-two.

Selected Sources

Information on Almeda Hitchcock and the Hitchcock family is in Mrs. Edward Hitchcock, *The Genealogy of the Hitchcock Family* (1894); M. Sheba, ed., *Prominent Men of Hawaii* (1900); Arthur Gove Day, *Hawaii and Its People* (1955); and Helen Maxon Hitchcock, *D. Howard Hitchcock; Islander* (1987). Biographical information on Hitchcock is in June Hitchcock Humme, "Almeda Eliza Hitchcock—Wahine Loio, or Lady Lawyer" (20 *The Hawaiian Journal of History* [1986]). Lelia J. Robinson includes Hitchcock in "Women Lawyers in the United States" (2 *Green Bag* [1890]). See also Mari J. Matsuda, *Called from Within* (1992).

Ada Harriet Miser Kepley

Ada Kepley, popularly remembered as an eccentric temperance reformer, was the first woman in the United States to earn a law degree. Like many of the female lawyers of the late nineteenth century, Kepley used her legal knowledge to advance the reform agenda of the nineteenth-century Woman Movement. While being a pioneer woman lawyer brought her notoriety, her professional status also helped to publicize the cause of women's rights.

Ada Harriet Miser Kepley was born on February 11, 1847, in Somerset, Ohio, to Henry and Ann Miser. With her two sisters and one brother, Kepley's childhood was a happy one. Her parents spent a great deal of time with their children, often gathering the family together to read stories. When she was thirteen, the Misers moved to St. Louis, Missouri, where Kepley attended grammar school and two years of high school, completing her studies in 1866. That year, the family moved to Effingham, Illinois, where Ada Harriet Miser met the locally well-known attorney, Henry B. Kepley. The couple was married in November of 1867.

Henry Kepley encouraged his wife to take an active interest in his professional work. In 1868 she began studying law in his office. His encouragement may have been shaped in part by a need for a clerical assistant with some legal knowledge. Ada Kepley was not content to remain in such a position. Her interest in a legal education was sharpened by this introduction to the law; she thirsted for more. In 1869, she began a more formal program of study, enrolling in the one-year law course at Union College of Law (Northwestern University). When she graduated with a LL.B. degree in June of 1870, she became the first woman to graduate from a law school in the United States.

Ada Kepley did not shy away from a good fight. Her resolute personality and legal training seemed to forge in her a fierce determination to overcome all opposition to the causes she championed. Kepley faced her first obstacle shortly after graduating from law school when she was denied admission to the Illinois bar. Assisted by her husband, Kepley challenged the ruling by drafting a bill banning sex discrimination in professional occupations. The act was passed by the Illinois legislature in 1872, subsequently allowing women to be admitted to the Illinois bar. Kepley herself did not apply to the bar until 1881 when she was quickly admitted.

The battle for admission to the bar now won, Kepley turned her attention to other fronts. During the 1870s she assisted in her husband's legal practice but increasingly devoted more of her time to suffrage, equal rights, and temperance work. In 1881, she took a step into the public arena from which she would not turn back when she ran for state attorney general on the Prohibition Party ticket. With little chance of winning, Kepley used the publicity generated by the campaign to educate the public about important reform issues. Her candidacy forced people to think about issues, especially women's rights to vote and to serve in public office as professionals, and kept the agenda of the temperance reformers at the forefront of the campaign. Kepley demanded steadfast loyalty to all the causes of which she was a part. When the Prohibition Party dropped suffrage from its platform, she abandoned the group stating: "I left it when they threw the women's ballot plank out and did not return till it was replaced."

Kepley was best known for her work in the temperance movement. She maintained a correspondence with leaders of the national Woman's Christian Temperance Union and served in a few elected WCTU positions, but her most important work was done in her hometown of Effingham. In 1884, the elected male officials of the town of Effingham denied the female-dominated WCTU access to local buildings for their meetings. Kepley, with her husband's aid, outwitted the board of supervisors by purchasing the Southern Methodist Church and converting it into a public meeting house called "The Temple." The building served as the headquarters for the local WCTU and was used as a meeting place by different temperance groups and churches that lacked their own facilities. Kepley launched a multipronged attack to advance the temperance movement by involving youths in her programs. She organized a local youth group called the "Band of Hope" where children learned about the dangers of alcohol and the value of temperance. Whenever a public temperance event was held, Kepley marshaled her young troops and made sure that a contingent was present at all parades and picnics sponsored by the WCTU. Childless herself, Kepley's actions to incorporate children into the temperance movement can be read as another extension of women's domestic responsibilities into the public sphere.

Kepley's temperance activities included efforts to restrict the passage of obscene material through the postal system and the publication of the first temperance newspaper in Effingham, "The Friend of Home," from 1885 to 1896. The monthly journal provided a controversial forum in which to wage her fight. Undeterred by public agitation against her, Kepley took a cue from social purity reformers who published lists of men who visited prostitutes as a way to shame them into changing their habits. She began to spy on the local saloons to see who visited them and published lists of the men who patronized the establishments. The gesture stirred many a domestic and ecclesiastical quarrel, and Kepley herself was the target of an assassination attempt by a local liquor dealer's son.

Kepley drew strength and support from the women's networks to which she belonged. She regretted that her membership in the Equity Club had been delayed when she had failed to submit a letter the first year, and found the correspondence club a good place to seek support for the way in which she put her legal training to work. At home, in addition to her work with the WCTU, she belonged to the Daughters of the American Revolution and the Eastern Star and was a founding member of the "High Cult Emerson Club," a woman's reading circle established in 1883. Her activities in the Emerson Club led her to join the Illinois Federation of Women's Clubs, and in 1895 she represented the Effingham club at the annual meeting. In 1892 she was ordained a minister in the Unitarian Society.

Following her husband's death in 1906, Kepley secluded herself in a farm he had owned in a nearby county. Desperately in debt, she pursued a writing career in the hope of making enough money to make ends meet. In 1912, she published an autobiographical book, *A Farm Philosopher: A Love Story,* primarily dealing with her temperance work. During the first World War, Kepley wrote a patriotic song called "My Sweetheart Over the Sea Who fought For Liberty." Neither effort proved lucrative in spite of published pleas to her friends and associates to buy the materials in order to help relieve her of her debt. The popular and only partially true legacy of her eccentricity in thought, word, and deed on behalf of reform was reinforced in the last years of her life when she was living in abject poverty on her late husband's farm. She often appeared in town looking frail and ill and wearing outdated fashions while attempting to give candy to small children. She died a pauper at St. Anthony's Hospital in Effingham County on June 13, 1925.

Selected Sources

An understanding of Ada Kepley's life is best derived from her autobiography, *A Farm Philosophy: A Love Story* (1912). A biographical essay on Kepley is in Frances Willard and Mary Livermore, eds., *A Woman of the Century* (1893). She is included in John William Leonard, ed., *Women's Who's Who of America* (1914–15). Lydia Hoyt Farmer discusses Kepley in *The National Exposition Souvenir: What America Owes to Women* (1893). She is also included in Lelia J. Robinson, "Women Lawyers in the United States" (2 *Green Bag* [1890]) and Ellen J. Martin, "Admission of Women to the Bar" (1 *Chicago Law Times* [1886]). Additional information on Kepley is in Mrs. Peggy Pulliam, "Effingham's Fighting Female," in Hilda E. Feldbake, ed., *Effingham County Illinois—Past and Present* (1968). Additional information is available from the Vandalia Historical Society, Vandalia, Illinois.

Laura A. Woodin LeValley

Laura Woodin LeValley's life balanced the traditional patterns of Victorian womanhood with the unconventional decision to practice law. Born in Granville, New York, to Daniel and Sarah Smith Palmer

Woodin, she grew up in Romeo, Michigan, where she was educated at a local private school, Dickenson Institute. LeValley then embarked on the study of music, first at Falley Seminary in Fulton, New York, and then at Sherwood's Musical Academy in Lyons, New York. Her strong musical training earned her a reputation as a skillful music instructor.

While LeValley's education prepared her for work that was appropriate for women of her social class, she ultimately chose a less traditional path. Though her brother became a merchant, she was attracted to the legal career of her father, and he welcomed her into his law office. She studied stenography, became a notary public, and helped her father, particularly in the prosecution of United States claims.

With her father's encouragement, LeValley entered the law school of the University of Michigan in 1880. She was popular with her classmates and was elected vice president of her senior law class. She graduated in 1882, but because of her experience in her father's office, she was prepared to pass the bar exam before she graduated and was admitted to the bar of Michigan in 1881.

While she was a law student at the University of Michigan, LeValley met a classmate, David Wilford LeValley. He graduated in 1881, and they married in December, 1881, shortly after she graduated. They settled in East Saginaw, Michigan, and practiced law together. Their law practice mirrored the sexual division of labor in traditional Victorian marriages. He was a circuit court judge who spent much of his time in court. She was content to assist her husband in the office just as she had helped her father.

With the birth of her two daughters, LeValley devoted less time to law and more time to her family and to traditional womanly pursuits. She was a religious woman who worked for years in the Sunday school of the First Congregational Church in Saginaw, Michigan, before she became a Christian Scientist. She was active in a number of women's clubs including the Daughters of the American Revolution and the Drama League of America. She organized the University Club for alumnae of the University of Michigan, which she described in her letter to the Equity Club.

In 1912, LeValley moved with her husband to Ann Arbor. She died December 9, 1918, in Pontiac, Michigan.

Selected Sources

There is biographical information on Laura LeValley in Frances E. Willard and Mary Livermore, eds., *A Woman of the Century* (1893) and John William Leonard, ed., *Woman's Who's Who of America* (1914–15). LeValley is included in Mary Cooley Bassett, *Lineage Book of the Daughters of the American Revolution* (1911). Lelia J. Robinson, "Women Lawyers in the United States" (2 *Green Bag* [1890]) has information on LeValley. An obituary of LeValley is in the *Pontiac Daily Press Gazette* (December 9, 1918). Additional information is available at the Bentley Historical Library, University of Michigan, Ann Arbor, Michigan.

Ce Dora Lieuellen

Ce Dora Lieuellen was born June 9, 1854, and grew up in Clinton, Ohio. The youngest of six daughters of a farming family, she spent her childhood doing the housekeeping duties traditionally reserved for young girls as well as the farm chores typically performed by boys.

While her childhood deviated from the traditional path for a girl of her generation, Lieuellen's parents held conservative views of women's place and did not approve of higher education for women. But Lieuellen's unconventional childhood set her at odds with her parents' views on women, and she left home to secure her own education at the National Normal School in Bedford, Ohio. In 1886, she joined the faculty of the Central Normal School of Ladoga, Indiana, and moved to Danville, Indiana, when the school relocated there in 1888. Lieuellen lived in Danville for the next eleven years of her life, teaching a number of subjects at Central Normal School, including history, geography, rhetoric, and composition. During her years as a teacher in Danville, Lieuellen undertook a number of activities that earned her a reputation as a woman of independence in a community where most women adhered to the traditional views of Victorian womanhood. Motivated by her love of education, she read law on her own and in 1886 she became the first woman to gain admission to the Indiana bar. She organized a suffrage society even though the majority of women of Danville refused to join and deliberately avoided marriage because she did not want the burden of domestic duties.

Though Lieuellen was a maverick among the women of Danville, Indiana, she was greatly admired and respected by her students and colleagues at Central Normal School, and they lamented her departure in 1889 to study law at the University of Iowa. But ill health prevented Lieuellen from going to Iowa, and she went to Florida instead, where she hoped to organize a law school and teach law at the Florida Normal College of Sulphur Springs.

Ultimately, Lieuellen never practiced law nor taught it. But she never strayed from her commitment to education for she worked as an instructor for the agents of insurance companies around the country. Lieuellen died January 22, 1917, at the age of sixty-two at the home of one of her sisters in Bellafontaine, Ohio.

Selected Sources

Information on Ce Dora Lieuellen is sparse. It includes a news article on her departure from Central Normal School, "Miss Ce Dora Lieuellen" (Hendricks County *Republican* [August 1, 1889]); an obituary, "Former Instructor Dead" (*Danville Gazette* [January 25, 1917]); and an obituary notice in the *New York Times* (January 23, 1917). She is included in Lelia J. Robinson, "Women Lawyers in the United States" (2 *Green Bag* [1890]). Additional information is available from the Hendricks County Historical Society, Danville, Indiana.

Belva Ann Bennett McNall Lockwood

Belva Lockwood, who broke the gender barrier to become the first woman admitted to the bar of the Supreme Court of the United States, stood at the center of many of the nineteenth-century reform efforts dedicated to checking the abuses that occurred when the nation was transformed from an idealistic republic of farmers into an enormous industrial and political world power. Abolitionist, pacifist, suffragist, civil rights activist—she strove to preserve for all Americans the ideals that were basic to the nation's founding. Lockwood believed in and fought valiantly as a lawyer and a private citizen for the basic principle of equal rights for all. By far the most recognized of the first generation of female lawyers, her achievements stand out as bold and courageous; they are the accomplishments of a rugged pioneer. Yet all of her actions, public and private, were rooted firmly and simply in her deep allegiance to the fundamental doctrines of American political culture—equality, liberty, and justice for all.

Belva Lockwood, the second child of Lewis J. and Hannah (Green) Bennett, was born in a log cabin on October 24, 1830, in Royalton, Niagara County, New York. At the time of her youth, religious enthusiasm rocked the hills and valleys of upstate New York. She took her Bible reading literally and attempted to reenact many of the stories she read. Although her attempts to walk on water, raise the dead, and move a (small) mountain were unsuccessful, her faith in human ability, especially her own, was not shaken. Later in life she stated that while she could not move mountains, she had found that removing them to be just as effective in changing the environment around her.

Lockwood attended a rural one-room schoolhouse until age fifteen when she became the school's teacher. In 1848, she married a local farmer, Uriah H. McNall, and a year later gave birth to her daughter, Lura. McNall suffered a farming accident and died in 1853 leaving Lockwood a widowed and single parent at age 23. Her broad reading introduced Lockwood to the idea that a college education had fortified many a successful person to meet the challenges of life. In 1854, she sent her daughter to live with her parents in Illinois and enrolled in the scientific program at Genesee Wesleyan Seminary in Lima, New York. Graduating with a B.S. degree with honors in 1857, she accepted a position as preceptress of Lockport (New York) Union School. Earning half the salary of the male schoolteachers who worked for her, it took Lockwood six months to save enough money to bring her daughter home. For the next nine years she worked as the principal of girls' schools in New York state. Her experience in demanding a fair salary and advocating an expansion of women's educational programs to include gymnastics and public speaking had sparked her interest in equal rights. At a teachers' institute in 1860, Lockwood met Susan B. Anthony and became allied with the women's rights movement.

The challenges of life in upstate New York had grown routine for the energetic young woman. Throughout the Civil War she had spoken openly in favor of emancipation and began to understand that the seeds of social change were being planted in the nation's capitol. In 1866 she and her daughter moved to Washington, D.C. Upon arriving there she opened a school for girls, but spent most of her time exploring the halls of the government. In 1868, she married Dr. Ezekiel Lockwood and gave birth to a second daughter, Jessie, in 1869. The child died two years later.

The vibrancy of Washington, D.C., life fed Lockwood's increasing dissatisfaction with life as a schoolmarm. Again, her reading suggested the course her life should take. Great men, she read, had a thorough knowledge of the law. Lockwood decided to enter law school and gain such wisdom for herself. She enrolled at the National University School of Law with fifteen other women but only Lockwood and one other woman completed the program to graduate in 1873. Her male classmates protested that the value of their degrees would be lessened if shared with a woman and Lockwood was not allowed to participate in the graduation ceremonies. Her diploma was also withheld until Lockwood wrote to President Ulysses S. Grant, ex-officio president of the university, to demand that he award it to her. She received it in the mail a few weeks later. Immediately after, she became the first woman admitted to the bar of the District of Columbia.

Lockwood's request to be admitted to the United States Supreme Court was not as simple. She petitioned for admission several times but it was not until 1879, after drafting a bill that was sponsored by Senators Sargent of California and Samuel Hoar of Massachusetts, that the law was changed. On March 3, 1879, Lockwood became the first woman admitted to the bar of the United States Supreme Court. A few weeks later she also became the first woman admitted to the bar of the Court of Claims. Within months of her own admission to the bar of the Supreme Court, Lockwood proved her commitment to equal rights and shocked the nation's highest court again when she presented Samuel Lowery, the first Southern black lawyer, for admission in 1880.

Shortly after graduating from National University, Lockwood opened a practice in Washington, D.C., specializing in financial claims against the government. Through her husband's connections as a former Union Army surgeon and her own activities, Lockwood attracted a large number of clients, mostly Union soldiers and sailors, seeking government pensions. Her practice became so busy that she found it most efficient to ride a large tricycle around the city to meet appointments. Her legal victories included equal pay for equal work for government employees, pensions for mothers and widows of soldiers killed or injured in the Civil War, and, in 1906, a five million dollar claim for the Cherokee nation against the federal government for lands it had taken from the tribe in the 1830s.

Operating in the whirl of activities in the nation's capitol, Lockwood's reputation spread across the land. In 1884, the Equal Rights Party of California nominated her for president of the United States. She accepted the nomination and ran on a platform laced with the most progressive reform programs of the day including equal rights for all citizens, uniform marriage and divorce laws, temperance, and international peace. She polled 4,149 (male) votes, an achievement that won her the honor of being the first woman to receive votes for president of the United States. The campaign initiated a breach between Lockwood and the female suffragists who supported mainstream party candidates they believed had a greater likelihood of being elected. Lockwood was renominated by the Equal Rights party in 1888, but the novelty had worn off and her candidacy received little attention.

The volatile presidential campaign of 1884 propelled Lockwood into the national limelight. A much sought-after lecturer, Lockwood traveled the country advocating for reforms advanced in her campaign platform and on such topics as women in professions, breaking up Indian reservations, the role of government, and the need for university extension programs. Each appearance increased her popularity and brought forth people who wished to file claims against the government. Lockwood sent the claims to her daughter, Lura McNall Ormes, who ran Lockwood's law office for her.

The enormous loss of life and physical destruction caused by the Civil War prompted Lockwood's commitment to pacifism. Her persistent call for world peace and a system of international arbitration was proclaimed loudly against cries in the United States on behalf of manifest destiny and white supremacy. She served as a delegate to the first International Peace Congress in 1889, became a member of the nominating committee for the Nobel Peace Prize, and an editor for *Peacemaker,* the journal of the Universal Peace Union of which she was a founding member. A staunch defender of pacifism, Lockwood was a strong voice during the Spanish-American War of 1898, and continued to advocate international arbitration as hostilities grew in Europe in the 1910s.

Her life and achievements beckoned other women to pursue their dreams. In 1880, Emma Gillett, another future Equity Club member, followed Lockwood's example and attempted to enroll at National University. By that time, the university had closed its doors to women.

Lockwood's belief in the power of women's association encouraged her to assist the aspiring law student. She opened her office and tutored Gillett in the law until she was admitted to Howard University Law School. The two women remained friends and shared a lifelong interest in promoting equal rights for women, each frequently referring questions and requests for information or invitations to speak to the other.

Many of Lockwood's achievements paved the way for other like-minded women. Her admission to the bar of the United States Supreme Court, the cases she won, the ideas advanced in her lectures, and her presidential candidacy all opened doors for women. Yet, few of the reforms that captured Lockwood's attention and channeled her energies came to successful completion during her lifetime. However, when she died in Washington, D.C., on May 19, 1917, she believed that enough change had occurred to insure that American society would be radically different from the world in which she had lived. Three years later the Nineteenth Amendment to the United States Constitution was passed granting women the right to vote.

Selected Sources

There is a great deal of information available on Belva Lockwood. Detailed information on Belva Lockwood is in Edward T. James, ed., *Notable American Women* (1971). Additional biographical sources include Frances E. Willard and Mary A. Livermore, eds., *A Woman of the Century* (1893); John William Leonard, *Woman's Who's Who in America* (1914–15); and Phebe A. Hanaford, *Daughters of America* (1882). Lockwood is also included in Lelia J. Robinson, "Women Lawyers in the United States" (2 *Green Bag* [1890]); Ellen Martin, "Admission of Women to the Bar" (1 *Chicago Law Times* [1886]); and Dr. Louis Frank, "The Woman Lawyer" (3 *Chicago Law Times* [1889]). Lockwood's autobiographical articles, "My Efforts to Become a Lawyer" (*Lippincott's* [February, 1888]), and "How I Ran for the Presidency" (*National Magazine* [March, 1903]), are very useful. Lockwood's letters and papers have been preserved in archives throughout the United States including the State Historical Society of Wisconsin, the State Historical Society of North Dakota, Swarthmore College Peace Collection, the Sophia Smith Collection at Smith College, and the George Arents Research Library at Syracuse University. Throughout her adult life Lockwood's activities received the attention of the media. Articles about her were printed in national and local papers and professional and popular magazines including the *New York Times,* the *Washington, D.C., Star,* the *Woman's Journal, Chicago Legal News, Lippincott's Monthly Magazine,* and *Harper's Weekly.*

Leona Taylor Lounsbury

Leona Taylor Lounsbury's life is the story of a nineteenth-century woman whose ambitions to practice law were destroyed by the demands of marriage and motherhood. Lounsbury was born in 1854. She studied law at the University of Michigan and graduated in 1881. While at law school, she became a leader among her classmates, serving as vice president of the Jeffersonian Society, a literary and debating club for the law students. At the University of Michigan, Lounsbury was well on her way to preparing for a legal career, but two events occurred that changed the course of her life. First, just before she graduated from law school, her closest friend died. The loss caused her such grief that she felt physically and emotionally unable to contemplate law practice. But the loss of her close friend was offset by her relationship with John W. Lounsbury, a fellow classmate in the law school. In 1881, after they graduated together and she was admitted to the bar of Michigan, they married and moved to Omaha, Nebraska.

Lounsbury went west with her husband, fully intending to practice law with him. Instead, they established a traditional Victorian marriage. He practiced law while she had a baby within a year of their arrival in Omaha and settled down to the life of marriage and motherhood. While Lounsbury adored her daughter, her dashed professional expectations were not compensated by the joys of her domestic life. Instead, she confessed in her letter to the Equity Club that her unending household responsibilities made her feel like a "voluntary prisoner" in her home.

John Lounsbury's early death left Lounsbury a widow after only seven years of marriage. While she needed to support herself, she did not take the opportunity to begin a law practice, probably feeling unable to take on the professional responsibility with a young child. Instead, she supported herself and her daughter, Edith, by taking in boarders, describing herself as a "Land Lady" in the 1900 census. By

1910, Lounsbury sold and leased real estate and Edith, who had finished her education, was a stenographer at a local bank.

Despite the disappointments and trials of her life, Lounsbury never forgot the excitement and hopes of her law school days. In 1911, she journeyed back to the University of Michigan to participate in the thirtieth reunion of her law school class where she reunited with her classmate and fellow Equity Club member Cora Benneson.

Selected Sources

There is little information on Leona Lounsbury. She is in *1881 University Pallidium* (1881) and in Lelia J. Robinson, "Women Lawyers in the United States" (2 *Green Bag* [1890]). Lounsbury is listed in [Bureau of the Census], State of Nebraska, 1885, Omaha, Douglas County, Nebraska, p. 23; United States Bureau of the Census, Twelfth Census of the United States, 1900, Omaha City, Nebraska, Sheet 6; id., Thirteenth Census of the United States, 1910, Omaha City, Nebraska, Sheet 8B. All census documents are from the Nebraska State Historical Society, Lincoln, Nebraska. Additional information is available at the Bentley Historical Library, University of Michigan.

Ellen Annette Martin

Ellen Annette Martin, the only daughter of three children of Abraham and Mary (Burnham) Martin, was born on January 16, 1847, in Kiantone, New York. Her father, a self-taught and prominent local attorney, frequently discussed legal issues and courtroom events with his children, including his daughter. The experience of learning at her father's feet in the company of her two brothers sparked an interest in pursuing a legal career, but also planted in her mind the idea of full equality between the sexes. At age twenty-four, single and well read, Martin decided to begin a career in the legal profession. She worked as a clerk, reading law in her spare time, for two years in the Chautauqua County firm of Cook and Lockwood before enrolling in the University of Michigan Law School in 1873. She graduated in 1875, was admitted to the Michigan bar that year, and upon moving to Chicago, joined the Illinois bar in 1876.

Martin, although unmarried, did not travel to Chicago alone.

Joined by Mary Fredrika Perry, a fellow law student at the University of Michigan, the two opened a legal practice together in the city and lived together with Perry's family in Lombard, a nearby suburb. The firm of Perry and Martin specialized in real estate law and was one of the first female law partnerships in American history.

In the early years of the joint partnership, Perry and Martin often took charity cases for poor women. The practice continued until Perry became ill after spending too much time out-of-doors on a winter day. As a result, Perry's cold developed into pneumonia and she died in 1883. Martin resolved never to take another charity case and advised other women to do likewise, suggesting that they support charity work through the donation of money rather than legal services.

After Perry's death, Martin continued to practice and kept the office open under the original name of the firm until 1915. She continued to live in Lombard as well, and was a frequent visitor to Perry's family, the Vances. Perhaps it was Mr. Vance's position as an electoral judge in the town of Lombard that sparked Ellen Martin's resolve to challenge the lack of woman suffrage there. She used her legal expertise to study and analyze the Illinois state constitution and the local charter on voting qualifications. On April 6, 1891, Martin packed her green bag with an extensive brief and a set of law books and went to the Lombard polling place to vote in a municipal election. Confident that she had found a legal basis to vote, Martin explained to the judges that the Lombard City Charter guaranteed the vote to "all citizens." The three male judges were unwilling to suspend the election to hear her prepared briefs and subsequently yielded to her demand. She cast her vote and left, becoming the first woman to vote in Illinois.

Fortified by her success, Martin canvassed the town and found fourteen other women who wished to exercise the right to vote. Among the female voters were Mrs. C. B. Vance, wife of Judge Vance, and their married daughter, Mrs. C. L. Towne. Both women were direct descendants of Mrs. Sarah B. Latham who voted at Mendham, New Jersey, when such practice was allowed under New Jersey law in the late eighteenth century. Due to Martin's careful legal argument, the judges accepted the women's votes. A tempest ensued when male voters began to express their wrath that women had been allowed to vote. The Lombard town magistrates quickly took steps to deny the right to vote in general elections. News of the women-voting episode reached the state capitol and in June, 1891, the 37th General Assembly of Illinois passed the School Act allowing women to vote for local public school officials. While the act restricted the number and type of municipal elections in which women could vote, it at least set the stage for practice and precedent of women voting at all. Martin's achievement at the polls brought her much praise and notoriety. In 1891, the Equality Club of Jamestown, New York, recognized her for her bravery and the advancement of the women's suffrage movement. At home in Chicago, the Queen Isabella Association, a social group of professional women that Martin helped to establish, honored her by naming her chair of the Legal Committee.

Ellen Martin knew the difficulties facing women who chose to pursue a professional career. She advised other young women to take support from whatever source, but especially encouraged the development of female networks that offered young women role models and mentors. Throughout her life she participated in efforts to bring women together, most notably by her connections with the Equity Club, the fifteen women voters of Lombard, and the Queen Isabella Association. She followed closely the progress of women lawyers, and in 1886 she wrote an essay for the *Chicago Legal News,* "Admission of Women to the Bar," surveying the efforts of women to gain admission to the bar throughout the United States. In 1893, the year of the Columbian Exposition, Martin worked with fellow Equity Club members Catharine Waugh McCulloch and Florence Cronise to recruit women lawyers to visit Chicago where they would have a chance to meet one another in person while witnessing the wonders to be seen at the Exposition.

In 1915, Martin closed the firm of Perry and Martin and returned to Chautauqua County, New York. She died on April 27, 1916, at her brother's home in Jamestown, New York.

Selected Sources

There are a number of articles by or about Ellen Martin in the *Chicago Legal News* from 1875 into the early twentieth century. They include her essays "Admission of Women to the Bar" (11 *Chicago Legal News* [1879]) and "The Women Voters at Lombard" (23 *Chicago Legal News* [1891]). Her obituary is in the 48 *Chicago Legal News* (1916). Martin is included in James B. Bradwell, "Women Lawyers of Illinois" (32 *Chicago Legal News* [1900]), and in Lelia J. Robinson, "Women Lawyers in the United States" (2 *Green Bag* [1890]). Additional information on Martin is in John William Leonard, *Woman's Who's Who of America* (1914–15) and in John P. Downs and Fenwick Y. Hedley, *History of Chautauqua County and Its People* (1875). Papers of Ellen Martin are in the Bentley Historical Library, University of Michigan, Ann Arbor, Michigan and in the Lombard Historical Society, Lombard, Illinois.

Rebecca May

Universities in the western sections of the United States opened their doors to women earlier than their eastern counterparts. Many women who aspired to be lawyers enrolled at the University of Michigan Law School not only for its outstanding curriculum but also because the female community of women lawyers and law students living in Ann Arbor offered them a well-established support system. In the 1880s, many of the women who graduated from the University of Michigan resided in town for a year or two after graduation, staying in part because of the female network and friendships available from the presence of a critical mass of young women attorneys and law students. One of four members of the law school class of 1887, Rebecca May enjoyed the benefits of the already thriving bonds of female association in Ann Arbor when she enrolled as a law student in the university in 1884.

A native of Pekin, Illinois, Rebecca May took advantage of the expansion of opportunities for women in the professions when she left home to attend the University of Michigan. Almost immediately she found a vibrant community of intelligent and like-minded women with whom to share her ideas, aspirations, and opinions. A group of seven women, including two University of Michigan graduates, attended law school lectures together and, in the fall of 1886, formed a social club. May was one of the women law students who encouraged the group to expand its mission and its membership by becoming a correspondence club. In 1887, the suggestion achieved fruition when the Equity Club was formed.

The friendships made at Ann Arbor endured the challenges caused by distance when the members of the group began to move out of the town. May graduated from the University of Michigan in 1887 and shortly after moved to Topeka, Kansas, and was admitted to that state's bar. She opened a solo practice but abandoned it a year later when she was called home to help care for a family member who had been taken ill. Her friends, especially those she had made while living in Ann Arbor, did not abandon her. In 1890, fellow law school classmate and Equity Club member Lettie L. Burlingame invited May, who was still not working as an attorney, to move to Joliet, Illinois, to start a partnership. Within a few weeks of extending the invitation, however, Burlingame became ill, and she died seven months later. Burlingame's untimely death closed the door on an opportunity that would have allowed May to resume legal work and still live close enough to home to assume family responsibilities as needed.

It is not known whether Rebecca May ever returned to the legal profession. More than paving the way to a professional career, May believed that the most important aspect of her legal education was the mental discipline she learned from her studies of the law. To May, the training in piano playing and domestic arts imposed on young girls in the Victorian era seemed utterly useless and potentially harmful. Contrary to prevailing opinion, she believed that the rigors and disciplines of formal study would improve women's mental and physical health. May's opinions about academic training for women and girls reflected contemporary women's efforts to reform the educational opportunities and experiences available to members of her sex.

Selected Sources

Information on Rebecca May is sparse. She is included in Lelia J. Robinson, "Women Lawyers in the United States" (2 *Green Bag* [1890]). Lettie Burlingame's correspondence with her is in Olive C. Burlingame, ed., *Lettie Lavilla Burlingame: Her Life Pages. Stories, Poems, and Essays* (1895). Additional information is available from the Bentley Historical Library, University of Michigan, Ann Arbor, Michigan.

Catharine Gouger Waugh McCulloch

Catharine Gouger Waugh McCulloch, born on June 2, 1862, was the firstborn child and only daughter of Susan and Abraham Waugh of

Ransomville, New York. When Catharine was five years old, the family moved to New Milford, Illinois, where farming opportunities proved more profitable than the hardscrabble life that western New York had offered. At the age of sixteen she was selected to be a school teacher in a nearby district but decided to enroll in Rockford (Illinois) Female Seminary instead, receiving her diploma in 1882. For the next year and a half she assumed an exhaustive schedule as a temperance speaker throughout northwestern Illinois. In October of 1884 she began working in the Rockford law firm of Marshall and Taggart, embarking on her legal career. By the following September she rejected the informal process of "reading law" in favor of a formal legal education and enrolled in the Union College of Law (Northwestern University) from which she graduated in 1886.

McCulloch's entry into the male-dominated classrooms of the law school was eased by the maternal presence and friendly advice of her classmate, Catharine V. Waite, a woman of fifty-six who had enrolled at Union simultaneously with McCulloch. Waite's humor and hospitality helped the young McCulloch to overcome her shyness with the male students and in the classroom. During the year at Union, Mrs. Waite took advantage of her social position as a matron and introduced McCulloch to several male suitors, including Frank McCulloch, her future husband. McCulloch and Waite both joined the Equity Club and shared an interest in the work of the suffrage movement.

McCulloch was admitted to the Illinois bar on November 9, 1886, and attempted to establish a legal practice in Chicago. Frustrated by the prejudice of male attorneys toward women lawyers, she left Chicago and opened a practice in Rockford. While living in Rockford she continued her studies at the now fully accredited Rockford College, and received both a bachelor's and a master's degree in 1888 for her thesis on "Women's Wages." That same year, McCulloch travelled to Washington, D.C., to attend the meeting of the International Council of Women and was present at the formation of the International Women's Bar Association when Catharine V. Waite was elected its first president. During her visit to Washington, D.C., she had the opportunity to meet several notable women lawyers and fellow Equity Club members including Belva Lockwood, Ada Bittenbender, and Emma Gillett.

Much of McCulloch's legal practice involved charity work for poor women clients. Some of the older male attorneys cautioned her against such activity and also suggested that she give up her speaking engagements on behalf of suffrage, temperance, and women's rights. McCulloch found their "advice" tiresome and explained that while all young attorneys received some measure of criticism and advice, she believed that young women were more often subjected to it than were young men. Still, McCulloch had found some young male attorneys who were legitimately interested in her work. Indicative of her ideas about cooperation between the sexes, McCulloch suggested to the Equity Club that men who were sympathetic to the work of women lawyers be awarded honorary memberships in the group.

The idea of companionate relationships between men and women was new to people of the late nineteenth century, but it was readily accepted by McCulloch and her husband, Frank McCulloch. The couple was married in Rockford on May 30, 1890, by the Reverend Anna Howard Shaw, a leading female minister of the period. Their honeymoon was spent in South Dakota, where McCulloch had agreed to conduct a series of lectures for the local suffrage groups prior to making wedding plans. Upon returning to Illinois, the two opened a joint practice, McCulloch and McCulloch, in Chicago. Initially much of the firm's work involved clients of Mr. McCulloch, but the situation was remedied over time as Catharine McCulloch attracted clients of her own. Having been a victim of discrimination by the male-dominated society of the Chicago legal profession when she attempted to enter it in 1886, Catharine W. McCulloch was quick to acknowledge that her marriage to an attorney made her own professional life easier. McCulloch combined her professional career with a deep commitment to family life. Between 1891 and 1905 she gave birth to four children while launching a busy practice and increasing her involvement with a variety of political, social, and educational groups.

Catharine McCulloch's interest in women's rights activities were supported by her husband. In 1890, with his encouragement, she accepted the position of legislative superintendent of the Illinois Equal Suffrage Association, a responsibility she had inherited from her mentor, Catharine V. Waite, and one she held until 1912. During her tenure she used her legislative connection to win passage of two pieces of legislation affecting women: an act in 1901 granting women equal guardianship rights with their husbands over their children and, in 1905, an act to raise the age of consent from fourteen to sixteen years of age. McCulloch established the Mississippi Valley

Conference of the National American Woman Suffrage Association in 1912 in an effort to reshape the group's East Coast orientation. After the Nineteenth Amendment was passed, she joined the newly formed League of Women Voters in 1923 and became chair of its Committee on Uniform Laws Concerning Women. She participated in a number of other women's organizations involved with issues of importance to her including the Women's Christian Temperance Union, the Chicago Commons Settlement House, the Illinois Conference of Charities and Correction, the Illinois Woman's Democratic Club, and the Women's Bar Association of Illinois, serving terms as president for several of these groups. McCulloch was a devoted alumna of Rockford College. She served a lengthy term as one of the school's directors, and she was a major financial supporter and occasional commencement speaker. Her service to Rockford was rewarded with an honorary LL.D. from the college in 1936. Her lifetime of accomplishments were all the more impressive given that she also raised four children.

In the late 1930s, Mr. and Mrs. McCulloch traveled around the world studying social legislation and the legal system in other countries; she was particularly impressed with the customs in the Soviet Union where women held an important role in the country's legal system. Frank and Catharine McCulloch celebrated their fiftieth wedding anniversary on May 30, 1940, surrounded by their four children, grandchildren, and many friends. That same year the Illinois Bar Association named the McCullochs "Senior Counsellors" in recognition of their many years of legal practice together.

Catharine Waugh McCulloch died of cancer on April 20, 1945, while a patient at the Evanston (Illinois) Hospital; Frank McCulloch survived her by two years. They were interred side-by-side in Graceland Cemetery, Chicago.

Selected Sources

Useful biographical essays on Catharine McCulloch are in Edward T. James, ed., *Notable American Women* (1971) and in Frances E. Willard and Mary A. Livermore, eds., *A Woman of the Century* (1893). McCulloch is also included in Lelia J. Robinson, "Women Lawyers in the United States" (2 *Green Bag* [1890]); Ellen Martin, "Admission of Women to the Bar" (1 *Chicago Law Times* [1886]); and James B.

Bradwell, "Women Lawyers of Illinois" (*Chicago Legal News* [June 2, 1900]). For insight into her early professional years, see Nancy Cott, "Women as Law Clerks: Memoir of Catharine G. Waugh," in Domna Stanton, ed., *The Female Autograph* (New York Literary Forum, 1984), 12–13. McCulloch's papers are at the Schlesinger Library, Radcliffe College, Cambridge, Massachusetts.

Martha Kellum Pearce

Many of the women who entered the male-dominated professions in the late nineteenth century often found satisfying work in applying their training to social reform issues of the day, particularly those that affected women. They joined such crusades as the woman suffrage movement, temperance, and the quest for equitable marriage and divorce laws. Martha K. Pearce, a founding member and the organizational backbone of the Equity Club, combined her legal training with her literary talent and drew on her extensive personal knowledge of the lives of Equity Club members to fashion a life's work in social purity campaigns. Pearce's efforts to correct and improve inadequate and unjust sexual assault laws sought, somewhat paradoxically, to preserve the tenets of Victorian womanhood while presenting a women's rights argument on the need for greater attention to the hazards imposed on women's health by these dangerously ineffective laws.

A native of Gambier, Ohio, Pearce enrolled in the law school of the University of Michigan, receiving the LL.B. in 1883, and was immediately admitted to the bar of Michigan. Pearce's love of literature and writing began to emerge while she was a law student at the University of Michigan. She served as vice president of the Jeffersonian Society, a literary and debating society of law students. Upon graduation, she chose literary and social reform work over a legal practice, and remained a resident of Ann Arbor for several years.

With other women lawyers and students, Pearce was instrumental in the founding of the Equity Club in 1886. When the Ann Arbor group came upon the idea of inviting women lawyers from around the world to join their circles through a network of correspondence, Pearce's interest in letter writing as a form of literature garnered her the position of corresponding secretary of the Equity Club. Her love for the literary and belief in the power of women's networks combined with her administrative talent were critical in sustaining the four-year existence of the organization.

Pearce's work as corresponding secretary involved attending to the numerous details of maintaining an active membership. She wrote letters of invitation to women lawyers, responded to inquiries about the group, collected and recorded dues, reminded club members of regulations and missing letters, prepared an annual report, and circulated the body of letters to all active members each year. Although she enjoyed reading and responding to all of the letters that came through her hands, she was frustrated by the amount of attention needed to monitor the administrative work of a correspondence club. By 1889 she moved to Chicago, began writing for the Woman's Christian Temperance Union, and sought to expand her career. She continued to serve as corresponding secretary through 1890 when no other member could be persuaded to assume the duties, but relinquished them thereafter.

The work as corresponding secretary allowed Pearce access to some of the intimate details of the lives of Equity Club members. Through their private letters to her, Pearce incorporated her knowledge of circumstances of Equity Club members, without reference to the individuals, into her writings on the need for social purity reform. In 1891, she published a leaflet in the Woman's Christian Temperance Union's "Social Purity Series" entitled "Some Legal Aspects of the Question." The essay compared the laws and social reform efforts of the United States and England. She demonstrated that the English had been at work on issues of social purity for a greater length of time and with better results than American efforts. Additionally, she showed how the law did not adequately protect women from men and urged women to work especially for the preservation of the purity of young girls by seeking to raise the age of consent and creating strict laws against perpetrators of rape and sexual assault.

If the detail work of corresponding secretary frustrated her, Pearce also knew that the position offered her a pulpit from which to articulate her views. She was the only Equity Club member who had a chance to comment publicly on the annual letters before they were distributed to the membership. She used her annual reports to the Equity Club to challenge the statements written by others and encouraged her "sisters-in-law" to work for charity and social reform.

Pearce's ability to generate debate within the correspondence club did not detract from her belief in the need for a close network of female support. She encouraged the exchange of photographs among Equity Club members as a way to introduce a more tangible level to the written conversations they shared. It was she, more than any other member, who held the Equity Club together, giving it continuity, direction, and inspiration over the course of its four years.

SELECTED SOURCES

Information on Martha Pearce is sparse. She is included in Lelia J. Robinson, "Women Lawyers in the United States" (2 *Green Bag* [1890]) and in Ellen Martin, "Admission of Women to the Bar" (1 *Chicago Law Times* [1886]). Her essay "Some Legal Aspects of the Question," published by the WCTU in 1891, is useful for her views on temperance, women, and the law. Additional material is available at the Bentley Historical Library, University of Michigan, Ann Arbor, Michigan.

Lelia Josephine Robinson [Sawtelle]

To attempt to become a female attorney in Victorian Boston required an extraordinary amount of patience, endurance, and skill for those women who sought to scale the peak of social stigma placed before women who entered the public sphere. Lelia J. Robinson, the pioneer female law student and attorney in Boston, entered the fray armed only with a persistent desire to be an attorney and a thorough legal education. After an early period marked by barriers and frustrations in her effort to establish her legal career, Robinson's perseverance paid off. She was able to manage a modest practice in Boston as well as finding the time to serve as a role model and mentor to her younger colleagues. Blending her own self-confidence with a commitment to the fundamental importance of women's networks, Robinson cut a path for herself and other women through the dense and foreboding woods of the male-dominated legal elite of Boston.

Lelia Robinson was born in Boston on July 23, 1850, to the family of a well-established trader. Her education in Boston's public schools provided her with an academic training particularly emphasizing expository writing. At the age of seventeen, she married Rupert J. Chute, a tinsmith, and began a journalistic career working for several of Boston's newspapers. Unlike most of their Victorian counterparts, the Robinson-Chute marriage ended in divorce. Charging Chute with adultery, Robinson's petition for divorce and her request to resume her maiden name were granted by the Supreme Judicial Court in 1877. The social stigma emblazoned on divorced women was so great that Robinson felt the need to shroud her marriage to Chute in silence. It was never mentioned in her autobiographical writings and none of the eulogies or obituaries included the information.

In 1878 Robinson enrolled at the Boston University School of Law. The only woman in a school of one hundred and fifty students, Robinson was on her own in attempting to assess how to behave properly and most advantageously in such a situation. She found that being open and outgoing with her classmates allowed them and her to ignore her gender and get on with the business of being law students. Robinson often stated that the three years spent at law school were among her most rewarding and productive. In 1881, she became the first woman to graduate from the Boston University Law School receiving the LL.B. cum laude and placing fourth in a class of thirty-two students.

Having successfully crossed the uncharted social territory of law school, Robinson attempted to apply for admission to the Massachusetts bar. No woman had yet attempted to pass the bar in the Commonwealth and Robinson's petition received a fair degree of attention from the most prominent legal officials. The briefs she prepared on her own behalf advanced an equal rights argument for her case. Ironically, she had to enlist the support of a male colleague, former Attorney General Charles R. Train, to argue the case before the Supreme Judicial Court. The court asked the Executive Committee of the Bar Association of the City of Boston to file a brief in opposition to the petition. While waiting for Chief Justice Gray's decision, Robinson bided the time by opening an office in Pemberton Square, Boston. Although she fully expected that her petition would be denied, the gesture was indicative of her steadfast resolve and persistent optimism that some day she would be a practicing attorney. The petition was denied in November, 1881.

As the new year opened, Robinson found support for her cause within the Massachusetts legislature. A bill to enable women to be admitted to practice law on the same terms as men was submitted to the House in January, 1882. Robinson passed the bar examination and was admitted to practice in Massachusetts shortly thereafter.

A pioneer willing to face the difficulties of being a first, Robinson, nevertheless, recognized the limits of her new role. In the first three and half years of her Boston practice, she only appeared in court once to argue a claim for separate maintenance and custody for a deserted wife in probate court. Like many of her sisters in the first generation of women lawyers, Robinson initially relied on office practice or claims work to earn her living as an attorney. This choice meant that she did not have to deal with the scrutiny women faced when they entered the public sphere of the courtroom.

News of the success and acceptance of women lawyers in the Western territories sounded deeply in the ambitious young woman's heart. In 1884, Robinson moved to Seattle in the Washington Territory and opened a practice. With the encouragement of Judge Green of Seattle, she began to engage in court work that included the risky task of arguing cases before mixed juries of men and women. The liberality toward the "woman question" in the West allowed her to acquire experience in trial work and increased her self-confidence as a lawyer well beyond what her Boston experience had offered. A year later, when it became clear that her family would not be able to join her in Seattle, Robinson packed her bags and returned to the East Coast. The decision to leave a burgeoning and rewarding practice was not easy, for it punctured her dream of an active legal career.

The journalistic training of her young adulthood helped Robinson traverse the chasm of doubt facing her upon her return to the provincialism toward women in the East. The next two years were spent writing *Law Made Easy: A Book for the People,* published in 1886. A summary of the law of contracts, real property, wills, marriage, divorce, criminal law, and torts, the book allowed Robinson to combine her skill as a journalist with her legal knowledge to make the law accessible to the general public. The following year found Robinson back in the midst of Boston attorneys working as a legal stenographer to an established lawyer that served as a refresher course on the methods of practice in Massachusetts. Her legal skills did not go unnoticed, and before the year was out, her employer encouraged her to open her own office.

Perpetually optimistic, Robinson believed that the environment for women attorneys in Boston had changed in the six years since her initial attempt to find her niche there in the early 1880s. By 1888, when she reopened her Boston practice, a small but strong community of women interested in the law had taken shape. Two women were enrolled at Boston University Law School, and Robinson herself was assisting two more women to learn the law in her own office. Robinson knew well the strength and support available through the network of female association. She had joined the Equity Club in 1887, finding there a place to express her views about women and the law and receiving encouragement from reading the stories of other women who struggled toward the same end. In 1888, joined by fellow Equity Club members and Boston University alumnae Jessie Wright and Mary Greene, the women lawyers and law students of Boston formed the Portia Club, a weekly dinner and discussion club. Robinson also helped to found the Pentagon Club, an association of women in theology, medicine, teaching, law, and journalism. Boston's growing community of professional women and her own increasing commitment to legal issues pertaining to women nurtured Robinson intellectually and professionally. In 1889, she published a book on family law, *The Law of Husband and Wife,* and began to open her office on Saturday afternoons to women, offering them free consultations on legal matters. Miss Alice Parker joined Robinson's practice in 1890 to assist her with an increasingly busy practice.

Reflecting on the decade since she had graduated from Boston University, Robinson felt the time had come to declare that the battle for women's entry into the legal profession had been victorious. She celebrated the era of women lawyers with an article on "Women Lawyers in the United States" published in the *Green Bag* in 1890. Comprised of short biographies of successful women lawyers, the essay clearly presented her message that women were equal with men. As in her own case, dozens of other women—through hard work, patient struggle, and mutual support— had become practicing attorneys. Their numbers were growing, and the reports of their successes could not be doubted. Women lawyers were here to stay.

Robinson's letters to the Equity Club often raised issues central to women's status in the legal profession. It was she who addressed such timely topics as whether women should wear their hats in the courtroom and to what extent women attorneys should dedicate themselves to charity or political work outside of their practice. Her 1889 Equity Club letter asked a question on the minds of many young female attorneys: "Is it practicable for a woman to successfully fulfill the duties of wife, mother and lawyer at one and the same time?"

Robinson answered her own questions, sometimes giving contradictory responses indicative of the confusion professional women faced when addressing these issues: she wore her hat in court, believed that women lawyers should not allow themselves to be lured away from their practice, and argued that marriage to another lawyer allowed for mutual understanding of the partner's commitment to the legal profession and to each other.

Robinson only partly followed her own advice; she allowed herself to be lured away from her practice to write articles about women lawyers and legal issues. Similarly, in selecting a marriage partner, she chose a man who supported her ambitions, but he was not a lawyer. On April 2, 1890, she married Eli Sawtelle, a piano dealer, a man whose pride in and support of Robinson's professional life manifested itself when he gave her a rolltop desk for her office as a wedding present. During their wedding trip to Washington, D.C., Robinson was admitted to the bar of the United States Supreme Court. Sawtelle and Robinson enjoyed a loving and companionable, if brief, relationship. Tragically, Robinson died only a year after her marriage from an overdose of medication while vacationing at his family homestead in Amherst, New Hampshire, on August 10, 1891.

A pioneer woman lawyer in nineteenth-century Boston, Robinson's life experiences were nonetheless typical of the first generation of women lawyers. Like other successful women lawyers in the nineteenth century, she was bright, articulate, formally educated, married, and committed to working as a practicing attorney. She was also deeply involved in female associations, finding mutual support among other professional women and frequently staying just a step ahead of her own sage and hard-won advice.

Selected Sources

There is a wealth of information on Lelia Robinson. The *Chicago Legal News* and the *Woman's Journal* followed her career from the 1880s through her death in 1891. Robinson recounts her experiences at Boston University Law School in 22 *Woman's Journal* (1891). Her friend Mary Greene wrote a biographical sketch of Robinson, "Lelia Robinson Sawtelle—First Woman Lawyer of Massachusetts" (7 *Women Lawyers' Journal* [1918]). A biographical essay of Robinson is in the 22 *Chicago Legal News* (1890). An obituary is in the 23 *Chicago Legal*

News (1891). Additional obituaries are in the 22 *Woman's Journal* (1891); the *New York Times* (August 11, 1891); and the Boston *Evening Transcript* (August 10, 1891). Robinson is included in Ellen Martin, "Admission of Women to the Bar" (1 *Chicago Law Times* [1886]). Robinson's book *Law Made Easy* is reviewed in the 1 *Chicago Law Times* (1886). The brief in support of Robinson's attempt to gain admission to the Massachusetts State Bar is reprinted in the 22 *Woman's Journal* (1881). An interpretive analysis of Robinson and her admission to the Massachusetts bar is provided in Douglas Lamar Jones, "'a woman is not entitled to be admitted as an attorney': *Lelia J. Robinson's Case* and the Entry of Women into the Legal Profession in Massachusetts," *300th Anniversary History of the Supreme Judicial Court,* ed. Russell K. Osgood (tentative title, forthcoming 1992).

Jane Mariah Slocum

By the end of the nineteenth century a significant majority of schoolteachers were single women. Teaching increasingly became a woman's occupation as men surrendered the task to pursue more financially lucrative positions. Educating young children in the classroom was also considered an extension of women's domestic responsibility, making teaching one of the few acceptable professions open to women in the Victorian era. Although Jane Slocum worked in the tradition-bound profession of teaching throughout her life, she was not fettered by any type of doctrinal beliefs that suggested what or how she should teach her students. She expanded the curriculum at the girls' schools where she worked to include courses not usually offered to young women including civics, economics, and political and social science. Furthermore, her ideas on women's special role in the social sciences were ahead of her time. Long before settlement houses and social housekeepers, Slocum advocated that women's understanding of the world would be enhanced through a study of social science, a subject of which they had intimate knowledge by virtue of their domestic responsibilities. The generation of reformers in the Progressive era would echo these statements about the need for proper training in social science in order to correct the social problems of their day.

Jane Mariah Slocum, born on May 1, 1842, was the fourth of six children of Samuel and Phebe Slocum. Her father's successful business ventures provided easily for the material needs of the large family and brought fame to himself when the New York town he had founded and selected to raise his family was named Slocumville to honor his civic contributions. Both parents were devout Quakers, strict in self-discipline and firm in ideas about self-improvement. They taught her to read when she was only two and a half years of age. At age fifteen, Slocum attended the New Friends Boarding School in Union Springs, New York, completing the three-year course just as the Civil War broke out. Slocum tried to enroll in the volunteer nursing corps, but her young age forbade her joining. The war interrupted her plans to attend Antioch or Oberlin College, so she chose to enroll for a year of study at the Howland Collegiate Institute for girls in Union Springs, New York.

Eager to demonstrate her patriotism and belief in equality, Slocum was one of the first people to volunteer to teach the newly freed slaves. She gained her first real teaching experience when she taught for eight months at a school built for freed black men and women in Yorktown, Pennsylvania. An attack of malaria kept her from continuing her work with freed slaves, so she moved instead to northern New York to teach in a private school in the small town of Philadelphia. Her alma mater called her to its faculty in 1866. Howland gave her plenty of room to experiment with courses. She established a department offering courses in government, politics, and economics, courses typically unavailable to young girls of the day.

By 1873, Slocum had been appointed principal of Howland and decided it was time to further her own education. She took a two-year leave of absence to study law at the University of Michigan. Her decision to earn a law degree was not done with the intention of becoming a practicing attorney. Rather, as she explained to Equity Club members in 1887, her goals were to gain a solid legal foundation for teaching social studies courses and to better understand coeducation through firsthand experience. Furthermore, she thought that a formal educational program would strengthen her scholarly discipline. With these goals in mind, Slocum completed the law school program while also attending lectures in political science and economics. In 1874, she became the fifth woman to graduate from the University of Michigan Law School.

Armed with a solid legal education, Slocum returned to Howland to continue teaching courses in civics and economics. Apparently, the trustees began to view Slocum's curricular innovations with skepticism. She relocated to Canandaigua, New York, to help found the Granger Place School for girls in 1876. Unfettered by the trustees, Slocum offered courses in civics, political economics, psychology, logic, and ethics while serving as vice president of the school. Slocum made many friends with her students and fellow faculty members. During her tenure in Canandaigua, she met and began a lifetime friendship with fellow Granger teacher Mary E. Post. In 1893, she took the opportunity to travel to New York City to apply her knowledge of social science to study the social conditions of the poor. She offered parlor talks and informal classes in social science at Carnegie Hall through the urban reform association, the Patriotic League.

In 1896, Slocum accepted a position as principal at Weiser Academy in Idaho. Four years later, she helped the Reverend Edward Paddock to found the Idaho Industrial Institute (later called the Intermountain Institute). The school's purpose was consistent with Slocum's egalitarian ideals: it offered a high school education to those for whom regular high school was inaccessible. Students did not pay tuition but were required to do daily chores and attend Sunday church services. Slocum served as the first female principal at the institute, where she developed a reputation as an outspoken supporter of suffrage and equal rights. She fostered her professional life through memberships in numerous organizations including the American Academy of Political and Social Sciences, the American Economic Association, and the University Extension Association.

The institute's physical accommodations were primitive compared to those Slocum had enjoyed in the wealthier community at the Granger School. In its first years the school had only one small wooden building to its name. Slocum and Post, who had traveled to Idaho together in 1896, lived in a tiny room and carried their own wood and water. Their former students and friends at Granger collaborated to raise $1,200 for Slocum's birthday that was used to build a small house. The cottage, named "Friends Lodge," stood among the buildings of the institute and became a haven of hospitality to students, friends, and alumni. Content amidst its academic surroundings, Slocum viewed "Friends Lodge" as a place where she could live and work the rest of her life. Slocum remained active at the Industrial Institute until failing eyesight forced her to retire from teaching in 1913. She remained an active member of the school's board of trustees and was able to witness the growth of the institute from a small one-room shack to a thriving complex. She died on August 10, 1924. Her burial was in Hillcrest Cemetery in a grave next to her lifelong companion Mary Post and not far from the educational compound she had helped to build.

Selected Sources

A useful biographical essay of Jane Slocum is in Frances Willard and Mary Livermore, eds., *A Woman of the Century* (1893). She is also included in John William Leonard, ed., *Woman's Who's Who of America* (1914–15). History of the Slocum family is in Charles Elihu Slocum, *History of Slocums, Slocumbs, and Slocombs of America* (1882). Slocum is included in Lelia J. Robinson, "Women Lawyers in the United States" (2 *Green Bag* [1890]). Slocum's obituary is in the Weiser *Signal* (August 11, 1924). Additional information is available from the Weiser Public Library, Weiser, Idaho; Intermountain Cultural Center and Museum, Weiser, Idaho; and Sophia Smith Collection, Smith College, Northampton, Massachusetts.

Marion Marsh Todd

Marion Marsh Todd's career exemplifies the significant extent of women's influence in the volatile realm of Gilded Age American political life. In an era before women won the vote, Todd pursued an active public life, using the powers of third-party membership, writing, and public speaking to influence the agenda of late nineteenth-century politics.

Born in March, 1841, Marion Marsh Todd was one of seven children of Abner K. and Dolly A. (Wales) Marsh of Plymouth, New York. Her parents, and especially her father, a minister of the liberal Universalist tradition, provided the basis of her early education. When the Marsh family moved to Eaton Rapids, Michigan, in 1848, Marion Marsh Todd entered the local public schools. A good student and quick learner, she completed preparation for a teaching career at Ypsilanti State Normal School by age seventeen. After ten years of teaching, she married Boston attorney Benjamin Todd in 1868.

The marriage proved to be a turning point in Marion Todd's life. With her husband's encouragement, Marion Todd expanded her public role as an orator and political activist, speaking on such issues as temperance, suffrage, and labor. Marion Marsh Todd transformed her classroom skills into one of public speaker and became a noted lecturer on reform issues. The birth of her daughter and a strenuous speaking schedule impaired her health, inspiring the family's decision to move to California in the late 1870s.

Marion Todd enrolled at Hastings Law School in San Francisco in 1879, shortly after Clara Shortridge Foltz and Equity Club member Laura de Force Gordon won admittance to the state school. Her husband's death in 1880 left her a single parent with limited resources. Although Todd did not complete the law school program, she passed the bar examination and was admitted to practice before the California courts in 1881. Todd enjoyed a busy and successful law practice in San Francisco for three years, until in 1883, having turned her attention to politics, she closed her law office.

Todd's training in finance, law, and political economics provided the intellectual framework for her work in reform politics. Excluded from positions of power and influence in mainstream political parties, women like Marion Todd were welcomed into third-party politics. Todd attended the 1882 California state convention of the Greenback Labor Party and was a principal contributor to the party's platform. Nominated for state attorney general on the Greenback ticket that year, she polled more votes than any another Greenback party candidate.

Todd returned to Michigan in the mid-1880s where she expanded her involvement in political work. She worked as a lecturer for several political parties and reform groups including the Greenbacks, Anti-Monopoly, Knights of Labor, and the Union Labor Party, all of which were dedicated to addressing the unequal distribution of wealth and power in American industrial capitalism. To support herself and her daughter, she earned money as a public speaker and author. In 1886, she published her first book, *Protective Tariff Delusions,* arguing that political pork barrels over tariff laws deprived American laborers of the fruit of their work. In other works—*Prof. Goldwin Smith and His Satellites in Congress* (1880) and *Pizzaro and John Sherman* (1891)—Todd integrated her knowledge of political economy with a more pedantic writing style to attack those whom she saw as the political instigators of the injustices prevalent in American society during the Gilded Age.

In 1890, Todd moved to Chicago to become editor of the *Express,* a national weekly reform newspaper. The position gave her a larger audience for her views and brought with it greater opportunities to implement her ideas on the need for social change. In 1891, she attended the organizing meeting of the People's (Populist) Party in Cincinnati. Her book on the railroad industry, *Railways of Europe and America* (1893, 1895), incorporated the political agenda of the Populists with a solid understanding of the financial structure of the railroad firms. Praised by Populist leader Ignatius Donnelly, the work demonstrated the need for restructuring the railroad system in the United States to serve the public interest of the people rather than the private profits of the railroad.

At the end of her life, Marion Todd used the novel to reach a broader audience with her beliefs about the evils of capitalism and the need for social reform. Her stories, *Rachel's Pitiful History* (1895), *Phillip: A Romance* (1900), and *Claudia* (1902), documented the tragedy of human life wrought by the capitalist system. She criticized the churches for not rising to the challenge of social responsibility inherent in the mission of Christian love they preached, and she offered political and economic reforms as the most effective way to change the maligned social order of the era.

Todd used the media of public lecture, newspaper articles, and scholarly and popular books to articulate and deliver the message that American society was woefully off balance in the way it treated workers, women, and the disadvantaged. With greater power and influence than a single vote would have allowed, Todd's knowledge, opinions, and activism helped shape the agenda of third-party politics in the late nineteenth century.

Marion Marsh Todd appeared to have lived the rest of her life in Michigan, being a resident of Springport in 1914. The date and cause of her death is not known.

Selected Sources

Biographical essays on Mary Todd are in Edward T. James, ed., *Notable American Women* (1971) and Frances E. Willard and Mary A. Livermore, eds., *A Woman of the Century* (1893). Todd is also included in *Who's Who in America* (1912–13), and John William Leonard, ed., *Woman's Who's Who of America* (1914–15). Lelia Robinson refers to her in "Women Lawyers in the United States" (2 *Green Bag* [1890]). A summary of Todd's publications with newspaper comments is included in Todd's *Rachels Pitiful History* (1895).

Catharine Van Valkenburg Waite

Enthusiasm and courage comprised the spirit of the generation of middle-class Americans born and raised in the expanding western region of North America during the nineteenth century. The opening of new territories held promises of advancement for men and women and those who enjoyed the privileges of education and class could pursue their dreams in the wide-open spaces of the Great Plains. Catharine V. Waite's character embodied this spirit as she participated in the different professions and the social movements of her day. While she accomplished her personal ambitions as author, lecturer, educator, and publisher, she was not able to witness what she considered the primary goal for women—equal access to the polling place. But her struggles to secure the vote for women placed her among the frontline suffragists and created a legacy for the generation of young women who followed her.

Born in western Ontario on January 30, 1829, Catharine Van Valkenburg Waite was the elder child and only daughter of Joseph and Margaret Van Valkenburg. When Catharine was seventeen years old, the family moved to Iowa where she began to teach school. In 1849, she enrolled in the female department of Knox College in Galesburg, Illinois, transferring to Oberlin and graduating from the coeducational college in 1853. A year later, on April 26, 1854, she married Charles Burlingame Waite, a young man she had met while enrolled at Knox College.

The Waites moved to the Chicago area where Charles Waite conducted a busy legal practice. Catharine V. Waite settled into a life of domesticity, bearing six children, five of whom reached adulthood. In addition to her domestic responsibilities, Waite taught for two years, 1857 to 1859, at Chicago's Union Park Seminary. After the family moved to Hyde Park in 1859, she opened the Hyde Park Seminary, a girls' school, to provide educational opportunities for her own children as well as her new neighbors' children.

Between 1862 and 1866, the Waite family followed Charles Waite's legal career to a one-year appointment as associate justice of the

Supreme Court of the Utah Territory and then to Idaho City, Idaho, where he opened a law office and dabbled in politics. Catharine V. Waite did not sit idly by while her husband developed his career. In Utah she took advantage of the opportunity to observe Mormon society, particularly women's role in plural marriages. Her concern for the dangers to women caused by polygamy sparked her interest in reading the law and provided her with enough material to publish a book, *The Mormon Prophet and His Harem,* when the family returned to Chicago in 1866. The book was reissued in popular form in 1882, as *Adventures to the Far West: And Life Among the Mormons,* the year Congress outlawed polygamy.

After being denied admission to Rush Medical College in 1866, Waite reopened the Hyde Park Seminary, operating it until 1871, and began to take an active interest in the post–Civil War woman suffrage movement. She and her husband helped to found the Illinois Equal Suffrage Association in 1869, and she served as its president in 1871. The year of her presidency found her serving as one of the first of a series of nationwide test cases of the recently passed Fifteenth Amendment to the United States Constitution. A similar and better-known test case was advanced by Susan B. Anthony in New York in 1872. The case involved Waite's application to vote in a Hyde Park election, an act that if successful would have forced the state of Illinois to change its constitution and allow women to vote. Even after Judge Waite submitted carefully worded arguments on his wife's behalf her application was denied. Waite's activism as a suffragist ended with this decision, but she continued to work on behalf of suffrage, serving as legislative advisor to the Illinois Equal Suffrage Association until she relinquished the post to her protégée and fellow Equity Club member, Catharine Waugh McCulloch, in 1890.

The decades of the 1870s through the mid-1880s found Waite busy raising a family, running the family's publishing firm of C. V. Waite and Co., assisting her husband in his writing efforts, and managing the family's real estate interests while Judge Waite travelled abroad. In 1885, Catharine V. Waite decided that the period of independent reading of the law was over and the time for formal legal training had dawned. Since the family's brief visit to Utah she had taken up an interest in law, claiming that she preferred reading Blackstone to the contemporary novelists. Undaunted and probably challenged by the youthful population surrounding her in the law school classroom Waite, at the age of fifty-six, enrolled at the Union College of Law in Chicago, later the Law School of Northwestern University, and graduated in 1886. She served as a role model and mentor to her younger colleagues, particularly befriending the shy and intelligent Catharine G. Waugh. The two shared an interest in suffrage work and both joined the Equity Club. Waite's status as a matron helped Waugh overcome some of the social obstacles facing a single young woman in the male-dominated culture of the law school. Later in life, Waugh credited Waite with introducing her to her husband, Frank McCulloch, another student at Union College of Law.

Immediately after her graduation, Waite was admitted to the Illinois bar but never practiced law. With law degree in hand, an established reputation as a publisher and a noted author, Waite began to publish the quarterly *Chicago Law Times* in November, 1886. The paper offered a more progressive tone than Myra Bradwell's *Chicago Legal Times*. During its three-year existence, Waite used the paper to argue for social and legal reforms, discussing such topics as abortion, insanity, and divorce. Her firm convictions and well-written articles won her national attention. In 1888, she was elected president of the International Woman's Bar Association at a meeting of the International Council of Women in Washington, D.C., where several members of the Equity Club including Belva Lockwood, Ada Bittenbender, Emma Gillett, and Catharine G. Waugh were present to help elect her.

By 1890, when she was sixty-one years old, Waite had stopped publishing the *Chicago Law Times* and resigned from suffrage work. For the next twenty years she devoted her time to her children and grandchildren. Judge Waite passed away in 1909 and four years later, Catharine V. Waite, suffering from heart disease, died at her daughter Lucy's home on November 9, 1913.

Selected Sources

A biographical essay on Catharine V. Waite is in Edward T. James, ed., *Notable American Women* (1971). Additional biographical information is in James B. Bradwell, "Women Lawyers of Illinois" (32 *Chicago Legal News* [1900]) and James Grant Wilson and John Fiske, eds., *Cyclopedia of American Biography* (1889). Information on Waite is also in Lelia J. Robinson, "Women Lawyers in the United States" (2 *Green Bag* [1890]); Ellen Martin, "Admission of Women to the Bar" (1 *Chicago Law Times* [1886]); and Elizabeth Cady Stanton, et al., *History of Woman Suffrage* (vols. 2–5 [1881–1922]). Catharine Waugh McCulloch wrote an unpublished biographical sketch of her friend that is in the McCulloch papers at the Schlesinger Library, Radcliffe College, Cambridge, Massachusetts. An obituary of Waite is in the *Chicago Legal News* (November 15, 1913).

Sarah Killgore Wertman

Sarah Killgore Wertman, the first woman to graduate from the law school of the University of Michigan and the first woman admitted to the Michigan bar, was also one of the first professional women to face the dilemma between the traditional Victorian woman and her desire to be a professional. Like many of the pioneer professional women of her day, Sarah Killgore Wertman found that working under the shelter of her husband's law firm allowed her to combine her legal career with her duties as wife and mother.

Sarah Killgore Wertman was born on March 1, 1843, to David and Elizabeth Killgore. Raised in Jefferson Clinton County, Missouri, she was tutored at home by her mother and father until she enrolled at the Ladoga Seminary. After graduating in 1862, Sarah Killgore Wertman taught school for several years not far from her parents' home. Wertman's parents held considerable influence over her life choices. Her father, a prominent attorney in Jefferson County, encouraged her to study law. An example of pious Victorian motherhood, Elizabeth Killgore's influence appeared at a later point in Sarah Killgore Wertman's life.

In 1869 Sarah Killgore Wertman enrolled at the Union College of Law in Chicago. She transferred to the University of Michigan in 1870 and became the first woman to graduate from the law school in 1871. A short time later she became the first woman admitted to the Michigan bar. Three years of academic work in the male bastion of law schools took their toll on Wertman's health, rendering her an invalid for more than a year. Her Christian upbringing, combined with her long illness, tempered any maverick spirit she may have held as a pioneer in the legal profession. Wertman held rigidly to middle-class, Christian values of the era. She believed firmly that women's chief role as lawyers was to introduce the purity of Christian love to the bar, extending women's moral agency from the private to the public sphere through their professional accomplishments.

Four years after her graduation, Wertman married Indianapolis attorney Jackson S. Wertman on June 16, 1875. The couple moved to Indiana and opened a joint practice. However, because women were not admitted to the Indiana bar at this time, Mrs. Wertman's work was restricted to office practice. She specialized in real estate law while her husband assumed the legal work involving public courtroom appearances.

By 1878 the Wertmans had moved to Ashland, Ohio, and started a family. During the years in Ohio, Wertman gave birth to three children, one of whom died in infancy. The mantle of motherhood upon her, Sarah Wertman followed the example of her mother and stayed at home to raise her family. When her son and daughter had reached their teens, Sarah Wertman turned her attention back to her career. She was admitted to the Ohio bar in 1893 and returned to her husband's law office where she practiced real estate law.

The Wertmans followed their children to Seattle in the early years of the twentieth century, establishing a home there by 1905. Sarah Wertman chose not to practice law with her husband, a decision that was confirmed when his death removed the protective covering of her professional identity. At the end of her life she lived with her son in Seattle, keeping an interest in University of Michigan alumni affairs and a heavy schedule of religious reading. She died in 1935.

Selected Sources

A biographical essay on Wertman is in Frances E. Willard and Mary Livermore, eds., *A Woman of the Century* (1893). Additional biographical information is in "First Woman Lawyer of Country Resides in Seattle" (*Daily Journal of Commerce,* Seattle [June 6, 1925]); "Michigan's First Woman Lawyer" (63 *Michigan Bar Journal* [1984]); and Donald Thompson, "Sarah Killgore Law Graduate" (*Montgomery County* [December, 1988]). Wertman is included in Lelia J. Robinson, "Women Lawyers in the United States" (2 *Green Bag* [1890]). Additional information on Wertman is available from the Bentley Historical Library, University of Michigan, Ann Arbor, Michigan.

Jessie Elvira Wright Whitcomb

Jessie Wright Whitcomb, one of two children of William J. Wright, a Presbyterian minister and mathematics professor, and Julia McNair Wright, a much-published author, was born on September 24, 1864. Whitcomb's fertile imagination and natural intelligence were nurtured by her highly educated parents and through adventures with an older brother and many childhood friends—mostly boys. She received little formal schooling during her childhood years in New Jersey, Ohio, and Pennsylvania. Independent reading was supplemented by a two-year tour of Europe, extended conversations with her parents, and brief forays into public school and private seminaries. Whitcomb's parents encouraged her to learn on her own and to pursue whatever topic of interest appealed to her. This sense of family interaction and vitality remained with her throughout her life.

Whitcomb graduated from the University of Vermont in 1884, where she was elected to Phi Beta Kappa and started a chapter of Kappa Alpha Theta, a woman's sorority. She became the second woman to graduate from the Boston University Law School, following fellow Equity Club member Lelia J. Robinson and preceding Mary Greene, another member of the Equity Club. Whitcomb received the LL.B. cum laude in 1887. In a letter to the Equity Club in 1888, Whitcomb explained that she entered the profession out of a personal interest in law, having thought little about the position of women in law, and without "any single high-toned credible motive." After marrying law school classmate George Herbert Whitcomb on November 15, 1888, the couple moved to Topeka, Kansas, and opened a joint practice after Whitcomb was admitted to the Kansas bar in 1889. The practice of law provided little satisfaction to the energetic young attorney. She devoted most of her time to establishing a household and tending to the administrative details of the law firm. Nevertheless, she fully expected to return to work at Whitcomb and Whitcomb following the birth of her first son in 1891. Her husband thought otherwise and announced to her that he had entered a partnership with friend and neighbor Tyler Frederic Fuller, subsequently dissolving their shared practice.

Whitcomb devoted her energy and productivity to her family. She raised six children, became personally involved in the schools they attended, and took them to the family's summer home in the Rocky

Mountains each year. The summer home proved to be the most nurturing place for the growing family. The children were encouraged to explore the out-of-doors and had a hand in designing and building the growing assortment of buildings on the family's property. Here, in the pristine setting of the family's vacation place, Jessie Whitcomb was able to create the type of warm and stimulating home life for her children that had marked her own childhood years.

Outside of the immediate family, Jessie Wright Whitcomb became a highly respected Sunday school teacher and noted author of children's books including *An Odd Little Lass, A Story for Girls* (1898), *As Queer As She Could Be* (1895), and *Curly Hood* (1889). Her interest in travelling took her to Europe, South America, and back to Vermont twice, once in 1921 when she was the first woman to deliver the Founder's Day address at the University of Vermont. In 1924, after her last child and only daughter had been married and her husband's career as a judge had been firmly established, Whitcomb began an extended trip to Hawaii, Japan, China, and the Philippines. News of her husband's illness reached her while visiting her son in Manila. She left immediately, but upon arriving in Seattle and learning that he had recovered, she decided to travel to Alaska to visit another son and his family before returning to Topeka.

Independent in her relationship with her husband, she devoted most of her life to creating a stimulating educational environment for children, a commitment shaped in part by a friendship she shared with educational philosopher John Dewey when they were both young adults in Vermont. The Whitcomb children and grandchildren always came first in her life, but her interest in children extended to the teaching of Sunday school classes at the First Presbyterian Church of Topeka and to teaching a second grade class of Chinese students while visiting that country. In addition, she contributed to family magazines including *Youth's Companion* and *Mother's Magazine*. Following her death on April 22, 1930, Mrs. Whitcomb was eulogized "as a great mother, whose heart was big as her brain, big enough to be interested in all Childhood."

Selected Sources

The best source on Jessie Wright Whitcomb is her memoir, entitled "Reminiscences," in the Kansas State Historical Society in Topeka.

There is information on Jessie Wright Whitcomb and her husband in William E. Connelley, *History of Kansas: State and People* (1928). Useful information on her life is also available in two memorials written shortly after her death. Rev. Stephen Sewall Estey, "A Pastor's Tribute" (1930) is available in the Kansas State Historical Society. "In Memoriam: Jessie Wright Whitcomb" was published by the Topeka, Kansas Bar Association in 1931. She is also included in Lelia J. Robinson, "Women Lawyers in the United States" (2 *Green Bag* [1890]). Additional material on Jessie Wright Whitcomb is in the Kansas State Historical Society, Topeka, Kansas.

Margaret Lyons Wilcox

In the latter half of the nineteenth century, many children from poor and lower-class families found that access to education opened the door to social and economic mobility. After the Civil War, women took advantage of the opportunity to attend colleges and universities opened by the passage of the Morrill College Land Grant Act in 1862. The legislation had not designated that land grant universities be restricted to male students, thus allowing women access to a level of higher education previously unavailable to them. A college degree and professional training earned in the public universities offered women a variety of career choices. Margaret Lyons Wilcox, the daughter of Irish immigrants, was trained in a normal school for a career as a school teacher, a role she found particularly satisfying. The opportunity to earn a law degree opened new doors to her professional development. Wilcox found that legal training increased her status in her chosen profession of education. Her marriage to another attorney placed her in a socioeconomic class significantly different from the one of her childhood in the country home of her widowed mother.

Margaret Lyons Wilcox was born on August 26, 1852, in the rural Wisconsin town of Wilmot. Her father's death when she was ten years old left the family of four daughters struggling to make ends meet. The family scrimped and saved to put young Margaret through school, and at age fourteen her success as a scholar won her a teaching job in a neighboring district and added a little money to the family's budget. In 1871, Lyons enrolled in the Wisconsin State Normal School at Whitewater, earning her teaching certificate in 1874.

Immediately she was offered a position in the public school system of Milwaukee and moved there with her mother. In the late 1870s she met and married Levi Peter Wilcox, a fellow school teacher. The two decided that in order to secure their future they would need to further their education.

In 1880–81, the Wilcoxes attended the University of Wisconsin in Madison, transferring to the University of Michigan in Ann Arbor in 1882. Both Margaret and Levi Wilcox received the bachelor of arts degree from the university's literary department in 1885, and then enrolled in the university's law school, earning their LL.B. degrees in 1887. During their years as law students, they were one of two married couples enrolled in the law school.

Shortly after receiving their law degrees, Margaret and Levi Wilcox were forced to live apart while Margaret returned to Milwaukee to care for her dying mother and Levi took a position with a law firm in Chicago. Her mother's death in November, 1887, did not signal the end of Margaret's time apart from her husband. She remained in Milwaukee working in the public school system until 1889, when she moved to Chicago to live with Levi.

The politics imbedded in the public education system had been a catalyst in Margaret Wilcox's initial interest to pursue the study of the law. She believed that knowledge of public affairs, attainable through legal education, would enhance her ability to operate within the political labyrinth of the public school system. Her law degree carried greater weight in increasing her salary than in furthering any hope she had of correcting political misconduct in the schools. Beyond her own experience though, her belief in the practical application of a legal education led her to advocate for the role of women attorneys in social reform work and argued for the special moral role women lawyers had for society in general and women in particular.

Wilcox's memories of her childhood in a poor country home played an important role in her decision to remain a school teacher after graduating from law school. With both a bachelor's degree and a law degree, combined with her years of experience as a school teacher, Wilcox could earn more money working in the public schools than she could as a young woman attorney just entering the profession. A dedicated member of the Equity Club, Wilcox was one of the club's founders and a member of its executive committee. She used the correspondence club to express her thoughts about the utilitarian aspects of legal education and the need of women clients for women attorneys. Wilcox also asked her sisters-in-law probing questions about financial compensation for established female attorneys. The responses she received must have confirmed her belief and provided additional defense of her decision that school teaching offered her better security than the law.

Apparently, Margaret Lyons Wilcox never joined her husband in a legal practice, though she was known to have assisted him in office work for a short period of time after moving to Chicago. In 1901, the Wilcoxes reported to the University of Michigan that they were living in Chicago where Levi practiced law and Margaret taught school. Wilcox believed firmly in women's right to professional education. As a devoted schoolteacher it is likely that she imparted this belief and a strong dose of encouragement to ambitious young girls who came under her tutelage.

Selected Sources

The sources on Margaret Wilcox are sparse. She is included in Lelia J. Robinson, "Women Lawyers in the United States" (2 *Green Bag* [1890]). An obituary notice is in the Milwaukee *Sentinel* (November 19, 1887). Wilcox is listed in the *Catalogue of the State Normal School at Whitewater* (1871). Additional information is available from the Bentley Historical Library at the University of Michigan, Ann Arbor; the Division of Archives at the University of Wisconsin-Madison; the University of Wisconsin-Whitewater; and the State Historical Society of Wisconsin, Madison.

Mary Hickey Wilkinson

In 1873, shortly after Myra Bradwell was denied admittance to the Illinois bar, Mary B. Hickey Wilkinson graduated from the law school of the University of Iowa, the first law school in the United States to admit women. Born in 1841 to an Irish immigrant who settled in Jasper County, Iowa, Mary Hickey Wilkinson seemed undaunted at the potential difficulties facing her as the first and only woman in a law school class of fifty-six students.

Within weeks of her graduation from the University of Iowa, Mary Hickey Wilkinson married Joseph Wilkinson of Vermont, Illinois. As she assumed the mantle of wife, she discarded the recently achieved privilege to practice law and devoted her energies to her husband and family. The family moved frequently, living in the town of Virginia, Illinois, in 1877, then in Hutchinson, Kansas, by 1890, and finally moving to Pomona, California, in the mid-1890s. Economic opportunity was probably the motivating factor in the decision to move so often. Joseph Wilkinson's income was sufficient to finance the frequent relocations and Mary Wilkinson reported to the Equity Club that her contemplation about initiating a legal career seventeen years after law school did not spring from any "need that urges me to cast about for an opportunity to start."

During her life, Mary Hickey Wilkinson kept alive a practice of reading the law and maintaining an interest in legal matters. Her ruminations about returning to the legal profession never materialized in a law career for herself. However, the fruit of her intellectual interest in the law did not die on the vine. In 1896, her son, William Josiah Wilkinson, followed in his mother's footsteps and received an LL.B. from the University of Iowa. He pursued a career in finance in Pomona, California, probably not living too far away from his influential mother, also a resident of Pomona until her death on April 10, 1925. Well-versed in the tenets of middle-class Victorian motherhood, she kept herself out of the public eye while creating opportunity for her family.

Selected Sources

Biographical information on Mary Wilkinson is in Teresa Opheim, "Portias of the Prairie: Early Women Graduates of the University Law Department" (67 *The Palimpsest* [1986]); Lelia J. Robinson, "Women Lawyers in the United States" (2 *Green Bag* [1890]); and Ruth Gallaher, *History of Legal and Political Status of Women in Iowa* (1918). Wilkinson is included in H. J. Thornton, "Coeducation at the State University of Iowa" (45 *Iowa Journal of History and Politics* [1947]). Additional information is available from the State Historical Society of Iowa, Iowa City.

Women Lawyers in Europe: Eliza Orme, Marie Popelin, and Emilie Kempin

The Equity Club's desire to support the activities and aspirations of women in the legal profession extended to the small but highly trained group of European women lawyers. The low status of women lawyers in Europe first became apparent to American women with Equity Club member Mary A. Greene's 1889 translation of Dr. Louis Frank's essay "The Woman Lawyer," published serially in the *Chicago Law Times*. The article provided a lengthy discussion of the customs, traditions, and arguments against the public appearance of women in courts of law, including citations from Roman law and Catholic canonical law as well as contemporary regulations against women being admitted as advocates in the courts of various European countries. Three European women lawyers, mindful of their relative isolation in their chosen profession, answered the Equity Club's invitation to join their numbers. Within the welcoming embrace of the professional association, Marie Popelin of Belgium, Emilie Kempin of Switzerland, and Eliza Orme of London found a sororal network of sympathetic ears. Kempin found that her association with American women did provide an opportunity for her professional development when her European brothers closed the door to her promising legal career.

Essentially, European women were allowed to pursue graduate education in law and earn the prestigious degree, doctor of laws. Legal education in European universities required extensive training in classical law of Greece and Rome, training not required of attorneys in the United States. Upon completion of their formal education, women were allowed to work in attorneys' offices drawing up various documents such as wills and deeds, but were consistently refused admission to the order of advocates, the equivalent of being admitted to the bar in the American system. Consequently, women lawyers in Europe could never appear to argue a case in court. Many American women lawyers such as Mary Greene, having been admitted to the bar, often chose office practice over courtroom practice. The choice, while shaped by social norms of the day, was also a voluntary one. The fact that American women had such a choice speaks to one of the significant differences between the legal status of women in the republic of the United States of America and that of women in Europe, a land when monarchs still ruled and traditional customs seemed to prevail over legal precedent and social progress.

Eliza Orme

While Greene's translation of Frank's essay introduced the status of European women lawyers to a broad audience, some members of the Equity Club already had personal knowledge of the situation. Jessie Wright's tour of Europe following her graduation from Boston University Law School in 1887 included a visit to the office of Eliza Orme and M. E. Richardson, a partnership of two women attorneys in London. Eliza Orme had a reputation as one of the ablest women in England. She was the first woman to receive the degree of LL.B. from London University. She worked on the English Labor Commission and was a leader among women in English politics. Wright spent an interesting afternoon visiting with Orme in her well-appointed office on the second floor of 27 Southampton Building in London. Orme explained that the firm's practice was limited to preparing documents and paperwork for barristers and solicitors, legal work for which they were paid half of what their clients charged. Occasionally, the women drew up wills and deeds for private parties, but were not allowed to appear in court. Orme sent a telegraphic message to the Equity Club *Annual* in 1888: "Cordial Greetings. Will write letter next year. Orme." Her practice may have been extraordinarily busy, or the success of American women lawyers reported in the 1888 *Annual* too great an emotional weight to bear, or both, for while the Equity Club members were delighted to include her as one of them, Orme never corresponded with the Equity Club again.

At the time of Wright's visit, no woman in England had applied to become a barrister, the office that would allow them to argue cases before a judge. Orme and Richardson both felt that it was important to wait until six or seven women had completed their degrees and the group could apply together for admission. A critical mass of women attorneys likely appeared within a few years of Wright's visit. However, their quest to become barristers was lengthy and frustrating. It was not until nearly three decades later, in 1914, that a movement among male barristers began to show positive signs of admitting women to practice in their profession.

Marie Popelin

A 1876 Belgian law opened the doors of graduate education to women. A decade later, Marie Popelin completed the course of study for the doctor of laws, graduating from the University of Brussels in 1888. Along with the men in her graduating class she requested admission to the order of advocates in October, 1888. The denial of her petition precipitated Dr. Louis Frank's interest in the case of European women lawyers and provided the basic material for his article. Her appeal was likewise denied one year later. Taking the oath constituted the second of three steps on the path to becoming a practicing attorney in Belgium. Until the oath was administered Popelin could not enter the third phase of legal training, the probationary period that provided a hands-on education in courtroom practice under the direction of an established attorney.

Writing to the Equity Club in 1890, Popelin explained the procedure for becoming an advocate in Belgium and the arguments raised against her request. Those arguments included established social customs against women's public appearances and concerns about women's physical condition. Popelin noted that Belgian women who had pursued professional education in medicine and pharmacy had reaped the fruit of their training becoming doctors and pharmacists. Popelin, prevented from practicing law in Belgium, declared her own education "sterile."

Emilie Kempin

Emilie Kempin of Zurich, Switzerland, met a similar professional fate upon completing her legal training. Entering the School of Jurisprudence at the University of Zurich at age thirty-two, with three young children at home, Kempin became an expert in Roman Law, receiving the LL.D. after completing the four-year course in 1887. Twice she applied for admission to the order of advocates and each time was rejected on the legal basis that only those holding active citizenship—an honor extended only to men in Belgium—could be advocates. Unlike Popelin, Kempin did find work related to her training. A leading male jurist of the day, Dr. Meili, invited her to join him in his office where she drew up wills, deeds, and other legal documents.

An endless round of paperwork did not satisfy Kempin's professional and intellectual aspirations. Sacrificing her family life for her profession, Kempin emigrated to the United States in 1888 in search of opportunities to practice or teach law. New York City social reformer, Mrs. Leonard Weber, invited Kempin to help her run the Arbitration Society, a "legal dispensary" for the city's poor. Kempin prepared arguments for other attorneys to present before the court but the necessary legal talent did not appear to aid them in this effort. Very few women had been admitted to the New York bar—which had only been opened to them in 1886—and few men could be persuaded to join in the unremunerative work as legal advocates for the poor. The unsuccessful effort induced the two women to close the Arbitration Society and found the Women's Legal Education Society. The new organization served as an avenue both to educate women about their legal rights and to prepare women for pursuing a formal legal education. The society offered "parlor lectures" to members twice a week until enough demand for a more in-depth and formal program encouraged Kempin and Weber to find an institution to house the class.

In 1890, New York University offered the society a home for its Women's Law Class and hired Kempin to give the lectures. Drawing on models of adult education classes, the lectures were offered to nonmatriculants in the evenings when working women would be able to attend. Students received a vigorous introduction to the law as Kempin's lectures covered nearly every topic in the legal education curriculum including elementary jurisprudence, contracts, wills, sales, personal and real property, trusts, equity, corporations, and constitutional law. At the end of six months' instruction, the students were examined by Kempin and other faculty at the university. A special "graduation" ceremony was held for those who completed the course. Several of the "graduates" went on to enroll at the university's law school and to become successful attorneys.

Kempin found teaching law an agreeable and satisfying task. She readily accepted an offer from New York University to teach Roman Law to male students enrolled in the law school during the 1890–91 year. She complained that the men failed to pay the respect to her that she had received from her women students. Kempin returned to Zurich to spend the summer with her husband and children. A teaching offer from the University of Berne, the desire to be with her family, and, perhaps, the ungrateful reception of the male law students at New York University, all persuaded her to remain in her native Belgium where she pursued an active scholarly career.

European women lawyers were not admitted to the order of advocates until the first decade of the twentieth century, nearly thirty years after American women began to practice law in the nation's courts. The bonds of female association stretched across the Atlantic Ocean but were neither strong nor influential enough to effect changes in the legal traditions and social customs of European society. European women appreciated the sympathy extended by American women attorneys but found it did little to improve their situation either home or abroad. For American women, the status of women lawyers in Europe served as a constant and glaring reminder of the battle they had won in the not too distant past. Perhaps the wounds were still too tender to probe too deeply in considering the on-going battle on the European front.

Selected Sources

Useful information on Orme, Popelin, and Kempin is in Dr. Louis Frank, "The Woman Lawyer," translated by Mary A. Greene (3 *Chicago Law Times* [1889]).

Of the three women, materials on Kempin are most available. The *New York Times* followed her career in the Women's Legal Education Society and the Women's Law Class in 1889 and 1890. The papers of the Women's Legal Education Society and the Women's Law Class are in the New York University Archives in New York City. Also useful is *"For the better protection of their rights": A History of the First 50 Years of the Women's Legal Education Society and the Women's Law Class at New York University* (1940). Kempin is included in Lydia Hoyt Farmer, *The National Exposition Souvenir: What America Owes to Women* (1893). On Popelin see John Gilissen, *Introduction Historique Au Droit* (1979). On Orme see 14 *Chicago Legal News* (1914) and Jessie Wright's letter to the Equity Club (1888).

Index

Adams, Charles K., 69
American Bar Association, 2
American Medical Association, 13
American Medical Women's Association, 13
Anderson, Mary, 162
Anderson, Olive San Louie, 32
Angell, James B., 5, 8, 69
Anthony, Susan B., 137
Ashton, Carrie, 133
Atkinson, Edward, 131

Benneson, Cora Agnes, 21, 136, 233; at University of Michigan, 8, 206; and Equity Club letter, 1887, 44–45; biographical sketch of, 205–7; with Woodrow Wilson, 207; applies to Harvard University, 207; at Bryn Mawr, 207
Bennett, Edmund H., 141
Billings, Addie Melvina Stephenson: and Equity Club letter, 1888, 88–90; biographical sketch of, 208–10
Bittenbender, Ada Matilda Cole, 37, 92, 134, 270; first woman admitted to Nebraska bar, 20, 212; and WCTU, 21, 212; on charity, 25–26; and Equity Club letter, 1888, 90–91; and Equity Club letter, 1889, 151–54; on sexual relations in marriage, 152–53; biographical sketch of, 211–13; and women's suffrage, 211
Blackstone, William, 132, 190
Blair, Henry W., 154
Booth, Henry, 107
Boston University, 13, 17, 64, 168, 228, 273; admits women, 4; few women at law school, 9; Whitcomb at, 141–42, 168, 273; Greene at, 168, 228; women at law school, 169, 186, 201; Robinson at, 258
Buffalo Law School, 4
Burlingame, Letitia Lavilla A., 1, 5, 6, 76, 81, 88, 106, 164, 220, 251; and women at University of Michigan Law School, 9–10; at University of Michigan, 10–11, 214; and founding of Equity Club, 11; on equity law for women, 16; and hat debate, 30; and personal health, 35; death of, 35; and Equity Club letter, 1887, 46–47; and Equity Club letter, 1888, 91–93; and Equity Club letter, 1889, 154–57; biographical sketch of, 213–16

Campbell, E. M., 169
Campbell, James V., 7, 68
Case and Comment, 32
Chambers, Eliza Anne: and Equity Club letter, 1887, 48; biographical sketch of, 216–17; at Howard University, 216–17
Chicago Law Times, 19, 20, 164, 270, 279
Clarke, Edward H., 35–36; on women's health, 31–35
Colesworthy, Lydia, 169
Columbia University, 3

Cooley, Thomas M., 43, 68, 112, 190; and women at University of Michigan Law School, 7–8, 12
Cornell University, 7
Cousins, Phoebe, 136
Crim, Ella, 182–83
Cronise, Florence, 23, 80, 84, 155, 174; on charity, 24, 158; and Equity Club letter, 1888, 94–95; and sister, Nettie C. Lutes, 94, 158–59; and Equity Club letter, 1889, 157–59; and Equity Club letter, 1890, 182–84; biographical sketch of, 217–19
Cronise, Nettie. *See* Lutes, Nettie Cronise

Douglas, Corinne Williams, 5, 11, 46, 88, 120; founding member of Equity Club, 3; marriage of, 27–28; and Equity Club letter, 1887, 48–50; at University of Michigan, 76; and birth announcement of son, 93; biographical sketch of, 219–22; and Grover Cleveland and Edwin Stanton, 220
Dynamic Sociology, 86, 152

Equity, 79; as legal concept relevant to women, 15–16
Equity Club, 46, 51, 214, 255, 276–77; founding of, 1, 11, 76–78; significance of, 1–2; founding members of, 3; as a women's institution, 11, 13; naming of, 14–16, 78–79; and relations with men, 14; membership requirements of, 16; and membership by year, 17; characteristics of members of, 18–21; and ties to Woman Movement, 19, 21; and topics discussed in letters, 22; and hat debate, 23, 30; and sexual rights of married women, 23, 31–37; and charity in women lawyers' lives, 23–26; and marriage and legal career, 26–30; and women in courtroom, 28–30; and women's health, 30; constitution of, 87–89; motto of, 149, 181
Equity Club Annual, 17–18, 26, 34, 82, 83, 84, 87, 171

Fall, Anna Christy, 169–70, 201
Fall, George Howard, 170
Field, Walbridge A., 163
Foltz, Clara Shortridge, 20, 129, 226, 266
Foster, Ellen J., 136, 143
Frank, Louis, 164
Frieze, Henry S., 5–6

Gillett, Emma Millinda, 21, 23, 29, 58, 84, 135, 154, 164, 216, 244, 270; and founding of Washington College of Law, 20, 224; on charity, 24, 161; on marriage, 26, 162, 185; on women's health, 34, 160–61, 162; at Harvard University, 96; and Equity Club letter, 1888, 96–97; and Equity Club letter, 1889, 159–62; and Equity Club letter, 1890, 184–85; biographical sketch of, 222–25; with Alice Paul, 224; with Ellen Spencer Mussey, 224; and women's suffrage, 224
Goodell, Lavinia, 116
Gordon, Laura de Force, 14, 20, 21, 129, 266; and Equity Club letter, 1887, 50–51; biographical sketch of, 225–28; and women's suffrage, 226; and Hastings College of Law, 226
Gougar, Helen, 92, 137
Green Bag, 32, 260
Greene, Mary Anne, 13, 17, 124, 170, 201, 260, 273, 279; at Boston University Law School, 9, 168–69, 228; as first woman admitted to Rhode Island bar, 20; and Equity Club letter, 1887, 51–53; and Equity Club letter, 1888, 97–99; and Equity Club letter, 1889, 163–65; and Equity Club letter, 1890, 186–

87; at Lasell Seminary, 187; biographical sketch of, 228–30
Greene, Roger S., 121
Greenleaf, Simon, 190

Haddock, Mary Emily Humphrey, 165; marriage of, 27, 29, 100–101, 231, 232; and Equity Club letter, 1888, 100–102; at University of Iowa Law School, 101, 232; biographical sketch of, 231–33
Hall, Mary, 136
Harlan, Edward, 107
Harrison, Clara B., 57
Harvard University, 3, 207; Gillett at, 96; Bowdoin prize at, 128
Hastings College of Law, 4, 14, 20; and Laura de Force Gordon, 266
Hat debate, 23, 30, 127, 177–78, 260–61
Haven, Erastus, 5
Hemenway, Alfred, 98
Henry, Patrick, 130
Higginson, Thomas W., 123, 125
Hitchcock (Moore), Almeda Eliza, 5, 11, 17, 19, 46, 76, 81, 88, 220; founding member of Equity Club, 3; at University of Michigan, 6–7; as first woman admitted to Hawaii bar, 20; death of, 35–36; and Equity Club letter, 1887, 53–56; and WCTU in Hawaii, 56; and Equity Club letter, 1888, 103–4; and Equity Club letter, 1889, 166–67; and Equity Club letter, 1890, 188–89; biographical sketch of, 233–35
Howard University, 18; Emma Gillett at, 96, 223, 245; Eliza Chambers at, 216–17
Hubbard, Emma L., 68
Hulett, Alta, 116
Hutchins, Harry Burns, on equity, 15, 79

International Council of Women, 79, 132; McCulloch at, 133–37

Kaahumanu, 54
Kamehameha, 54
Kempin, Emilie, 81, 83; and Equity Club letter, 1888, 104–6; biographical sketch of, 281–83; and legal reform and education, 282; at New York University, 282–83
Kent, James, 132
Kepley, Ada Harriet Miser, 23; first woman to earn law degree, 19; on charity, 25; and Equity Club letter, 1888, 106–8; and Equity Club letter, 1889, 168; biographical sketch of, 235–38
Kepley, Henry B., 106, 107

Law Made Easy, 64, 259
Law Notes, 32
LeValley, David, 110
LeValley, Laura A. Woodin, 29, 84; and marriage, 27; and Equity Club letter, 1888, 109–10; biographical sketch of, 238–40
Lieuellen, Ce Dora: and Equity Club letter, 1888, 110–12; and Equity Club letter, 1890, 189–91; at Florida Normal College, 189; biographical sketch of, 240–41
Lockwood, Belva Ann Bennett McNall, 21, 96, 216, 223, 270; as pioneer woman lawyer, 19, 120; and Equity Club letter, 1887, 56–59; on Emma Gillett, 58; at WIBA, 135; as author in *New York Illustrated American*, 201; biographical sketch of, 241–46; meets Susan B. Anthony, 242; at National University School of Law, 243
Lounsbury, Leona Taylor: and Equity Club letter, 1887, 59–60; biographical sketch of, 246–47
Lutes, Nettie Cronise, 94, 158–59, 218, 219
Lyons, Mary, 81

McCulloch, Catharine Waugh, 11, 19, 21, 29, 35, 77, 84, 98, 119, 269, 270; on charity, 25, 174; and hat debate, 30; and Equity Club letter, 1888, 133–37; at International Council of Women, 133–37; and Equity Club letter, 1889, 173–77; in private practice, 173–74; on women's health, 175; marriage of, 184, 191–92, 253; and Equity Club letter, 1890, 191–92; on Robinson's marriage, 192; biographical sketch of, 251–55; at Union College of Law, 252; and women's suffrage, 253–54
McCulloch, Frank, 19, 191, 192, 252, 270
Mansfield, Sir William Murray (Lord), 71
Marriage, 3, 26, 60, 184; and legal career for women, 26–30, 109, 171, 260–61; of Douglas, 27–28; of Haddock, 27, 29, 100–101, 231, 232; sexual relations in, 36–37, 86, 152–53; of Bittenbender, 152–53; views of Gillett on, 162, 185; of McCulloch, 184, 191–92, 253; and women's legal status, 185, 253; of Robinson, 200–201; of Hitchcock, 234; of Kepley, 235; of LeValley, 239; of Lounsbury, 246; of Whitcomb, 273–74; of Wilcox, 276; of Wilkinson, 277–78
Marshall, John, 71
Martin, Ellen Annette, 5, 36, 68, 84, 156, 159; on women's health, 33–34, 114, 156; and Mary Fredrika Perry, 33–34, 114–115; and Equity Club letter, 1888, 112–16; on charity, 114–15, 165; biographical sketch of, 247–50; and women's suffrage, 248–49
Massachusetts State bar, admission of Lelia J. Robinson to, 20
May, Rebecca, 5, 46, 76, 88, 153, 220; as founding member of Equity Club, 3; at University of Michigan, 10, 11, 250–51; and Equity Club letter, 1887, 61–62; on women's health, 61; and Letitia Burlingame, 215, 251; biographical sketch of, 250–51
Meili, Dr., 105, 281
Merrill, Mary, 6, 46
Michigan State bar, 20
Michigan State Board of Regents, 5
Michigan Teachers Association, 4
Moore, Charles C., author of "The Woman Lawyer," 32
Mussey, Ellen Spencer, founder of Washington College of Law, 20, 224

New York University, 4
Northwestern University, 4, 132, 235, 270, 271; Ada Kepley at, 19; Catharine Waugh McCulloch at, 252

Orme, Eliza, 81, 143–44; and Equity Club letter, 1888, 117; biographical sketch of, 279, 280
Ormes, Lura M., daughter of Belva Lockwood, 57

Parker, Alice, 186, 200, 201
Pearce, Martha Kellum, 5, 13, 14, 17, 36–37, 46, 47, 89, 93, 104, 133, 143, 152, 192, 220; and founding of Equity Club, 3, 11, 76–78; at University of Michigan, 7, 10–11; as corresponding secretary of Equity Club, 17–18; on women's health, 34, 84–86; and Equity Club secretary's report, 1887, 62–63; and Equity Club secretary's report, 1888, 75–87; on naming of Equity Club, 78–79; on Emilie Kempin, 83; on sexual relations, 85–86; and Equity Club secretary's report, 1889, 150–51; and Equity Club

secretary's report, 1890, 182; biographical sketch of, 255–57
Pearson, Eleanor B., 128
Pentecost, Hugh O., 131
Perry, Mary Fredrika, 68, 115, 248; in Webster Society, 8; and Ellen Martin, 33–34, 114; health of, 34, 114, 333
Phillips, Wendell, 69
Poët, Lydia, 44
Pomeroy, J., 111
Popelin, Marie, 164; and Equity Club letter, 1890, original French version, 193–96; and Equity Club letter, 1890, English translation, 196–99; biographical sketch of, 281
Portia Club, 170, 186, 229, 260
Portia Law School, 18

Ray, Charlotte, 135n
Richardson, M. E., 143
Robinson (Sawtelle), Lelia Josephine, 17, 21, 22–23, 29, 84, 93, 143, 151, 159, 163, 164, 165, 184, 187, 191, 273; as first woman graduate of Boston University Law School, 9; as first woman admitted to Massachusetts state bar, 20, 258; on marriage, 26, 27, 192; and hat debate, 30, 92, 127; death of, 35–36, 261; and Equity Club letter, 1887, 63–67; and Boston University, 64, 126–27, 201; and Mary Greene, 98, 228; and Equity Club letter, 1888, 117–28; on marriage, 118; and marriage of Margaret Wilcox, 118; and experience in West, 121–22, 125; and women lawyers in Boston, 124; and Equity Club letter, 1889, 168–71; marriage of, 186, 200–201, 261; and Equity Club letter, 1890, 200–201; biographical sketch of, 257–62; and divorce, 258–59; as author of *Law Made Easy,* 259
Rogers, Henry W., 92
Roper, Susannah, 68

Santini de Sio, 44
Sex in Education, 31–32, 34–35
Slocum, Jane Mariah, 5, 21; and Webster Society, 6; at University of Michigan, 7; and Equity Club letter, 1887, 67–70; biographical sketch of, 262–65
Stiles, I. N., 171–72
Stockbridge, Mary, 67; and Webster Society, 6
Strickland, Martha, 68, 124; as secretary of Webster Society, 6

Tappan, Henry, 5
Thomas, M. Carey, 31
Todd, Marion Marsh: on charity, 25; on marriage, 26; and Equity Club letter, 1888, 128–32; and Equity Club letter, 1889, 171–73; biographical sketch of, 265–68
Torrey, Henry W., 128

Union College of Law. *See* Northwestern University
Union Signal, 63
University of California, 20, 104, 210, 226
University of Chicago, 106–7
University of Iowa, 4, 241; Haddock at, 101, 232; Wilkinson at, 20, 203, 231, 277
University of Michigan, 2, 3, 12, 14, 78, 104, 124–25, 215, 276; admits women, 4–5; opposition to women, 5; Wertman at, 5, 19, 271; few women law students at, 8–9; female friendships at, 10; medical school, 13; members of Equity Club as graduates of, 16–17; Benneson at, 43, 206; Wilcox at, 71, 276; Slocum at, 67–69, 263; women at law school of, 76; University Club at, 109; Burlingame

at, 214; Douglas at, 220; Hitchcock at, 233–34; LeValley at, 239; Lounsbury at, 246; Martin at, 247; May at, 250–51; Pearce at, 255
University of Pennsylvania, 4

Van Hoosen, Berth, M.D., 13

Waite, Catharine Van Valkenburg, 19, 20, 93; and Equity Club letter, 1888, 132–33; at Union College, 132, 270; and Woman's Inter-National Bar Association, 132, 135, 270; and McCulloch, 252; biographical sketch of, 268–71; and women's suffrage, 269
Walter, Edward Lorraine, 43
Washington College of Law, 18; founding of, 20; as all-white school, 224
Washington University, 4
Waugh, Catharine. *See* McCulloch, Catharine Waugh
Webster Society, 6, 8, 68
Wertman, Sarah Killgore, 21, 23; as first woman graduate of University of Michigan Law School, 5, 19, 271; and Equity Club letter, 1888, 138; biographical sketch of, 271–72; marriage of, 272
Whitcomb, Jessie Elvira Wright, 13, 19, 280; at Boston University Law School, 9, 141–42, 168, 273; in Boston, 98; and Equity Club letter, 1888, 141–45; and Orme, 143–44; marriage of, 165, 169, 191, 273; and Portia Club, 260; biographical sketch of, 273–75; and John Dewey, 274
Whiteling, Sarah J., 150–51
Whiting, Mary C., 46–47, 76
Wilcox, Margaret Lyons, 46, 81, 84, 88, 165, 220; as founding member of Equity Club, 3, 5, 17, 220; at University of Michigan, 10, 11, 71, 276; and hat debate, 30, 177–78; and Equity Club letter, 1887, 70–72; marriage of, 118, 276, 277; and Equity Club letter, 1888, 138–41; and Equity Club letter, 1889, 177–78; and Equity Club letter, 1890, 201–2; biographical sketch of, 275–77
Wilcox, Peter L., 118
Wilkinson, Mary Hickey: as first woman graduate of University of Iowa Law School, 20, 231; and Equity Club letter, 1890, 203; biographical sketch of, 277–78; marriage of, 277–78
Willard, Frances, 137
"The Woman Lawyer," short story by Charles C. Moore, 32–33
Woman's Inter-National Bar Association, 132, 135, 136, 270
Woman's Journal, 8, 123, 206
Women doctors, 12–13
Women Lawyers' Journal, 1
Woman's Christian Temperance Union, 21, 25–26, 80, 140, 153, 183, 212; Bittenbender and, 25–26, 153, 212; in Hawaii, 56; and Kepley, 108, 236, 237; and Billings, 210; and Burlingame, 215; and McCulloch, 254; and Pearce, 256
Women's health, 3, 45, 61, 84–86, 114–15, 156, 160–62
World's Columbian Exposition, 182, 192, 219
World's Fair. *See* World's Columbian Exposition
Wright, Jessie Elvira. *See* Whitcomb, Jessie Elvira Wright

Yale University, 3
Young, Ernest, 128